Teaching the Whole Musician

Teaching the Whole Musician

A Guide to Wellness in the Applied Studio

Paola Savvidou

OXFORD
UNIVERSITY PRESS

Oxford University Press is a department of the University of Oxford. It furthers
the University's objective of excellence in research, scholarship, and education
by publishing worldwide. Oxford is a registered trade mark of Oxford University
Press in the UK and certain other countries.

Published in the United States of America by Oxford University Press
198 Madison Avenue, New York, NY 10016, United States of America.

Library of Congress Cataloging-in-Publication Data
Names: Savvidou, Paola, author.
Title: Teaching the whole musician : a guide to wellness in the applied studio / Paola Savvidou.
Description: New York : Oxford University Press, 2021. | Includes bibliographical references and index.
Identifiers: LCCN 2020048704 (print) | LCCN 2020048705 (ebook) |
ISBN 9780190868796 (hardback) | ISBN 9780190868802 (paperback) |
ISBN 9780190868826 (epub) Subjects: LCSH: Musicians—Health and hygiene. |
Musicians—Wounds and injuries. | Overuse injuries—Prevention.
Classification: LCC ML3820 .S28 2021 (print) | LCC ML3820 (ebook) |
DDC 780.71—dc23
LC record available at https://lccn.loc.gov/2020048704
LC ebook record available at https://lccn.loc.gov/2020048705

DOI: 10.1093/oso/9780190868796.001.0001

1 3 5 7 9 8 6 4 2

Paperback printed by Marquis, Canada
Hardback printed by Bridgeport National Bindery, Inc., United States of America

Contents

Preface

Over the past fifteen years of teaching I have learned that my rigorous training and preparation for the profession of a pedagogue desperately needed augmentation in several other dimensions that I never thought relevant to the work of teaching piano. I found myself in situations where I had to encourage a perfectionist six-year-old who lay on the bench for the entire lesson because she was so hard on herself for the wrong notes she played, or comfort a college student who cried every week due to tendinitis pain and the fear that her career was over. And then I listened and gently empathized with the retiree who couldn't bear the loneliness in his apartment and described how piano was the only thing in his life that kept him going.

The process of learning music can bring enormous joy and also deep struggle as we face our own personal insecurities, often exacerbated by an internal voice of judgment. That competitive drive to reach higher levels of achievement can also lead students to over-practicing, injury, and other unhelpful habits. In the lesson, vulnerabilities must be met with love in a trusting and safe environment. We must realize that, as teachers, we are more than transmitters of technical and artistic skill. Music teachers have the capacity to be lifelong mentors—role models with the power to support and nurture a holistic vision for a life in the arts. And when we hold our students in that space of caring attention and acceptance, they will be better situated to thrive, shining brighter into their future.

Acknowledgments

Writing a book is much like raising a child. It takes the support of many individuals who contribute in different ways: loving encouragement, curious questioning, and professional advice. Through every step of this process I have relied heavily on a remarkable network of family, friends, colleagues, mentors, and healthcare professionals for their insight, expert advice, and honest feedback. I feel incredibly fortunate to work in an institution with a team of medical colleagues who don't even think twice about spending their time and energy answering questions and pointing me to the right resources. My deepest gratitude especially to Kristen Schuyten, Lexie-Muir Pappas, Allie Heckman, Bruce Edwards, Elizabeth Baldner, Marsha Benz, and Lisa Camfield. A huge "Namaste" to my favorite yogini, Catherine Matuza, for reviewing the sections on yoga and for generously serving as the model for the companion website videos. And thank you to my illustrator, Amber Huo, for the beautiful images.

One of my favorite parts of this process was connecting with students, faculty, and medical professionals through interviews. Your insights have opened my eyes to more perspectives and raised even more questions to explore in the future. While I wish to keep students and faculty names anonymous for confidentiality reasons, I would like to publicly thank Dr. Jeremy Stanek and Evan Engelstadt for their expertise on physical health and nutrition, respectively. I was able to develop these ideas in large part due to my position at the University of Michigan. I am grateful for the encouragement and support of my former and current supervisors.

Within piano pedagogy (my field of training), I continue to be inspired by brilliant colleagues who pave the way to new and exciting research in wellness: Vanessa Cornett, Jessica Johnson, Lesley Sisterhen-McAllister, and Brenda Wristen. Wellness for the performing artist would not have become a recognized field if it weren't for the pioneering work of people like Gail Berenson, Linda Cockey, Gerald Klickstein, and Judy Palac. I was inspired to view wellness from a mentorship perspective due to my own deeply impactful mentors: Jessica Johnson and John Salmon. They saw me not just as a student or a pianist, but as a human being, with equal doses of talents and struggles.

My friends and family were an enormous source of strength—lifting me up when I felt defeated and reminding me that I can only tackle one thing at a time (my mantra that my sister Dina ingrained into me since freshman year of college). Thank you, Amy, Alex, Chris, and Olivia, for proofreading parts of the book and reminding me that simplicity is more powerful than convoluted wordiness.

People tell me I have inherited my mother's strength and my father's determination. So, thank you, mom and dad for passing those traits down to me, without which I wouldn't have been able to finish this project. The pride of my sisters, Dina,

Margarita, and Chrysso, in my work has kept me motivated. Their passion and creativity in their work has energized me in my own process. My in-laws' loving support eased my moments of self-doubt. Thank you, Nancy and Johannes.

None of my work would be possible without the support of my husband Jonathan. And I am not just referring to the daily emotional encouragement and endless supply of dark chocolate, but the willingness to stay up until 2:00 a.m. night after night proofreading chapters of this book, followed by early wake-up calls by our darling little Oliver, so that I could continue editing. All this during the toughest year of our lives (2020—I'm sure many readers will relate). Thank you for your endless faith in me, love, and healthy dose of critical feedback.

Finally, thank you to Normal Hirschy of Oxford University Press for giving me this remarkable opportunity to write a book on the topic I am most passionate about, and to the rest of the team for seeing this project to fruition.

About the Companion Website

www.oup.com/us/teachingthewholemusician

Oxford has created a website to accompany *Teaching the Whole Musician*. Material that cannot be made available in a book, including movement exercises, meditation audio, and worksheets, is provided there. The reader is encouraged to consult this resource in conjunction with the chapters. Examples available online are indicated in the text with Oxford's symbol ⏵.

1

Setting the Foundation

What Is Wellness?

Perspectives on Health and Wellness

We all want to be well. But what does that mean? When I first encountered the term "wellness" as applied to the performing arts, it seemed obvious. Either you are well, or there is something wrong with you. Keep your body and mind healthy, and you will achieve wellness. If you can find that state of being, you will earn that fuzzy, warm feeling of happiness—the feeling you get sipping a warm beverage on a cold winter day. But wellness is not a piping hot pumpkin spiced latte. Over the past decade, I have come to learn that this dichotomous attitude oversimplifies the complexity of pursuing wellness, and, when accepted widely, has devastating effects on our ability to cultivate student-centered pedagogy. Pursuing wellness requires us to think beyond just our physical and emotional states. It evolves over time, and a disruption in one dimension can ripple through other, typically stable aspects of our lives. These disruptions can manifest in many different ways, and may exacerbate our struggles when moments of stress boil over at home, in the workplace, or even in public. This book aims to frame the interconnectedness of wellness in a holistic manner, so that we can better understand how to support individual students within our pedagogy. To begin to understand these concepts in ways that can help us as teachers, we have to unpack some simplistic notions, and define the basic dimensions of what it means to be well.

Wellness has received considerable attention in the media. Although enjoyable, this association with consumerism and fleeting moments of satisfaction does not nearly begin to address the depth of reflection and thoughtfulness required to lead a rich and fulfilling life. To further confuse matters, there is a lack of clarity on the differences between the terms *health* and *wellness*. Our first order of business, then, is to understand the differences between those terms and what they mean.

In the Western world, we generally consider *good health* to be the absence of illness (and, truly, we have made remarkable strides in medicine to treat and eradicate diseases). However, while the absence of illness suggests that you are in good health, it does not necessarily mean that you are living a fulfilled life and living up to your full potential. This is where wellness enters the picture. In Western medicine, as the patient, you are the receiver of treatment; in a wellness model, you are utilizing your strengths toward actively maintaining health and recovering from illness. Taking

Teaching the Whole Musician. Paola Savvidou, Oxford University Press (2021). © Oxford University Press.
DOI: 10.1093/oso/9780190868796.003.0001

ownership over recovery means increased self-reliance and more successful long-term outcomes.

This differentiation between the two terms is addressed in the definitions created by the World Health Organization (WHO). The WHO states in its constitution that health is "a state of complete physical, mental and social well-being and not merely the absence of disease or infirmity."[1] This is a more expanded definition than the view of health described earlier; the WHO definition of wellness addresses not only the physical, mental, and social dimensions, but also the level of fulfillment in one's life: "Wellness is the optimal state of health for individuals and groups. There are two focal concerns: the realization of the fullest potential of an individual physically, psychologically, socially, spiritually, and economically, and the fulfillment of one's role expectations in the family, community, place of worship, workplace and other settings."[2] This definition includes spiritual, financial, and occupational dimensions within the context of personal fulfillment.

Let's pause here for a moment and address what you may be thinking: What does wellness have to do with teaching music? The short answer is that, as music teachers, we play a significant role in the lives of young musicians as they prepare to launch into a profession that challenges them to develop a clear sense of meaning and purpose. Presumably, we want our students to succeed, and because music-making is not *just* a profession, but a line of work that is intimately connected to these personal identity factors, it is prudent for us to understand how we can support our students so they can, in turn, lead long-lasting and thriving careers in the arts. I should clarify that our students need to take responsibility for and ownership of their own wellness. They must ultimately take responsibility for the decisions concerning their long-term health and well-being. However, as students explore the complexity inherent in pursuing wellness, a process informed by numerous external factors, it should quickly become apparent that pedagogues have an important role to play. As teachers we have the capacity to positively impact our students' habits, mindset, and confidence. Beyond empowering them to take an active role in the pursuit of a fulfilled life in the arts, we know that helping others contributes toward transcendence: acting in ways that don't involve yourself only, but that contribute to a greater sense of good. Therefore, there may be personal satisfaction reasons, too, for helping our students, in that we can attain a greater sense of well-being for ourselves.

We will continue to explore the benefits of supporting our students' holistically throughout the book, but, for now, let's go back to the theories of well-being for a moment and untangle all their moving parts.

Theories of Well-Being

Theories in the field of wellness attempt to answer fundamental questions such as: Is merely having more positive than negative experiences a satisfactory measure for long-term happiness? Do people essentially achieve well-being when they get what they want? What if what they want is morally wrong? And how do intrinsic values, social relationships, and personal goals fit in? Obviously, since humans are complex beings, no singular theory can fully answer these complex questions. In broad terms, the existing theories fall under three main categories: (1) hedonism (preference for pleasure over pain), (2) desire-satisfaction (fulfilling personal wishes), and (3) objective list (measuring well-being against lists that include items such as friendships and knowledge). A fourth category, well-being theory, has emerged in the research of Martin Seligman, considered by many as the father of positive psychology, that encompasses elements of all three aforementioned categories. We will use Seligman's framework as a basis for exploring these theories.

Martin Seligman arrived at his well-being theory after rigorous research involving thousands of people. In his TED Talk, "The New Era of Positive Psychology," he discusses three types of lives: a life of pleasure; the good life; and the meaningful life. Let's take a closer look at these, as they each hold a key to understanding our sense of happiness and, by extension, our wellness.

A life of pleasure is one in which people seek experiences that will result in positive emotions. We all have the friend who is always up for a night out, one more game, or declining a rote task in favor of a fun activity. This terminology within the context of happiness is parallel to the *hedonic* approach toward well-being, which focuses on pleasure, happiness, and avoidance of problems or pain, and falls under the first category of theories mentioned previously.[3] For many people, it is more fun to go out for ice cream than it is to mow the lawn! And that makes sense because such experiences release the "feel-good" hormones in the body (such as dopamine, oxytocin, and endorphins), which elicit positive feelings. Although undoubtedly more enjoyable, exclusively opting for hedonistic pleasures may be not be as fulfilling as we think. We all encounter circumstances that challenge us to give up immediate, short-term pleasures in order to fulfill important personal and professional responsibilities. We may be much better served by balancing those dosages of pleasurable experiences against the commitment to intentionality that will lead to long-term personal growth and satisfaction.

In contrast to an existence rooted in pleasure, the "good life" is one in which people pursue activities that use their personality strengths, even if it challenges them. Some people excel at being organized and tidy. You may have a friend who never gets tired of helping you rearrange your bookshelf, cleaning off your desk, or unpacking those ancient moving boxes from the attic. In such cases where someone is able to focus on performing a task that simultaneously challenges them and activates a core strength, they may achieve a state of "flow." As described by Mihalyi Csikszentmihalyi, this theory posits that people are happy when they are immersed in an activity that matches their skill level.[4]

Within the "good life" we can see aspects of desire-satisfaction theories of well-being, which postulate that people are happy when their desires are fulfilled, no matter how much pleasure (or difficulty) is associated with achieving their goals. A counterargument for these theories is that a goal may be satisfying temporarily (for example, owning an extensive stamp collection), but may not contribute to long-term happiness. Moreover, one's personal wishes may be potentially inconsiderate, or even damaging, to others (e.g., if my goal is to watch every late-night talk show on TV, it could be interrupting my roommate's sleep and interfering with her success in school).

Finally, the "meaningful life," also called "eudaemonic well-being" in the formal research context, refers to the degree to which a person is leading a fulfilled life, finding meaning, and the quality of their social relationships.[5] It's a state of being that one has to work toward, rather than a fleeting feel-good emotion; it represents the act of living a life with greater purpose.

The theoretical distinction between a life of meaning and a life of pleasure has its limitations. People are complex beings, and, while they may be pursuing meaning in their personal and professional lives, that does not preclude them from also wanting to have pleasurable experiences, which is why Seligman built on these three types of lives to develop a theory grounded in a holistic approach to wellness. His well-being theory (WBT) is outlined in his book *Flourishing: A Visionary New Understanding of Happiness and Well-Being*. Indicators for the WBT include both pleasurable and fulfilling components, in addition to other unique predictors, i.e., positive emotion, engagement, relationships, meaning, and achievement (also referred to as PERMA). Measuring well-being against objective measures adheres to the third theory of objective lists mentioned at the beginning of this section. Positive emotions refer to emotions such as happiness and joy. Engagement has to do with the level of active involvement in daily activities. Connecting with others, feeling valued, and having meaningful relationships fall under the relationship category. Meaning suggests having a sense of purpose that is greater than the self, i.e., positively contributing to other people's lives. Finally, achievement is the desire to accomplish goals. This model may be more realistic for students who not only want to pursue their passion, but also wish to maximize enjoyment during their time in college. In the midst of the daily grind, perhaps pursuing enjoyable experiences as well may increase their overall sense of well-being.

Indeed, researchers in the field have validated this theory through rigorous empirical studies. The results show that PERMA can predict flourishing outcomes in individuals. For example, Coffey et al., in a longitudinal study in a college population, showed that sophomore PERMA can predict interviews for post-graduate opportunities in those students' senior year. The same study also found that the results of PERMA predicted better physical health and academic success two years after.[6] Knowing that positive emotions, engagement, connection, relationships, and meaning can gauge students' life satisfaction and longer-term success, could we, for example, encourage our students' full and positive engagement with their studies? Develop a meaningful teacher–mentor relationship with them? Foster a warm and supportive environment within the studio? Help them set goals to work toward so they can feel a sense of accomplishment? Many of us already practice these behaviors, so perhaps this gives you context for the work you are already doing with your students.

Several researchers have developed theories of well-being that are based on measuring fulfilled (or eudaemonic) lives against objective factors. Carol Ryff and colleagues at the University of Wisconsin–Madison, for example, identified six factors that encompass meaningful well-being: autonomy, environmental mastery, personal growth, positive relations with others, purpose in life, and self-acceptance.[7] Corey Keyes, sociologist and psychologist, developed a model that complements Ryff's eudaemonic perspective and expands on social interactions. Keyes's five factors that determine social well-being are social acceptance, social actualization, social coherence, social contribution, and social integration.[8] Ryan and Deci, professors of psychology and highly influential researchers on human motivation, embrace the concept of eudaemonia in their self-determination theory (SDT).[9] According to SDT, autonomy (making choices that are true to one's core mission and identity), competence (mastery), and relatedness (connecting with others, a sense of belonging) are three essential psychological needs for psychological growth, integrity, well-being, experiences of vitality, and self-congruence.[10]

SDT illustrates the importance of understanding the "order of operations" in pursuing wellness. It is much harder to achieve balance across the various dimensions if we are not pursuing activities that are rooted in our personal goals. In order to maintain balance across our physical, emotional, and mental health, we need to find meaning in our professional and personal lives. Consider what type of work fulfills you and aims to make your community better. Start there and look for opportunities to integrate such work into your professional life.

You would think that the eudaemonic approach of pursuing a meaningful life automatically means a happy and fulfilled life. Yet, finding happiness is not that simple. Ryan and Deci explain that "eudaimonic theories maintain that not all desires—not all outcomes that a person might value—would yield well-being when achieved."[11] My guess is that you elected a career path in music because it is meaningful to you and not because you were trying to avoid a more difficult path (i.e., pursuing a "life of pleasure"). As a result, you are also likely experiencing many stressful moments alongside those that trigger happiness. The reality is that a career in music comes with intense training, competition, and the stress caused by discipline in the face of uncertain outcomes. If left unchecked, these challenges may leave you unhappy, despite having achieved the very goals you once imagined.

From this short overview of well-being theories, we can deduce that it is a complex and evolving topic that does not have a singular answer to the question of what is well-being and how it is measured. Researchers have developed several instruments (mostly self-reported) that large public health organizations use in national surveys. These tools collect information on various indicators, such as predisposition to well-being (based on personality and genes), age, gender, income, and social relationships.

If we were to boil down the key components on which most theories agree, we might summarize that well-being goes beyond the mere absence of illness, to account for pleasurable experiences, fulfillment of desires, and/or meaningful concepts such as relationships and intrinsic values. Despite the complexity of this work, we can start exploring its practical applications within the applied lesson by discussing the eight dimensions of wellness—a relatable model that is easily adaptable to the music students' challenges.

The Eight Dimensions of Wellness

I was curious to determine how the students I interviewed defined wellness. I was struck by their wisdom and ability to, on the spot, distill such a broad topic into just a few sentences. Here are some of the definitions they came up with:

> Wellness is becoming aware of, acknowledging, and being able to put words to how I'm feeling; understanding why and which external factors are making me feel that way.
>
> Wellness is learning to take care of yourself as a human; checking, assessing and adjusting constantly. I don't think it's one thing, it's a journey.
>
> I would say having a sense of stability. I don't like using the word "balance" because I feel like musicians are never going to feel totally balanced. Feeling like you're able to focus and have the capacity to do the things that you want to do and the things that you value in life.

In these responses, the students touched on expressing emotions, self-care, and the fact that wellness is a way of life that enables us to reach our goals. Even though the word "balance" is used widely to describe wellness, I agree with the student who said musicians can never feel "totally balanced." I view it, rather, as having awareness of our strengths and weaknesses in each area of our lives within the constant interplay of growth and setbacks.

While many people understand the need for balance, they may also only perceive wellness as consisting of the physical and emotional dimensions alone, unaware of the several other components that contribute toward the larger equilibrium. We can look to an established model to account for the multiple modalities of our day-to-day well-being.

In the 1970s, Dr. Bill Hettler established six dimensions of wellness that account for the multidirectional nature of maintaining well-being. A cofounder of the National Wellness Institute (NWI), Hettler established the framework that health is not just a matter of preventing disease, but rather a process of making deliberate choices on a day-to-day basis toward the betterment of self; a way of life that empowers individuals to make choices toward improving each dimension based on their strengths and weaknesses.

Since the wider adoption of this framework, their number has increased from six to eight to include financial and occupational dimensions. The mere existence of eight dimensions doesn't mean that we are living a fulfilled life, however. The NWI defines wellness as "an active process through which people become aware of, and make choices toward, a more successful existence."[12] This definition speaks to the notion that we are active participants in our well-being. I view the eight dimensions as a way to organize the various aspects of our lives that we need to nurture. We can tease apart what troubles us and better understand our needs when thinking about each dimension individually.

Figure 1.1 represents the eight dimensions of wellness. The overlap between the petals suggests that one area affects the other, and together they make us whole. Think about a student, for example, who has a physical injury. It's not possible to avoid feelings of fear and anxiety and negative thought patterns. Perhaps it also affects income if she is unable to perform, and her social relationships if she is feeling a sense of shame about her injury and is avoiding her peer group. Because of the comprehensive nature of this approach, the eight dimensions of wellness model is now widely adopted on college campuses as a framework for on-campus services within the overarching goal of helping students become self-reliant in terms of health and well-being. Now let's look at the eight dimensions and think about common challenges music students face in each of these areas.

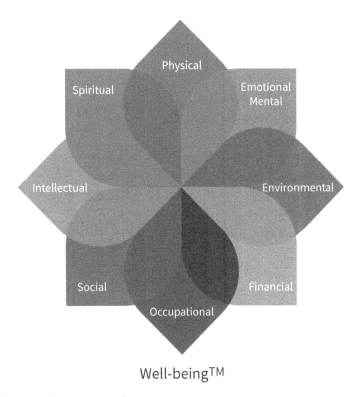

Well-being™

Figure 1.1. The eight dimensions of wellness.

Reproduced by permission from the University of Michigan Student Life.

Physical Wellness

Physical wellness refers to our physical body and what we do to maintain our strength and stamina to carry out our daily tasks with ease. Music students tend to resist the notion that they need to exercise. Too often we hear the excuse that "life is too busy, who has time to exercise?" While it is true that life is busy, especially when you are in school, taking care of your body gives you the strength to maintain your alignment for the long hours of practice. Exercising—whether running, yoga, baseball, or going for a long walk—is one way to support our physical wellness. Whatever type of exercise we choose, it must be tailored to our individual physique, lifestyle, schedule, and preference for type of activity. Making conscious choices about how to fuel our bodies helps to maintain energy levels and good health.

Emotional/Mental Wellness

In this model, emotional wellness is paired with mental wellness. Together they refer to the awareness of our feelings and the ability to manage stressful situations. We ask our students to tap into emotion as they make music, and we also need to honor the fact that emotional tumult exists in their lives beyond the lesson. Such situations include functioning in a competitive environment, prioritizing of a multitude of tasks, tackling a heavy workload, and anxiety related to performance. No doubt this is an area of critical importance that, unfortunately, many students struggle to manage.

Environmental Wellness

Environmental wellness is defined as the impact we have on our environment and the effect our environment has on us. The focus here is on how our environment impacts us. For example, students enrolled in academic institutions don't have much control over which practice rooms are available to them or the temperature in the performance hall. Elements such as a cold room can affect sensation in your hands, lack of proper humidity control can cause dryness in the throat, and a poorly lit practice room may cause the head to jut forward in order to read the music. Awareness of how our environment affects us allows us to make adjustments to minimize a negative impact (e.g., bring an extra lamp into the practice room or extra layers in the performance hall) and to be mindful of what we can and cannot change.

Financial Wellness

Financial wellness is an area that students commonly shy away from. Financial wellness refers to our relationship with money, the tools we develop for managing our budget, and the opportunities we seek to make money. Without exception, every semester of my wellness class includes a module on financial wellness, during which the students openly express that budgeting and planning for their financial stability are intimidating topics. It makes sense that this topic would be uncomfortable, not only because the music profession is not known for its cushy jobs, but also because we don't always have the time or resources to address this topic. In other words, thinking about money can be overwhelming. We must help our students overcome these feelings, which can greatly impact other dimensions of wellness. Although beyond the scope of this book, several resources exist to support artists' financial circumstances.

Occupational Wellness

The work we do and how it fulfills us falls under "occupational wellness." Most likely, students are not employed full-time in the music profession; however, they have already made the choice to follow a career in the arts, which will fulfill them and offer a sense of purpose. Because earning a degree has numerous requirements, it is important not to lose sight of that purpose while in college and to actively pursue activities that bring about inspiration and spark curiosity. Gigs and teaching opportunities while in school are a way to actively engage with creating a career in the arts and to be fulfilled from the joy of creating and sharing music with the community. This category is especially essential as it governs our satisfaction with life on a day-to-day basis.

Social Wellness

Social wellness depends on the degree to which one participates in healthy interpersonal relationships. While in-person relationships are the main source in which students develop a sense of social well-being, long-distance and digital relationships can equally contribute to one's social wellness, which can be impacted via the enormous amount of time students spend alone in a practice room. One can feel isolation and can get caught up in one's own thoughts for days at a time. Finding a social circle to connect with, friends to talk through problems with, a support network for times of stress, and socially enriching opportunities, create a sense of belonging.

Intellectual Wellness

The university setting is an ideal environment for nurturing intellectual wellness. Taking stimulating courses, learning how to think, and accessing educational resources all contribute toward students' ability to learn from different perspectives, challenge their own beliefs, and grow in their intellectual curiosity. Being able to apply new knowledge to affect behavior is a sign of intellectual wellness.[13] An example of this behavior is the ability to transfer practice techniques learned through one piece of music to another, more challenging work. This kind of growth, through perseverance, could lead to a strong internal locus of control.[14] An internal locus of control means that a person understands she is responsible for her own wellness, illness, or problems, instead of blaming others or external circumstances (i.e., external locus of control).

Spiritual Wellness

Defined as how we make meaning of our place and purpose and where we go for comfort, spiritual wellness completes the flower petals. Religion and church groups often provide spiritual fulfillment. For many musicians, music fulfills the need for spirituality. Further, mind/body practices, such as yoga or Tai Chi, are often described as having a spiritual component. Regardless of your spiritual orientation, accounting for this dimension of wellness may help develop connection to others, whether through a formalized religious organization, or more broadly through your own social pursuits. Beyond connecting with other people, spiritual practices can also contribute toward a greater sense of connection to self or with higher powers.

At the end of the chapter, you will find several assessments to use as a starting place for exploring wellness. These assessments may help you realize your strengths and identify areas that may need your attention.

Who Is the Twenty-First-Century College Student?

To understand how to support students in a holistic manner, it is advisable to explore the psyche of the twenty-first-century student. The sociocultural landscape has evolved immensely over the past few decades relative to our tertiary music curricula. How many teachers now use memes in classroom presentations to get a point across? How many utilize digital learning spaces, such as group video calls, in some capacity? How many of you have students who juggle holding a job while they study, or who serve as the head of their household while also pursuing their studies? The way we interact with technology, access information, and concern ourselves with the realities of today are significantly different from even a decade ago.

Despite the challenges of our changing landscape, there are resources available that effectively capture the state of college students' wellness. The American College Health Association (ACHA) is the leading organization advocating for college students' health. With a membership of approximately 1,100 institutions, ACHA advances our understanding of the challenges that students face through advocacy, research, and education. ACHA has created the National College Health Assessment (NCHA), which is a tool that universities use to collect information about their students' health habits, behaviors, and perceptions. In examining the most recent data available from the spring of 2019, we can gain perspectives on our students' views and the challenges they face. The data show information that we probably all know to be true because of our experiences: the top five impediments to academic performance are stress, anxiety, sleep difficulties, depression, and illness such as cold, flu, or sore throat. Within the previous twelve months prior to when the survey was conducted, 86.5 percent of students felt overwhelmed by all their responsibilities, 83.4 percent felt exhausted (but not from physical activity), 67.3 percent felt sad, and 60.9 percent felt overwhelming anxiety.[15] The negative impact on students' school-work included lower exam grades, disruption of thesis or dissertation progress, and incomplete or dropped courses.[16] Other studies confirm that the self-reported health status of students is generally low and is associated with emotional stress, psychosomatic ailments, and financial concerns.[17] The information presented here certainly sounds the alarm for students who need our support.

Viewing wellness through the lens of its eight dimensions means examining multiple areas of a student's life, e.g., nutrition, physical exercise, and sleep, to form a complete picture of the strengths or weaknesses that may be affecting the top five impediments noted in the preceding paragraph. When given the opportunity, we likely already encourage our students to eat well, exercise, and get enough sleep. Yet, when it comes down to it, what are they actually doing? Here are some data that will help answer this question: The NCHA 2019 assessment showed that only 4.3 percent of students eat the recommended five or more servings of fruits and vegetables per day. Only a mere 11.5 percent of the students surveyed get enough sleep on a daily basis to feel well rested in the morning; 45.2 percent of students get enough sleep between three to five days per week. As far as physical exercise is concerned, 45.6 percent meet the recommendations for moderate-intensity exercise, vigorous-intensity exercise, or a combination of the two. Of the total number of students surveyed, 58.4 percent have consumed alcohol within the last thirty days of the study.[18] The alarming part of alcohol usage is not the number of students who reported alcohol consumption, but the percentage who reported a negative experience when drinking alcohol. Approximately 50 percent of students who reported alcohol consumption noted that, in the last twelve months, they did something they regretted, got in trouble with the police, had a blackout, had sex with someone without their consent, considered suicide, or injured themselves or others. To deal with this widespread issue of students' reporting less-than-optimal health, health initiatives have started, such as the Healthy Campus 2020 in the United States by the American College Health Association and Healthy Universities in the United Kingdom.

It's impossible to know the cause and effect for every difficulty our students face. Lack of sleep may be the result of stress or, vice versa, insomnia may be causing stress. In any case, these facts present a sweeping image of what students are dealing with in the twenty-first century and can help us gain perspective for when students raise concerns about feeling tired or overwhelmed. Even accounting for these broadly applicable issues, music students face some particular wellness obstacles that demand further exploration.

Wellness Profile of the Music Student

Music students are unique within the general student population because they receive a large portion of their education through one-on-one interaction with their professor. Many other degree programs provide flexibility in the first two years prior to declaring a major, whereas music students are admitted into their program as incoming freshmen. This means that music students are often locked into a highly rigorous curriculum from day one. Music degrees are by no means the only demanding course of study available. And yet, examining prominent research around students' health illuminates the unique circumstances that challenge music students.

When compared with students in biomedical science and nursing, music performance students scored significantly lower for health responsibility (meaning behaviors to take care of themselves), physical activity, and spiritual growth, as well as self-efficacy and self-regulation.[19] A study by Spahn's team (a group of professors and researchers in performing arts medicine in Germany) compared music students' psychological and physical symptoms at the beginning of university study with students who are studying medicine, psychology, and sports.[20] Music students reported much higher levels of physical symptoms and anxiety than did medical and sports students. Overall, approximately a fourth of the 247 students investigated in this study were dealing with impairments that affected their playing. The results from these studies are certainly not comforting (hence the need for books like this one), but they do give us specific information about areas that need attention. Considering the limited resources committed to educational endeavors on this topic, instructors are finding themselves on the front lines of dealing with many of these issues.

Music students' life satisfaction is associated with "setting clear goals, autotelic experiences, and an optimal balance between challenge and skill."[21] Well-being, coping strategies, perfectionism, and sleep quality were among the areas researched in a study led by Araújo et al., which screened 483 undergraduate and graduate students from ten conservatoires in the United Kingdom and Switzerland.[22] When compared with their peers, music students rated higher in terms of their well-being and indicated lower levels of fatigue, even though, paradoxically, they rated lower in engaging health behaviors and stress management. Students generally report lower levels of fatigue, perhaps indicating that the fulfilling aspect of their daily lives is energizing rather than draining. They also have poorer sleep hygiene habits when compared with the general population; further, the fact that they do not engage regularly with physical activity may have a negative impact on their performance. Viewing this study in light of the previous discussion on eudaemonic well-being, we can see how living a meaningful life (i.e., a fulfilling, purposeful life) comes with stresses and its own set of challenges. Growth, musical and personal, comes with discomfort and a certain amount of stress, but in the grand scheme of life, the satisfaction of pursuing one's passion outweighs the temporary challenges.

Often, however, the line between the expected level of stress that is conducive to growth crosses over to more severe stress, which has long-term negative effects on students' health. While stress is inevitable in the pursuit of a meaningful life, it must be checked periodically and controlled by both internal and external mechanisms. As pedagogues, we play a special role in helping our students account for and mediate stress by encouraging activities that help them counteract their stress.

In terms of music students' physical health, playing-related musculoskeletal disorders are commonplace, as are fatigue, depression, and performance anxiety.[23] High levels of stress may be caused not only by students' busy schedules, but also by how students view their position in a perceived talent hierarchy within the school. Due to the public nature of performance, students know where they stand within their studio and within their department in terms of their talent and skill. Music schools foster an intensely competitive atmosphere for students, i.e., students are routinely ranked in a public hierarchy against their peers.

Perkins et al. investigated the perceived enablers and barriers that music conservatory students face in regard to their optimal health.[24] The researchers interviewed twenty recently graduated or currently studying students. The results divided the enablers and barriers into three categories: lifestyle, support services, and environmental. Enablers in the lifestyle category, as reported by participants, included awareness of health and well-being, the importance of their applied instructor as a support mechanism, and techniques they used to cope with mental health. Lifestyle barriers included physical playing-related problems, lack of time to eat well and to exercise, and alcohol intake. Other challenges related to day-to-day lifestyle included isolation and difficulties with the student-teacher relationship. Ninety-five percent of students interviewed identified support sources such as the Alexander technique, their applied instructor, medical professionals, and conservatoire welfare teams. Fifty-five percent felt that the conservatoire did not offer enough support for their health and well-being. Environmental enablers included experiencing emotionally impactful performances, growing as a person, and maintaining strong relationships. Barriers in this category included comparisons with other students, stress caused by a competitive environment, and a heavy workload. As with any study, these results provide a snapshot of a small group of students within a specific environment. My experience has shown that these outcomes can be applied in a broader context, particularly in identifying the applied instructor as the main source of support and physical injuries as a major barrier toward physical health.

Isolation is another contributing barrier toward students maintaining their wellness.[25] They spend a large amount of their time practicing alone, and the interaction they have with faculty is either one-on-one or in a classroom with minimal social interaction. The fact that students may not be reporting their injuries or expressing their struggles can make it difficult for teachers to know how and when to help them. Keeping quiet about injuries also prevents institutions from making curricular changes to provide training on wellness or to identify needs to train their faculty and staff on how to support their students. A piano student identified some of the difficulties aptly in her response to my question about challenges faced:

> As a pianist, I'm spending a lot of time alone. It's really easy to get secluded and become a loner, especially since there's less opportunity for pianists to meet other students since we don't get the experience of a large ensemble. You don't have those opportunities unless you really put yourself out there. It just feels really overwhelming to be at a school with so many resources and so many people but at the same time you feel isolated from students in other departments.

Her observation of being in a big place yet feeling alone points to the fact that living in a place with lots of people and resources does not automatically mean you are part of that greater network of people or that you are necessarily taking advantage of the available offerings.

Students know that engaging with healthy behaviors has a positive impact on their wellness, yet they still may choose not to act on that knowledge.[26] Simply having the requisite information available does not mean that they will choose to engage with it in ways that would be beneficial for their health. Academic administrators and educators must actively create environments in which health is considered a fundamental component of being a musician.

Working with music students requires an understanding of their individual backgrounds and a sensitivity to the realities they face at this critical time in their careers, which may be different in many ways from those of their teacher. Teaching the student as a whole person, beyond their musical skills and talents, reinforces the interconnectedness of all the areas of their lives and the importance of supporting their music studies through healthy behaviors in other areas.

The values of the institution and its actions to support students' wellness have an enormous impact on the students. Chesky, professor of music and prominent researcher in the performing arts medicine field, and his team recognized that music faculty "represent the primary channels for changing how music is taught and played in order to reduce performance injuries."[27] The authors also claimed that faculty involvement in students' performance health is crucial in order to ensure the success of medical professionals who are treating the students. In observing my own microcosm at the University of Michigan, I can attest to both of these aspects.

Since starting the wellness program here, several students have noted a shift in the school's culture. A greater number of students and faculty alike are choosing to discuss injuries, mental health concerns, and inquire about the resources available to assist them. On the medical side of the program, the healthcare professionals we work with have been able to secure greater levels of funding to develop new research within the performing arts and support more specialists. In fact, building collaborative opportunities that tap into medical science is key to identifying which wellness issues are most prevalent, treatable, and preventable. This isn't a novel concept, though, and we can look to some established models for how performing artists and medical professionals can work together to optimize our learning environments.

Performing Arts Medicine Overview

The roots of the performing arts medicine field can be traced back to the 1980s, even though other studies on musicians' health extend back to the mid-twentieth century. In the 1980s, pianists Leon Fleisher and Gary Graffman went public about their injuries. Well-loved books such as *A Soprano on her Head* by Eloise Ristad and *The Inner Game of Music* by Barry Green and Timothy Gallway, along with well-respected journals such as *Tension in Performance* by the International Society for Tension in Performance (ISSTIP), were published in the years that followed. Among its many contributions to the performing arts medicine field, ISSTP (founded by Carola Grindea in 1980) set up the first performing arts clinic at the London College of Music in Thames Valley University in 1990, created the first course on musicians' health, and put on the first International Forum of Health and the Performing Arts in 1997.

Martin Fishbein et al. completed the first large-scale research survey on medical problems of orchestral musicians in 1988.[28] Since the 1980s, the number of publications on the topic of musicians' health has grown by 400 percent.[29] During the 1990s, publications on the topic of performing arts wellness expanded to include somatic practices such as the Alexander technique and yoga. In 1989, a group of medical practitioners who were treating performing artists formed the Performing Arts Medicine Association (PAMA). PAMA has become a highly respected organization, leading education and research in the performing arts. Its membership includes medical professionals, educators in the performing arts, and administrators. The first *Medical Problems of Performing Artist* journal, published in 1986, preceded the official creation of the association. PAMA continues to be an active organization in sponsoring annual symposia and training sessions, publishing research, providing online resources, and maintaining an online referral directory of healthcare professionals working with performing artists. PAMA also collaborates with affiliate organizations, such as the Music Teachers National Association (MTNA), to present educational workshops. The first collaboration between PAMA and MTNA occurred in 2014, presenting a pre-conference day-long seminar in which healthcare professionals and musicians presented on the topic of musicians' health. MTNA continues its efforts to educate through an established wellness track at its Pedagogy Saturday pre-conference day. There are ample resources in the field, and yet there is no coordinated effort among institutions to adopt a single set of policies. Despite the reality that each institution must adhere to its own policies, as individual pedagogues we can look to national models to assist us in our own pedagogical efforts.

PAMA also collaborated with the University of North Texas System to develop a working conference (Health Promotion in Schools of Music) in 2004. One of the most important outcomes of this conference was a report that included initial recommendations for schools of music, which included a framework for approaching injury, consisting of prevention education and intervention.[30] Specific recommendations included the faculty understanding the importance of its role in students' performance health, developing an occupational health course for all music majors, educating students about hearing conservation, and providing education on healthcare resources available to students.

The *2009–2010 NASM Handbook*, published by the National Association for Schools of Music (NASM), first mentioned the need to include health and injury prevention information in music programs. In more recent versions of the *NASM Handbook*, the health standard was expanded to include the requirement of educating students on the "maintenance of hearing, vocal, and musculoskeletal health and injury prevention."[31]

NASM, in collaboration with PAMA, created a series of health advisory brochures on each area noted earlier, which can be used by institutions in the health education of their students. This information provides a starting point from which students can expand their knowledge on these topics and further their own understanding. Links to these brochures are available on the companion website ▶.

A recent survey, aimed at determining the type of wellness offerings music schools have available on their websites, showed that, out of 617 music schools, almost half do not include information on musicians' health.[32] Forty-seven schools offer classes in musicians' health, the majority of which are taught by faculty with backgrounds in somatic training. A mere 27 schools offer initiatives that go beyond the offering of one course. Through these findings, we can see that, even though educating students on injury prevention has become an NASM requirement, music schools have not adopted a standardized approach for delivering this information. As such, applied instructors play a powerful role in supporting their students' wellness, particularly in schools with limited offerings.

Students across the country are struggling to maintain their wellness in the face of the particular challenges of their craft. In order to thrive, aspiring artists need to find their own balance among the various dimensions of wellness. The artisan nature of musical training, foundationally based on the mentorship from an artist-teacher, means that pedagogues carry an essential role in the cultivation of their students' wellness, and it is to that subject that we will turn in the next chapter.

Toolkit: Assessing Your Wellness

Reflect on your own wellness as you complete the assessments in Tables 1.1–1.8. You may choose to make these assessments available for your students to help them identify their own strengths and weaknesses. Upon completion, note the areas that you can improve upon and decide on a small actionable step. These assessments are also available on the companion website (Worksheets 1.1–1.8 ▶).

Table 1.1 Physical Wellness Assessment

	Almost Never	Occasionally	Sometimes	Almost Always
I engage in moderately intense exercise on a regular basis (e.g., 3 to 5 times per week).	1	②)	3	4
I warm up/cool down before and after practicing.	1	2	3	④
I maintain a healthy weight for my height.	1	2	3	④
I maintain a healthy sleep schedule (between 7–9 hours per night).	1	2	③	4
I stay hydrated during the day.	1	2	3	④
I eat at least 5 servings of fresh fruits and vegetables every day.	1	2	③	4
I avoid drinking more than 2 alcoholic drinks per day.	1	2	3	④
I avoid taking mood-altering drugs.	1	2	3	④

Table 1.2 Emotional/Mental Wellness Assessment

	Almost Never	Occasionally	Sometimes	Almost Always
I maintain a positive outlook on life.	1	2	3	④
I have positive feelings toward myself.	1	2	3	④
I cope well with life's ups and downs.	1	②	3	4
It's easy for me to laugh.	1	2	3	④
I prioritize effectively.	1	2	3	④
I can express a wide range of feelings in a healthy way.	1	2	③	4
I maintain a balance between my personal needs, work, family, friends, and other obligations.	1	2	3	④
I avoid constant stress and worry.	1	2	③	4
I remain calm under pressure.	1	②	3	4

Table 1.3 Environmental Wellness Assessment

	Almost Never	Occasionally	Sometimes	Almost Always
I adjust my practicing environment to meet my needs (e.g., increase the lighting, bring an air purifier/humidifier).	1	2	3	(4)
I use the minimum amount of printing and paper products for classroom purposes.	1	(2)	3	4
I plan ahead for the temperature in a performance space.	1	2	3	(4)
I find opportunities to spend time outdoors, connecting with nature.	1	2	(3)	4

Table 1.4 Financial Wellness Assessment

	Almost Never	Occasionally	Sometimes	Almost Always
I feel in control over my finances.	1	2	3	(4)
I keep track of my income and expenses on a regular basis.	1	2	3	(4)
I pay my bills on time.	1	2	3	4
I actively save income every month.	1	2	3	4
I seek out opportunities to increase my income.	1	2	3	4
I know how to financially plan for the future.	1	2	3	(4)

Table 1.5 Occupational Wellness Assessment

	Almost Never	Occasionally	Sometimes	Almost Always
I am fulfilled by the profession I decided to pursue.	1	2	3	(4)
I balance my work with other areas of my life.	1	2	3	(4)
I know what skills I need to develop to be successful in my field long term.	1	2	3	(4)
I get satisfaction and enjoyment out of my work on a daily basis.	1	2	3	(4)
I work well with others.	1	2	(3)	4
I am able to find employment when I need it.	1	2	3	4

Table 1.6 Social Wellness Assessment

	Almost Never	Occasionally	Sometimes	Almost Always
I have at least one person in my life whom I trust.	1	2	3	(4)
I have a good relationship with my family.	1	2	3	(4)
I feel supported by the administration and faculty in my department.	1	2	3	(4)
I have friends at school or work that I enjoy spending time with.	1	2	3	(4)
I set aside time to spend with friends and family.	1	2	3	(4)
I am able to say "no" when I need to.	1	2	(3)	4
I give and receive equally in my relationships.	1	2	3	(4)
I consider my colleagues' feelings when I give them feedback about their performance.	1	2	(3)	4
I don't take feedback about my performance personally and I try to improve.	1	2	(3)	4

Table 1.7 Intellectual Wellness Assessment

	Almost Never	Occasionally	Sometimes	Almost Always
I actively seek out opportunities for growth.	1	2	3	(4)
I enjoy learning new skills.	1	2	3	(4)
I view problem-solving as an exciting challenge.	1	2	(3)	4
I collect facts before making decisions.	1	2	3	(4)
I know how to research topics that interest me, using the library and electronic resources.	1	2	3	(4)
I enjoy being intellectually challenged in my lessons and classes.	1	2	(3)	4
I seek to increase my understanding and knowledge of different topics by asking questions and researching.	1	(2)	3	4
I am open to new ideas.	1	2	(3)	4
I respect the viewpoint of others even if it is different from my own.	1	2	(3)	4

Table 1.8 Spiritual Wellness Assessment

	Almost Never	Occasionally	Sometimes	Almost Always
I make time to reflect on my life.	1	2	3	(4)
I integrate my spiritual practice of choice in my daily life.	1	2	3	(4)
I have a sense of greater purpose for my life.	1	2	3	(4)
I have strong values and beliefs that guide my life.	1	2	3	(4)
I am tolerant of other people's views on spirituality.	1	2	(3)	4

2

Parent, Teacher, Mentor, or Psychologist?

The Multifaceted Role of the Applied Instructor

As we explored in the previous chapter, while institutions are beginning to adopt policies and procedures that broadly support wellness, the individual private instructor is on the front lines of integrating those resources into their students' education. The nature of weekly one-on-one lessons cultivates an environment in which students can develop lifelong personal connections to their teachers, connections built upon a deep sense of trust. This powerful type of relationship will guide a student's musical development, shape her approach to music-making, and even influence her self-esteem and self-confidence. Applied instructors are thus uniquely poised to address and support their students' well-being.

You are likely to know before anyone else when physical pain or a mental health concern arises. However, due to the competitiveness of the music profession, students may fear that you will perceive them as weak when they openly share such concerns. Of course, we know that is not the case, but that fear does create a barrier for many students. If they don't seek help, the issue could worsen, thus requiring a more drastic resolution. By understanding the complexity of the student–teacher relationship and consistently noting any warning signs, the instructor may be able to detect discomfort, which might spark a productive conversation about the resources for seeking appropriate help. One effective way to address difficult topics is through a technique used in the field of social work called *motivational interviewing*. After we explore the student–teacher mentorship relationship, we will learn useful tools for utilizing this student-centered approach, as well as how to apply them to problem-solving scenarios, at the end of the chapter.

What Type of Teacher Are You?

In order to prepare for these types of conversations, we must first reflect on our own pedagogical journey. Consider how you got started in your career, whom you studied with, and who supported you along the way. Most likely, you are thinking about a mentor figure who advised you, supported you, listened to you, and affected the course of your life in significant ways. That mentor perhaps was a teacher, a friend, or an advisor who helped hone the vision of your future and encouraged you on your journey. This relationship no doubt had a transformative effect on you.

Teaching the Whole Musician. Paola Savvidou, Oxford University Press (2021). © Oxford University Press.
DOI: 10.1093/oso/9780190868796.003.0002

As you contemplate your own path, think about how key mentors have affected your own pedagogical practices. Did you have role models you admired and wished to emulate? Or experiences through which you determined how not to be? The following questions may help you further refine your role as a teacher, particularly as you consider your approach toward maintaining your students' wellness.

- What experiences have shaped your teaching philosophy?
- What do you value most in your teaching?
- As a role model, in what ways do you seek to model positive outcomes for your students?
- What are your primary concerns about your students' well-being?
- Where is there space in your classes/lessons for addressing wellness?
- What are some ways in which you currently address wellness?
- What are your students' backgrounds and the specific challenges they are dealing with?
- What are some common challenges your students face while in college? What tools do you need for helping them address those?
- What experiences with injuries and/or mental health issues can you draw from to relate to your students?

You may be finding that you are already a wellness-minded teacher and actively take steps to support your students. Or perhaps you're wondering how you can address this topic in your teaching. Wherever you are in your process, as long as you have your students' best interests at heart, you will be able to navigate the next steps for deepening your support toward your students' wellness.

The Teacher as a Mentor

Mentorship is not a new concept. Homer's *Odyssey*, in which the young Telemachus was entrusted to Odysseus's friend Mentor while Odysseus was away fighting in the Trojan war, first mentioned the word. Odysseus trusted the wise Mentor to protect Telemachus and to help him along the process of growing and becoming himself. Despite its ancient origins, mentorship's rise in prominence as a pedagogical concept is relatively recent. It wasn't until the 1970s that the word "mentor" was popularized and appeared in writings about improving business culture; later, the word was used in academia within the context of senior and junior faculty mentoring. In the music world, mentoring has been the primary training format for generations. Within the context of music education, mentoring between an established music teacher and a beginning teacher is a common practice. Further, several resources can be drawn from this topic to help us understand the benefits of mentorship and the role of the mentor.

Researchers have set forth three mentoring frameworks, which have laid the foundation for understanding the role of the mentor in a professional context. Broadly speaking, mentoring refers to the relationship between a mentor, who is generally older and more experienced, with a younger, less-experienced mentee. The aim of the relationship is to help mentees in their professional careers within the context of personal values and goals.

Research shows the importance of helping students identify their own unique goals and the power of the mentor to help them actualize even when they grow beyond the bounds of the institution. Kathy Kram developed a framework for understanding relationships in a workplace environment. Her book *Mentoring at Work* (1985) established the understanding of mentorship within a broader context and set a foundation for the research that followed. According to her definition, the mentor fulfills two roles: (1) career functions, e.g., offering support for advancement within the organization, sponsoring, protecting, and increasing the visibility of the mentee; (2) psychosocial functions, e.g., serving as a role model, providing acceptance and friendship, and supporting the mentee's personal growth and sense of self-worth.[1] Even though career and psychosocial functions are based on varying qualities of the mentor as well as the mentor's status within the field, according to more recent research, both functions play a predictive role in the mentee's job and career satisfaction.[2] Kram further established four stages in a mentoring relationship, which can easily be applied toward a teacher–student relationship within the applied lesson context[3]:

Initiation. The mentorship relationship is established. In a teacher–student relationship, each party gets to know one another. At this stage, the mentor provides more direct guidance.

Cultivation. In this phase, the relationship starts to shift toward a two-way sharing of ideas rather than a one-way path in which the mentor provides all the solutions. When students learn a new technique or style for the first time, they will need more guidance from the instructor. Over time, as their experience grows, they are able to contribute their own ideas and solutions.

Separation. Due to either the person moving on to a different location, or because of psychological reasons, the mentorship relationship may end when the student graduates and moves away. From experience, we know that many music teacher–student mentorship relationships survive beyond changes in location or degree attainment.

Redefinition. If the mentorship relationship was strong, the next phase would be redefining the relationship, even after separation. The pair may move on to a friendship or peer relationship.

The relationship between music teacher and student embodies these characteristics. Many teachers develop relationships that last well beyond the period of study. Another layer to the relationship is the mentee's stages of development, as defined by Laurent Daloz, who was instrumental in developing programs for traditional and nontraditional adult learners.[4] These three stages begin with an inward focus and move toward a more outward view. The first stage is surviving. In the case of our students, they are in a new environment and are coming to terms with their new and, often, overwhelming schedules. They are focused on themselves and how to stay on top of their day-to-day tasks. The second stage is striving. They have gotten a good handle on college life and are able to work toward their goals of improving and growing. During these first two stages, the mentee needs affirmation, encouragement, and motivation from the mentor. In the third stage, thriving, the student has gone through the bulk of her training or has already graduated and is more focused on the impact of the work. The student has gained independence and is finding professional success.

The third framework is Erik Erickson's theory of psychosocial development (1963), which presents key psychosocial tasks in eight different stages, ranging from infancy to the older adult. The seventh step in Erickson's theory is *generativity*, which refers to the need for people in middle adulthood to nurture others and contribute in a way that will benefit future generations. Therefore, if we ascribe to Erickson's theory, we can assume that faculty of that age group have a natural inclination to serve as mentors because of the innate need to ensure the success of the next generation of musicians.

The wealth of research developed in the past 50 years continues to explore the rich and complex relationships that affect our lives. A commonality among the frameworks for mentorship is that the mentor is usually part of the mentee's life for a short period of time. As the student moves into professional life, the teacher is present to support him but is not actively involved in his decision-making.

Daloz, in a beautiful definition of the longevity and evolution of this relationship, says: "Few teachers or mentors ever see a student through an entire journey. Rather, we accompany students along some legs of some of their journeys, and if we are to play our part well, we need to view their movement with a broader eye, to see whence they have come and wither they are headed."[5] Even though we may only be with our students for a short period of time, encouraging continued growth beyond our shared time together can help build confidence and provide the tools needed for a lifetime of success.

Characteristics of a Music Teacher Mentor

A primary goal of the mentorship relationship is for aspiring musicians to achieve independence and develop confidence in their abilities. Students rely on their teachers for improving their craft and for understanding how they measure up against other performers in their field. The professor will help the student to see her strengths and believe in herself. The student gains the musical guidance of someone who is established in the field, as well as emotional support while navigating through life in college and performance-related stresses. Beyond the college years, a mentor assists the student in preparing for his career path and helps connect him with contacts, thus expanding his professional network and employment opportunities.

The benefits of the mentorship relationship for the student are more obvious than the benefits for the teacher. The mentor presumably receives personal satisfaction in witnessing the progress of the mentee toward autonomy. Based on Erickson's idea of generativity mentioned previously, a mentor finds inherent value in passing on her knowledge and wisdom to the next generation. In a reciprocal relationship, the mentor may benefit from the students' ideas and perspectives as well. In many ways, this mirrors a parent–child relationship.

At the heart of mentorship lies the perception of the mentor (by the student) as a parental figure. One of my colleagues phrased this phenomenon by saying, "It's only natural for young people to put on (for better or for worse) their models for mentorship and guidance a familiar structure. So, psychologically speaking, anytime there is an imparting of information, one is driving from a memory bank of other ways that information has been imparted previously."

The teacher, then, becomes a person of critical importance in the life of the student. In a webinar for the Frances Clark Center of Keyboard Pedagogy, Dr. Julie Jaffee Nagel (psychotherapist, psychoanalyst, and musician) explains that teachers are "internalized" by their students. As she says, "You'll never forget your first piano teacher." The influence of what she has taught you (beyond the skill of playing the piano) will forever be imprinted in your memory. This points to the fact that caring for your students' overall well-being can have a long-lasting and positive impact on the students.

Reflecting back on your own experience with an incredible mentor, what exactly were the characteristics that made her so effective? Was it her teaching abilities combined with her faith in you? Was it the way she pushed you out of the bird's nest (so to speak) and into the world when you were nearing graduation? Or was it how he listened to you when you entered his office, overwhelmed and nearly in tears? My guess is that it's a combination of all these and more. Here, I have compiled key characteristics of a music mentor from existing resources on mentorship, as well as from my own interviews with colleagues and students.[6] As you read through these, you might consider the characteristics you exhibit and how they are perceived by your students.

Excellent musician. First and foremost, the student views the teacher as the expert in her craft. The teacher's performance ability is inspiring, exciting, and motivating. We often first see students absorb their teacher's performing style and mannerisms before they develop their own. At the graduate level especially, students seek out professors who are well known within their field. All the graduate students I interviewed mentioned that musicianship of the highest quality was of utmost importance in applying for schools. Some of them, who were also dealing with a past or present injury, were looking for a mentor with experience and success in retraining the fundamental technique of former students.

Effective teacher. An effective teacher is able to identify elements of his students' performance that are successful and to provide constructive criticism in a way that helps the student grow and flourish.

Trustworthy. A student who is away from home may view the teacher as a parental figure from time to time. Conversations about stress or fears about the future are not uncommon in a private lesson. A teacher-mentor is one who always has the student's interest in mind and can be trusted for confidentiality and advice. In reflecting back to her master's degree, one of the doctoral students I spoke with said: "I don't think I developed trust in my professor until the end of my first year. I had enough trust that I was going through the painstaking process of rebuilding my technique [after an injury], but it wasn't until the end of that first year that I trusted my teacher's guidance through it." While trust is fundamental in this relationship, it can take a while to build.

In a conversation about building trust within the studio, one of my colleagues reminded me that "trust requires testing." He went on to say, "I have to provide that measure of safety for the students to test the trust. Testing a trust means they have to know they're safe to disagree with me." These words illuminate the importance of the student finding courage to question and to try new things without fear of being judged. It also allows the student to feel comfortable making deeper and more personal connections with the music, thus leading to more engaging performances. Daloz eloquently phrases the need for trust in the process of growth when he says: "At the heart of development is trust, a willingness to let go, to listen to voices we too often struggle to shut out, to receive clear-eyed what the world has to offer. Such trust rarely happens in a vacuum. We need other people with whom to practice that trust."[7]

Knowledge of career possibilities. Gigs and job opportunities usually arrive in the applied instructor's inbox. From there, the instructor either reaches out to individual students or sends out a mass email to the studio. By connecting students to opportunities, the teacher helps them create their own contacts and network that will serve them down the road. Beyond the employment opportunities that come up during a student's degree, a mentor is able to offer guidance for the future, and connect the student with people who can support their professional advancement. An interviewee felt strongly that graduate students, especially, should be treated as potential colleagues: "Your professor should be someone who's going to help raise you to the professional level that they're at, so they see you as a potential colleague and not like someone who is never going to be as good as them." Indeed, the way to move our profession forward is to nurture our students to exceed both our expectations and our own successes.

Good listener. Lesson time is precious, and I believe we can all agree that we want to use every minute of it productively and effectively. Because of this, there may be a tendency for a one-way approach in which the teacher takes over the lesson, inadvertently leaving little time for the student to contribute. The students I spoke with expressed (in slightly different language) that they value a mentor who listens, invests in their emotional world, and can put herself in their shoes. Of course, we have our agenda for each lesson, for the semester, and the degree plan. That's our job! There are going to be times that the plan is disrupted, however. Perhaps the student is dealing with insomnia, anxiety, or an injury that threatens to derail an entire degree program. It is heartbreaking to hear that students have been told, "Your depression sounds like an excuse for not practicing," from a teacher who perhaps has never dealt with a mental health issue. It is our responsibility to listen and understand when students share difficulties, so we can provide appropriate guidance, connect them with resources, and adjust plans and expectations accordingly. Actively listening involves making eye contact, paying attention to what the student is saying and how she is saying it, and ensuring that what you heard is what she intended to communicate. Reflecting back (in other words, paraphrasing and repeating back) what the mentee said, in order to confirm your understanding, is an important step in proper communication and in giving her a sense that she is being heard (see section on motivational interviewing for more information about this process).

Professional status. The relationship begins either because the instructor recruited the student to the institution or because the student sought out the mentor because of her professional status. A professional status is important, as the mentor can use her influence to help mentees advance in their career and vouch for them when opportunities arise.

Vulnerability. "Vulnerability," in the words of a colleague, "is being authentic in [the students'] process of learning and acknowledging that I'm learning in some way, too." There will be times when you make mistakes (no one is perfect!), and it is significant for the students to know it is okay not to know everything. Where appropriate, it is important for students to see your humanity. It gives them permission to accept their own mistakes and sets an example for when it's their turn to be a mentor down the road.

Honesty. After living in the United States for over two decades, I have adapted the way I offer feedback in lessons, especially to younger children. I learned about the *sandwich* approach (praise-criticism-praise) and have worked on how to offer praise without sounding dishonest (especially when a student is still in the rough stages of learning a piece). Honest feedback and advice can still come from a place of love and support. There will be times when what you have to say is difficult to hear, but is valued, respected, and helpful in the long run.

Nurture. The incubation period of a student's life (i.e., the time while she is in school) is a time when the student needs a teacher's attention and care. Much like the parental role in early childhood, a teacher can help his students grow in confidence and self-efficacy during this time by providing the necessary conditions. In nature, nurturing also refers to providing sustenance or food. In the context of music lessons, the instructor provides intellectual stimulation for growth.

Ask the right questions. For long-lasting learning to occur, a student has to make her own mistakes and learn from those mistakes. The responsibility of the teacher is to help her identify the mistakes and work out her own solutions. Asking the right questions at the right time will create the necessary conditions for the student to gain insight into her own learning process and how she can improve. Open-ended comments such as "I like that idea. Can you expand on it a bit more?" or "Can you tell me more about that?" give the mentee space to express her thoughts and share concerns.

Show support. The need for support and trust is connected to the early years of our lives, when we needed to feel safe and secure in our parental environment in order to grow and move away from our comfort zone and into unknown terrain as we acquired more skills and knowledge. This need for a safe and supportive environment holds true in college as well. Students must feel that we trust in their abilities and potential for growth. Our support may be expressed by the words we use (e.g., "I know you can play this recital beautifully!") and through our actions.

An example of creating a supportive environment is in encouraging peer attendance in recitals. In my experience, studios and institutions differ in the way they cultivate expectations in terms of peer and departmental participation in student recitals. A poignant response by one of the students I spoke to addressed the need for support within the studio: "In my undergrad, it was an expectation that you were going to be at everybody's recital in your studio and everybody was really supportive. It's not quite like that here. There's more of a midlevel support." Personally, I want my students to feel like there's a full level of support, not a midlevel of support. Although you may not be able to single-handedly change the culture at your institution, perhaps you could encourage students to attend their peers' recitals and foster a culture of reliable support for one another.

Students in the performing arts tend to be highly motivated and overzealous. Often, they want to pursue projects that may not be directly linked to their applied lessons, but may need your support to achieve those. For example, your student may want to put on a concert in the community or initiate a local music festival. Another way of showing support is to allow students to explore these ideas by encouraging them and giving them the space to grow and develop independence.

Encourage. Mistakes will be made and egos will be hurt. It is all part of the learning process and the vulnerability of being a performer. A word of encouragement, e.g., "I believe in you" or "You worked hard and I know you have what it takes to perform a stunning recital," goes a long way in reminding the student that these roadblocks along the way can and will be overcome.

Provide a structure. Students rely on their professors to provide structure for their learning. Some students need more structure than others, depending on their ability to organize themselves. If a student is dealing with anxiety, that student may need more structure, with clearer instructions and specific assignments.

Challenge. In any learning environment, the teacher-mentor's role is to challenge students' preexisting beliefs and help move them in the direction of considering alternatives. The process of challenging the mentee can be difficult, as it requires entertaining the possibility that a current belief may be wrong or not the only way of viewing the world. It involves training students to ask challenging questions and inspiring a curiosity they will foster for the rest of their lives.

Provide a vision. The student may not know exactly how her career will look and is likely figuring out options while in college. More important than helping the student understand career options is to provide her with a vision of the strengths, values, and the type of musician she wants to become.

After reading these characteristics, you might identify with several of them in your mentor role. No matter to what degree you see these elements in yourself, the important thing is that your focus stays on nurturing and guiding your students' professional and musical growth. They will only thrive if they are in a trusting and supportive environment with a teacher who sees their potential, regardless of their background.

Creating an Inclusive and Supportive Studio Environment

Treating all students equitably, regardless of their background, race, ethnicity, socio-economic status, gender identity, and sexual orientation, should be the status quo in every institution. In the spirit of the topic of this book, I would expand this statement to include that students who deal with any type of physical or mental health issue should also be treated in a fair and equitable manner by their applied instructor, other professors, and administrators. Teaching strategies should be sensitive to students' physical limitations, injuries, and mental and emotional states.

Students in the same studio often and by association become friends and develop a support system for getting through their degree. Depending on the environment fostered by the applied instructor, studio relationships can be enriching and caring, or they can be a source of negativity that impedes growth and success. The most common complaint I hear from students is that their teacher, though not opposed to a healthy and supportive studio environment, does not actively foster one. In other words, it is not enough to simply say we believe in positive teaching environments; we must actively cultivate them every day.

My own mentors fostered friendships and a support system within the studio. During the endless hours spent in the practice rooms, it gave me a sense of comfort to know there was always a peer who wouldn't mind if I knocked on her door and asked to play for her or invited her to take a walk and have a cup of coffee. These small acts of support and friendship go a long way in building students' network of future colleagues they both trust and admire.

There are several ways through which a supportive and positive studio environment can be fostered. The questionnaire in Table 2.1 is a starting point for thinking about building an inclusive studio environment.

You may also consider including a statement in your syllabus regarding the importance of taking care of student wellness. Such a statement might look like this:
Musicians' Wellness Statement Sample

> Your well-being is a priority in your lessons. I encourage you to take care of yourself through adequate sleep, nutrition, hydration, exercise, and mindfulness practices. We will be learning exercises for warming up and cooling down before and after practice. I expect you will practice those on your own on a daily basis. If you experience any pain, discomfort, or stress related to practice or performance, feel free to contact me for support. We may be able to resolve minor issues in the lesson; however, I will always encourage you to seek help from a healthcare professional when needed.

Table 2.1 Inclusivity Questionnaire

Consider your responses to the following statements to gauge your studio environment.

My studio environment fosters inclusivity.	Agree	Neutral	Disagree
When students bring up mental health concerns, I am open to listening and supporting.	Agree	Neutral	Disagree
I frequently address physical posture and a healthy approach to technique.	Agree	Neutral	Disagree
Students are comfortable sharing concerns and difficulties with me.	Agree	Neutral	Disagree
Students are comfortable sharing concerns and difficulties with other members of the studio.	Agree	Neutral	Disagree
Students offer each other constructive and encouraging feedback.	Agree	Neutral	Disagree
I model supportive and encouraging feedback for my students.	Agree	Neutral	Disagree

At the end of the statement, you may include contact information for the campus health center, a mental health crisis line, and any other pertinent local resources.

There are several ways you can promote studio camaraderie and support. Here are a few ideas:

- Studio get-togethers: Opportunities to meet new students at the beginning of the year with a pizza party or a barbeque. Board games or outdoor games can break the ice and help students get to know one another. At the end of the semester, students will appreciate the opportunity to get together again to celebrate the end of the year.
- Promote a buddy practice system: Sometimes students may have difficulty organizing their day or may need an accountability buddy for effective practicing. Having a studio buddy can help students share ideas for scheduling and check in on their practicing goals.
- Studio activities: At the beginning of the semester, students are usually not ready to perform in studio class. This could be a nice opportunity to hold team-building activities, or introduce warm-up or stretching sequences (see Chapter 3 for ideas).
- Studio discussions: In addition to musically focused discussions in studio class (e.g., thoughts about recent performances, upcoming performances, and events), there could be wellness-minded ones that invite the students to share ideas on topics such as managing their practice schedules, what they do during practice breaks, sharing their favorite stretch, or what they plan to do for self-care the next day. These conversations build a sense of trust within the studio and encourage attention toward their well-being.
- Guest speaker: A presenter from the local healthcare community or campus could discuss topics such as physical health relative to performance or introduce

strategies for time management or self-care. Introducing local resources in this setting can provide students with safety and comfort in knowing that help is available, even if the students are not comfortable sharing their concerns with their applied instructor.

- Feedback in studio class: Giving students a chance to give each other feedback on their performance is obviously a crucial component of training their listening skills and ability to intelligently verbalize observations. How this feedback is delivered is important, particularly to students who may be dealing with physical or mental health difficulties. Students must be trained in the art of communicating their thoughts about the performance and giving constructive feedback mindfully. The instructor might offer tips and opportunities to provide both in-person and written feedback: how to phrase suggestions in a constructive manner, how to respond to feedback, and the importance of body language and eye contact.

You may already practice several of these; if so, I encourage you to keep these activities as part of your studio routine and explore more ideas for building an inclusive and supportive studio environment. Although these strategies are helpful for maintaining a positive environment, they may not be relevant to someone who is having difficulties in other areas. Therefore, while continuing to implement such practices, we also need to understand how to read and respond to a situation when students signal they are struggling.

When the Mentee Is in Trouble

Warning Signs

When a student brings up a concern, whether in the physical or mental/emotional dimension, the teacher must be equipped to discern the concern level and respond appropriately. Low-level concerns may be dealt with in the lesson through a productive conversation and raising awareness of resources on campus for pursuing further help. These types of concerns may have solutions that would be easy to find. For example, the student may have trouble with time management and fitting in enough practice time into his schedule. After talking through his schedule, it may be determined that he doesn't have to fit in a consecutive three-hour chunk into his day, but three one-hour long sessions are more productive and can more realistically be achieved.

Mid-level concerns involve more complex issues that may require the support of the mentor and that of a healthcare professional. Stress caused by such concerns may be affecting the student's day-to-day life in a significant way. An example of such a concern would be difficulty focusing because of insufficient sleep. A conversation about the importance of sleep and good sleep hygiene may be a productive starting point but will likely not resolve the issue completely. A suggestion to follow up with a healthcare professional is recommended in these types of concerns.

High-level concerns require immediate attention and action on the part of the mentor. The mentee might be in significant physical pain or emotional distress. A discussion of such issues in the lesson should provide the student with information, support, and encouragement toward reaching out for professional help. If the situation is an emergency or the student is threatening self-harm or harm to others, call 911.

The majority of circumstances, however, are not so drastic. Most likely you will be encountering low-level concerns that are subtle and may be productively addressed in a lesson, especially when they relate to music study. A simple question such as "How are you doing?" or "How are you sleeping lately?" might be enough to show care and invite the student to share and seek help without pushing boundaries and causing discomfort. Keep in mind that the student may not be comfortable with sharing personal information, or the student may want to, but fears that revealing a difficulty may affect his academic standing and his teacher's opinion. If the student chooses not to share information, I advise against probing unless you think there may be cause of concern or danger to the student. Examples of noticeable behavior that could be a cause of concern are as follows:

- Sluggish movements and yawning could indicate lack of sleep or dehydration.
- Rubbing shoulder or arm might signal pain or discomfort.
- Strained or tired-sounding voice could mean stress or fatigue.
- Quick and shallow breathing may indicate stress or anxiety.

When concerns arise, we must be ready to respond with language that is supportive, encouraging, and helpful for getting the students to where they need to be for further assistance. Motivational interviewing (MI) is an evidence-based practice used in various fields for eliciting positive change in habitual behavior. This approach is focused on helping the patient (or the student in our case) see the problem within the larger picture, to understand its causes for himself, and to tap into his own wisdom for developing solutions. Ideas from MI can be applied to a mentorship relationship as a way to facilitate the student's overall well-being. I suggest using this methodology as a way to problem-solve low-level concerns. I can't emphasize enough that we should avoid providing guidance beyond our expertise, but rather we should be ready to refer the student to services that will provide professional help.

Handling Student Concerns: Motivational Interviewing

Psychologist William R. Miller and collaborator Stephen Rollnick developed motivational interviewing (MI) in 1983 subsequently establishing it as a methodology.

Dr. Miller and Dr. Rollnick primarily worked with individuals with substance use disorders. Since its origins, MI has been applied in a variety fields, specifically toward the work of supervisors within corporate and academic settings, and, to an equal degree, informal professional advisors. The MI approach has been applied and tested in various circumstances and has proven to be an effective way to elicit behavioral changes based on internal motivation and an individual's values and beliefs.

Essentially, the practice of MI consists of a collaborative conversation between counselor and the patient about changing behavior through the process of identifying and resolving ambivalence about the behavior. Being ambivalent about change is considered a normal part of the process. The counselor treats the patient with respect and does not impose her own ideas about behavioral change. The techniques used in this conversation are designed to bring about the patient's own motivation and ideas for a specific behavior change. The foundational values of MI are called the MI Spirit, which refers to the qualities that permeate each conversation, rather than a set of prescribed intervention tools. The four components of MI Spirit are compassion, acceptance, partnership, and evocation (CAPE). From this point on, and where applicable, I will refer to the *client* as the *student* as I translate the MI model into conversations within the music lesson setting.

Compassion

Compassion refers to the ability to actively seek to understand another person's experiences and values without engaging in judgment. It means coming respectfully to a conversation about the difficulties the student is going through, working toward the student's benefit (not ours), and respecting her choices, even if we think those are different from what we would advise her to do.

Acceptance

Acceptance refers to affirming the student's ability to make change by highlighting her strengths, expressing accurate empathy through a process of reflecting meaning back to her, supporting autonomy by empowering her to rely on her strengths and to value her absolute worth and potential. In this approach, there isn't a single prescribed way of bringing about change, but rather multiple options based on each student's ideas and beliefs.

Partnership

This approach is different from other counseling approaches in which the counselor or therapist takes on the role of the expert and holds a more confrontational attitude toward the client's current behaviors (i.e., the old substance abuse model). In the MI model, even if opinions differ between the two parties, one can expect the projection of mutual respect, and a conversation centered around the student's point of view and experiences, thus supporting her autonomy no matter what.

Trust, as mentioned previously, is an important component of a partnership, which can often be difficult to accomplish in relationships that are hierarchical by nature (i.e., student–teacher relationship). In the applied lesson setting, conversations based on the MI model must be built upon a sense of trusting the student to make her own choices, without imposing your own values and solutions. Partnership is a collaboration, which means ensuring that the student is on board with the direction and speed of movement toward the goal. This makes it more likely she will follow through on the plan, rather than just smile, nod, and proceed to continue the previous behavior.

Evocation

The counselor is trained to draw from the motivation of the client for change. This is based on the foundation that, for change to be long-lasting, the person has to draw from her own ideas and skills to find solutions, thus increasing motivation and commitment to the new behavior. An example of a change in habit that is short-lived is joining a gym and committing to an hour's worth of weight-lifting per day when, in reality, a student's lifestyle does not match this change, or she may dislike going to the gym. The student might stick to the exercise plan for a while; however, because the change was not based on her individual exercise preference or schedule needs, it will not be a long-lasting change. Even if you start exploring external motivation in a conversation, the MI model can help you work with students to find their internal motivation.

Behavioral change in the context of the music lesson could apply to several different situations. Examples range from unwillingness to practice scales to a reluctance in scheduling an appointment with a physician when there is a physical injury. In these two circumstances, the teacher's approach would have to be different. In the first scenario, i.e., not practicing scales, a curricular requirement, would mean that the instructor has to use conversational techniques to try to understand what the barriers are, resolve those with the goal of the student eventually incorporating scales into her routine. In the second scenario, the instructor does not have the authority to require the student to visit a doctor, and there may be underlying reasons for not making an appointment that the student may not want to disclose. Having a conversation that explores the ambivalence, using MI spirit and techniques, may be beneficial in helping the student understand what is holding her back (even if the student chooses not to share) and to make decisions about next steps.

Elicit-provide-elicit (EPE) is a useful tool for providing advice in a non-expert, yet MI-adherent, way. The process follows a sequence that looks like this:

1. Find out what the person knows about ideas and options (e.g., "What do you know about warming up before practicing?" or, if the student is unaware of warming up strategies, "What do you see other people do to warm up?").
2. If, based on the student's response, the mentor believes there is an opportunity to add to what the student already knows, the mentor would ask for permission to share some ideas (elicit). To avoid coming off as the expert/person in charge (which can get in the way of partnership), these ideas would be framed as coming from other people who are in a similar situation as the student (e.g., "Would you be interested in hearing some other ideas for warming up that other students have used?").
3. If the student responds positively, then offer a menu of ideas (provide) (e.g., "Some students take a vigorous walk around the building before practicing; others follow a short video on YouTube; others create their own sequence based on where they normally get tight in the body").
4. Ask what the student thinks of all the ideas discussed and what, if any, options she is willing to try (elicit). It is important to take this next step to ask the student her thoughts instead of ending the conversation with the advice provided in the previous step (e.g., "What do you think about those ideas for warming up? What, if any, might you like to try?"). Notice you are supporting autonomy here as well.

Through the process of applying the EPE strategy, the instructor remains respectful of the student's ideas and wishes to move toward change, or not, while providing suggestions in a way that doesn't impose one specific solution to the problem that the student can say "no" to. It opens the opportunity for student choice. Again, when students choose their own solutions, they are more likely to follow through.

While MI may be a sophisticated technique that takes practice to master, one does not need to be a trained psychologist to leverage its power. In fact, we can look to the foundational skills of the practice to facilitate student-centered conversations—the basis for effective problem-solving.

Motivational Interviewing Foundational Skills

The foundational skills for MI are useful for any type of conversation that involves making a change. From simple issues to more complex ones, it provides an approach that is respectful and relies on the person's strengths and own ideas for change. These strategies spell out the word OARS: open-ended questions; affirmations; reflections; summaries.

Let us look at each of these skills individually.

Open-Ended Questions

Such questions allow for more elaborate answers that don't present themselves with a singular response or multiple-choice answers. They allow the teacher to gather information about the student and for the student to think deeper and in a way that is more exploratory rather than focused on a single solution or idea. Open questions also expand the response range to anything the student may be considering, things the mentor hasn't even thought about.

Affirmations

These point out the student's strengths and help her see that she has what it takes to bring about change and maintain a new behavior. This type of response often involves reframing previous successes in a new light to build confidence in the student about her ability to change. Affirmations are an important component of the process as they support self-efficacy. They also point out what's going well with the student. Quite often, advisors, mentors, and people in general focus only on what's wrong. Mining for strengths is an important component of MI. Affirmations are not praise. Praise is our judgment on an observation. Praise might be: "I like your technique today!" Affirmations typically start with "you," such as, "You've put a lot of effort into adjusting your technique."

Reflections

Reflections are akin to holding up a mirror for someone to see themselves. At certain points during the MI process, the teacher reflects back to the student what she is saying to express accurate empathy and to guide the student toward resolving ambivalence. The teacher points out what the student identifies as negative aspects of the current behavior and positive skills and outcomes of moving toward change. Different types of reflections may be used at any stage of the conversation. A reflection may mirror the student's feelings (e.g., "You're overwhelmed with all that's on your plate"); illuminate the ambivalence in her thoughts (e.g., "On one hand, you find scales boring, and on the other hand, you see that others you admire spend a fair amount of time practicing scales"); describe the meaning or a hypothesis about what she was saying (e.g., "You really aren't sure that practicing scales will help you improve your performance"); repeat an action step she wants to take (e.g., "If you could find a person to practice with, you might be interested in adding scales to your practice sessions"); or it may carefully omit aspects that did not seem as important.

Summaries

A summary is a collection of reflections that can be offered in the middle of a conversation as needed and is always provided at the end. The teacher highlights important aspects of the conversation and may check to see if she is understanding the student correctly or if the teacher left out anything important. A summary at the end of a meeting would include (1) some sustain talk (i.e., language indicating wish to continue previous behavior); (2) more change talk (i.e., language that signifies the student wants to make a change); (3) affirmation (i.e., highlighting the student's strengths); and (4) key question (e.g., "So, what do you think you'll do in the next couple of days?"). For example, if you've been having a conversation about where scales might fit into practice, a summary could look like this:

> So, in summary of our conversation today, scales seem like something that people do when they are first learning an instrument, and they don't excite you [sustain talk]. At the same time, you've noticed that several friends consistently use scales to warm up before their main practice begins, and you feel they are moving more quickly ahead in their abilities than you are [change talk]. You also would be willing to try warming up with scales over the next week and see how it impacts your practice [change talk]. You will set a time for five minutes for doing scales at the beginning of practice sessions [change talk]. You clearly have a will to do whatever it takes to reach your potential in playing [affirmation]. So, what do you think you'll do later today? [key question].

Such a summary is an effective way to wrap up the conversation and send the student off thinking about the changes she's been considering or planning for next steps.

Through the process of an MI-based conversation, the teacher is looking for change talk (e.g., "I would like to be a better performer") or dissatisfaction with the status quo behavior (e.g., "It bothers me that I can't perform that piece well"). The student expresses belief that she has the skills necessary to implement the change and is ready to start making an action plan to move toward that change. Whether the student is talking about preparatory change talk (i.e., is starting to think about change) or committed change talk (i.e., is ready to take steps toward change), the mentor can still reflect any type of change talk. If the student responds with sustain talk or discord (i.e., arguing, discounting, or interrupting), then it's a signal to the instructor to take a step back from talking about change and to evoke more discussion about the current behavior. This can seem counterintuitive, and you certainly wouldn't want to go back and talk about sustain talk if the student was giving you a lot of change talk. Further, if you get pushback from reflecting more about change or moving toward a plan, then follow your student back. Pushing just makes it more likely that she won't make changes. The mnemonic DARN CAT is a quick way to remember how the process for each change talk category works. Here is the breakdown of the preparatory change talk in a scenario about a student experiencing physical pain when practicing:

Desire (e.g., "I want to change. I want to be in less pain when I practice.")

Ability (e.g., "I am able to change. The pain is mild, and I know I could reduce the symptoms if I incorporate a warmup in my practice routine.")

Reason (e.g., "I have identified reasons for the change. I want to eliminate the discomfort I'm feeling in my body and prevent the pain from getting worse.")

Need (e.g., "The change needs to happen for some extenuating circumstance. This is my best opportunity to reduce pain and build better practice habits, when I have mentors and healthcare professionals around me at school. I won't always have this.")

And here is the outline of the change implementation process:

Commitment (e.g., "I am committed to making the change in my life. I am ready to add a daily physical warmup to my practicing routine.")

Activation (e.g., "I am motivated to start moving toward change. I set aside five minutes to practice my warmup before I start my practicing and have added it to my calendar.")

Taking steps (e.g., "I am ready to take steps toward change. I found a warmup video I like and plan to follow it before practicing twice this week.")

Most of us do not have a counseling or psychology background; therefore, we are not equipped to treat students (and, again, shouldn't attempt to do so) as a counselor. However, these tools remain accessible even to a nonclinical person and can be helpful in supporting better outcomes for our students in situations where difficulties are within our domain and can be resolved through a productive conversation. Several books are available on MI, as well as online courses and resources for further training on this topic that you may be interested in pursuing. You may be wondering how all this work could be applied in an actual conversation. Let's take a look at a common conversation topic that will inevitably come up at one point or another. The imaginary conversation that follows (which is not far from a real one) uses MI strategies to help students think through ways they can rely on their own skills to improve their practicing habits.

STUDENT: "I am having a difficult time fitting practicing into my day."

TEACHER: "You are very busy with a lot of homework and all the ensembles you are participating in." [meaning reflection, i.e., testing a hypothesis on what you think might be going on]

STUDENT: "Yeah, I'm overwhelmed."

TEACHER: "Tell me more about what makes it difficult to practice." [open-ended question]

STUDENT: "I am taking 19 credits this semester and three of my classes are not in the music building, which wastes time traveling back and forth. I also have a difficult time waking up early in the morning to practice, but, when I try to stay up late, I am too tired and unproductive."

TEACHER: "You have a large academic load, and that can feel paralyzing when you are trying to fit in your daily practice schedule and balance everything. You are still juggling your morning and night practicing and trying to work out what works best for you." [expressing empathy via accurate feeling and meaning reflections]

STUDENT: "Yes, I know that morning practice works best for me, but I just can't seem to make that work with my sleep and class schedule. It's too stressful to get through this degree. I'm not sure that it's possible for me to practice as much as I am expected to." [sustain talk]

TEACHER: "Getting enough sleep is getting in the way of your morning productivity and you'd like to know how other students manage it all." [meaning reflection]

STUDENT: "I stay up at night trying to finish homework, and, when I try to sleep, I worry that the next day will be just as stressful and difficult because I can't spend as much time in the practice room as I need to."

TEACHER: "A good night's sleep gives you energy and lowers your anxiety about all you have to do." [meaning reflection] "You are working hard to figure out your schedule and doing your best to stay on top of everything, while taking care of yourself." [affirmation]

STUDENT: "I'm trying, but nothing seems to be working." [sustain talk]

TEACHER: "You are trying hard to improve your situation and it hasn't been working so far. If you were to wave a magic wand, what would your ideal schedule look like?" [reflection and open-ended question]

STUDENT: "Well, I would wake up at 7 a.m., have a healthy breakfast, practice for two hours before my 10 a.m. class, and then fit in one more hour in the afternoon when I have a break between classes."

TEACHER: "You would have a sense of accomplishment if you could follow a schedule like that now." [reflection]

STUDENT: "I feel good about what I would be able to accomplish," [change talk] "but at the moment it doesn't seem attainable." [sustain talk]

TEACHER: "What would be the cons of changing your schedule to better fit in your practicing?" [explore sustain talk]

STUDENT: "It could also mean getting less sleep at night and feeling more tired during the day." [sustain talk]

TEACHER: "It would interrupt your current routine." [reflection] "What would be the pros of changing your schedule?" [explore decisional balance]

STUDENT: "It would help me make more progress on my rep and help my focus since I'm most fresh in the morning." [exploring pros and reason for change]

TEACHER: "Changing your schedule would improve your practice productivity." [reflection] "How did you work out your practice schedule when you were in high school?" [evoking change talk]

STUDENT: "I would practice for two hours every day after school. To get me through those two hours, I used to create rewards for myself. I would get to do something fun or have more time for self-care when I was done."

TEACHER: "You came up with a creative way to stick to your daily schedule." [affirmation] "How might you set up rewards for yourself now?"

STUDENT: "I love going for walks, but I often feel like I don't have time because I should be practicing. Maybe I can let myself go for a short walk after I've finished my practicing for the day." [ability]

TEACHER: "Going for a walk would feel like a treat and may help lower your anxiety, too."

STUDENT: "I think that it would help me get through the semester. I'll be able to play my instrument much better if I can spend more focused time being able to apply all the things we talk about in my lessons. I want to do well in my performance exam, and I need to be better about figuring out my practice schedule. Exercising a bit might help me sleep better, too." [need for change/exploring motivation for change and commitment]

TEACHER: "That makes a lot of sense. When do you think you'll be able to try out this new schedule?" [activation]

STUDENT: "I need to get through the end of this week first and I'll start next week." [taking steps]

TEACHER: "I'm wondering if there's a little piece of your plan you might be able to implement sooner?" [taking steps]

STUDENT: "I'll try to go to bed earlier on Sunday night and set up my alarm for 7 a.m."

TEACHER: "This is important enough to you that you want to do something now. What if you have trouble falling asleep because you are stressed? How will you handle that?"

STUDENT: "I don't know. That's hard for me. Do you have any ideas?"

TEACHER: "I'm not an expert on sleep, but if you want I can share a couple of things with you that have worked for other students in the past." [elicit]

STUDENT: "That would be great."

TEACHER: "Some ideas are breathing exercises before sleeping, taking about an hour before bedtime away from electronic devices while doing calming activities, shifting dinner time to earlier in the evening, and making meditation a regular practice." [provide] "Do any of these sound like they might be things you'd like to try?" [elicit]

STUDENT: "Thanks. I think scrolling through the news and social media right before sleeping stresses me out, so I'll plan to put my phone away for a while before I sleep."

TEACHER: "You already identified a potentially helpful solution. And if you find none of those is helping you, the counseling center on campus might also be able to help you with several other strategies related to sleep."

STUDENT: "Yeah I might try that. Thank you."

Table 2.2 Motivational Interviewing Practice

Respond to these questions in a way that follows the MI principles.

"I try to organize my week more effectively, but I keep failing."

"I'll never be able to perform in public after that horrible performance last week. I just can't control my nerves."

"I didn't do well in my theory exam. At this rate I'm going to flunk out of college."

"I always need to have an alcoholic drink before my performances, otherwise I can't play."

"All my friends seem to be depressed and it's dragging me down."

While this example reflects a particularly common scenario, the fundamentals inherent are widely applicable. Through using open-ended questions, reflecting meaning back, and helping the student realize pros and cons for a change in behavior, the teacher was able to activate the student to find her own solutions. By following the MI model for the preceding discussion, we can see how the student moved from feeling overwhelmed by the problem, and not knowing how to even begin tackling it, to finding a solution by reaching into her own wisdom.

Table 2.2 presents other common scenarios you might deal with. You might try working through them using the OARS strategies described earlier. At the end of the chapter, in Table 2.3, you will find possible responses to the given scenarios. It's not unusual to feel awkward when starting to use MI foundational skills—and, just like scales, lots of practice is how you will improve.

Setting Boundaries

As much as a supportive relationship is needed to guide students along their journey, it is important to also set boundaries with regard to our time commitment and when we need to refer to a healthcare professional. This ensures maintaining a professional relationship, protects our time and energy (especially for the empaths among us who tend to carry the burden of our students' stress), and utilizes professional resources that can provide the necessary assistance. It is difficult to predict when a student will come to her lesson and need to share a concern. I've been caught off-guard when certain conversation topics came up; in retrospect, it would have been helpful if I had phone numbers and websites more readily available. Letting your students know when and how they should contact you and when they should expect

Table 2.3 Motivational Interviewing Practice

Examples of possible MI responses.

Student: "I try to organize my week more effectively, but I keep failing."

Examples of possible MI responses:

- "You're frustrated you aren't getting results yet."
- "While you haven't figured it out yet, you are putting effort toward organizing to make it easier to study and get assignments done."
- "You want to find out what other students have done to successfully organize."

Student: "I'll never be able to perform in public after that horrible performance last week. I just can't control my nerves."

Examples of possible MI responses:

- "It can feel like you are the only one to have this type of experience."
- "You are looking for ways to calm your anxiety so this doesn't happen again."
- "You'd like to know how other musicians have worked through performance anxiety."

Student: "I didn't do well in my theory exam. At this rate I'm going to flunk out of college."

Examples of possible MI responses:

- "You're feeling stuck."
- "It's disappointing not to do as well on an exam as you planned."
- "It's hard to know ahead of time that study practices that allowed you to be successful in high school don't always work in college."

Student: "I always need to have an alcoholic drink before my performances, otherwise I can't play."

Examples of possible MI responses:

- "You've found alcohol to relax you before playing."
- "You're feeling like alcohol is your only option right now."
- "If there were strategies besides alcohol to help you calm yourself, you would try them."

Student: "All my friends seem to be depressed and it's dragging me down."

Examples of possible MI responses:

- "It's hard to stay in a good mood when others around you aren't."
- "You have tools to keep your spirits up that your friends don't have."
- "You are struggling to find ways to be there for your friends and to keep your own spirits up."

---

to hear from you if you are unavailable would be helpful for them (and for you to protect your time). Some students expect that you will be available to them 24 hours a day; while that may be true for some of us, it is not a measure of our commitment to the students if we are available at all times as opposed to during work hours. In fact, having healthy boundaries and knowing when to refer our students to other professionals is just as important as mastering the mentorship techniques described earlier.

Referring

None of us has all the answers, and it is impossible to predict all of the issues that may arise. Just as we help our students understand the power of knowing when they need help, we also need to recognize when it is time to direct them to appropriate resources. Beyond problem-solving conversations, we have a responsibility to be knowledgeable of healthcare resources on campus or in the community. Usually, university campuses have a health center where students can make an appointment for acute injuries. If the health center is not able to treat the injury, the student may be referred to a specialist. Knowing the specialists in the community (e.g., hand or TMJ specialists) may be helpful in this regard. Other ideas for contact information to have on your syllabus or readily available are nutrition clinics, sleep and apnea centers, free programs for stress reduction, psychological counseling services, and a list of apps on topics such as mindfulness, fitness tracking, hydration reminders, time management, and organization. Maintaining a comprehensive resource list and even distributing it to the students at the beginning of the semester can ensure that students are at least aware of practitioners, health centers, and other information that is available within reach. It also sends a signal to the students that their well-being is valued and that the teacher is on their side.

***

The unique circumstance of musical study, driven by the mentor and mentee relationship, poses challenges and opportunities for cultivating wellness in our pedagogy. Mentors play a critical role in the development of every musician. They encourage, challenge, support, and, by integrating motivational interviewing within problem-solving conversations, can foster self-confidence and growth that their students will undoubtedly need in the real world. Using the strengths of a mentorship relationship as the foundation for addressing wellness, we will now shift our focus to common physical injuries, one of the most critical aspects we are likely to encounter in our lessons.

3

"Is It Tendinitis?"

Common Physical Injuries

Pain is the most common signal that something about our physical activity is not right. It is a natural, built-in warning mechanism that should be honored and taken seriously. Unlike injuries caused by obvious incidents or blunt trauma (such as a fall or a car accident), pain related to music-making activity usually develops gradually over time. The onset of an injury may feel like benign discomfort. Over time and without intervention, what began as a seemingly minor injury can become disabling. It may interfere with the ability to practice or perform, and might even disrupt daily life. For some musicians, the constant presence of minor discomfort becomes the status quo to the point where they may not even recall ever playing or singing without some level of pain.

Since performing arts medicine became established as a field, there have been numerous studies investigating musicians' physical injuries. Researchers have examined an array of topics, including injury causes (e.g., relationship to instrument, age, size, and sex differences) and treatment efficacy. This has led to a wealth of resources on instrument ergonomics, vocal health, hearing health, and medical explanations of common injuries suffered by musicians. In this chapter, I will discuss an overview of common musculoskeletal, vocal, and hearing injuries; their causes, treatments, and warning signs; and prevention strategies for the instructor to support.

In the one-on-one lesson where we observe our students' physical movements every week, we might be more likely to encounter physical injuries. We have a responsibility to be knowledgeable about relevant, discipline-specific topics to best serve our students. Through mentorship, we can encourage our students to develop injury-prevention habits and guide them to appropriate healthcare resources when needed. I would like to caution, again, that most of us are not healthcare professionals and should not be giving medical advice on injuries. If a student is experiencing pain that does not diminish after a day or two, it is best to refer him to a healthcare professional. Pedagogues have weekly opportunities to observe their students in action; developing an understanding of biomechanics is one of the most important injury-prevention strategies an applied teacher might consider adopting. Even though the work of calibrating movement toward optimal physical performance is central to one's pursuit of a healthful life as a performer, the specifics of anatomy, as well as causes and treatment of injuries, are topics that are often unaccounted for in

Teaching the Whole Musician. Paola Savvidou, Oxford University Press (2021). © Oxford University Press.
DOI: 10.1093/oso/9780190868796.003.0003

music degrees. This is why we will now spend some time focusing on relevant physical structures and how they are affected by injuries.

Basics of Body Structure

It is unfortunate that most musicians are not required to take a class on basic body mechanics. A foundational understanding of how the body is constructed can go a long way in preventing injury. That knowledge is key to one's ability to maintain a healthy approach toward performance, while also avoiding pitfalls such as excessive practice and faulty technique. The anatomical structures responsible for physical movement are the bones, joints, and muscles. The nervous system is responsible for muscle movement and is affected by both thoughts and emotions, as well as environmental factors (such as a perceived threat, which can stimulate tightness in the muscles). This section frames some key foundational information about these systems, which, in turn, will inform the discussion on musculoskeletal injuries that we will explore later in the chapter.

Bones and Joints

Two hundred and six bones comprise the framework of the human body. Bones are designed to protect vulnerable internal structures. Their cartilaginous ends are formed in such a way as to join together with other bones. The various types of joints have their own degrees of flexibility and limitations (see Figure 3.1). Knowing what each joint should and should not do can prevent movement beyond the normal range of motion.

Ball and socket joints are more mobile and often less stable than other joints. The glenohumeral joint in the shoulder is a type of ball and socket joint and is arguably the least stable joint in the body. The end of the humerus bone of the upper arm is in a ball-like formation that sits in a cup-like socket. Due to this formation, the arm is free to move in almost any direction. This incredible mobility afforded by the design of the joint means that one has to be mindful of supporting the motion of the shoulder and arm with stability from the torso.

Hinge joints are limited to movement in one direction up to approximately 180 degrees. Examples of hinge joints are the knee joint, articulated by the fibia, tibula, and the patella; the joint between the humerus and the ulna at the elbow; and the interphalangeal joints in the fingers. Gliding joints are formed in flat areas, such as between the wrist's carpal bones. Bones can move in different directions along the plane of the joint. Saddle joints allow for flexibility in movement, as they comprise a saddle-shaped bone meeting a convex, complementary bone. The base of the thumb is an example of a saddle joint. The shape of the joint is what allows the thumb to

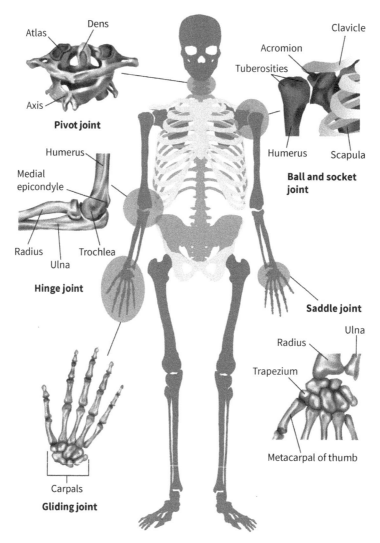

Figure 3.1. Types of joints.
Figure by Amber Huo.

have its opposing quality and to move in multiple directions. Joints only function when they are powered by their engines, and those engines are the muscles.

Muscles

Muscles are responsible for moving the bones. When they contract, they cause movement. The part of the muscle that contracts and relaxes is called the *muscle belly*. Muscles attach to the bones via tendons. Tendons are covered by protective sheaths that release synovial fluid, allowing the tendons to move easily without friction. Synovial fluid is used during movement and replenished during rest. Fasciae, which are bands of fibrous connective tissue primarily made of collagen, separate and surround muscles and other structures. Ligaments, made up of strong connective tissue, surround the joints and connect bone to bone.

Pairs of muscles that work together are called agonists and antagonists. Agonist muscles are able to move bones in only one direction. They rely on their antagonist muscles, which work in opposition to them, to return the body part back to its original position. Think, for example, about the muscles of the upper arm. When the biceps contract, the arm bends, but the biceps cannot return the arm to its extended position. The triceps have to contract for that to happen. If both muscles contract at the same time, they provide stability in the joint. However, this co-contraction could potentially lead to fatigue of the muscles. A set of muscles that commonly suffers from long-term co-contraction in musicians is the forearm flexors and extensors (see Figure 3.2). If you try curling your fingers to form a tight claw with your hand, you will notice that both the flexors and extensors of the forearm are contracting. While it may appear that extreme contractions of the hand go beyond musical study, in reality, they form the core of much of what we physically have to do to play our instrument. We hold our hands in clutching positions. When maintained over long periods without an understanding of the detrimental effects, this can lead to injury. The good news is that understanding how these issues develop can empower us, as performers, to counteract the tendency to hold these positions with undue tension.

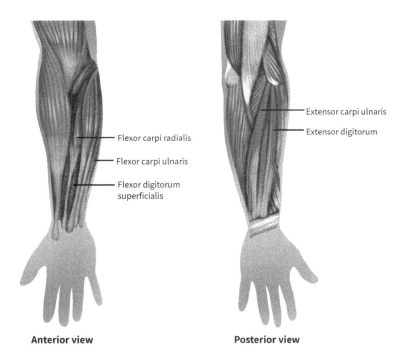

Flexor carpi radialis

Flexor carpi ulnaris

Flexor digitorum superficialis

Extensor carpi ulnaris

Extensor digitorum

Anterior view

Posterior view

Figure 3.2. Forearm flexors and extensors.
Figure by Amber Huo.

When muscles alternate contraction of the agonist and antagonist, blood pumps in and out of the muscle in a way that can sustain movement for a long period of time. This type of muscle movement is called *dynamic effort* and is typically utilized by performers who use a large range of motion when they perform (e.g., percussionists). Holding the muscles without much movement is called *static effort*, which is exemplified by performers who hold their instrument in a static position or maintain upright postures. Static effort is more problematic because the blood vessels are restricted in the muscles, so a fresh blood supply cannot easily reach the muscle to replenish essential nutrients. Muscles get fatigued after prolonged use and need time to replenish the essential nutrients (such as glucose and oxygen) that allow them to function well. Contracting the muscle for long periods of time means the blood may not be able to keep a constant flow of nutrients, causing waste products, such as carbon dioxide and lactic acid, to build up. The muscle then starts to send pain signals, indicating that it needs to rest. Anyone who has spent hours practicing his instrument can relate to this feeling of fatigue and even pain after hours of holding certain positions.

Micro-abrasions and tearing of the muscle fibers and tendons may occur when we don't give our muscles sufficient time to rest. Pain and, potentially, injury can develop due to chronic repetition of a specific motion. Hydration, maintaining a dynamic posture, stretching, and rest are effective ways to allow the muscles to recover, especially after heavy usage in the practice room. But try as we may to take care of our muscles and their surrounding structures, we have to take into consideration that muscles move because the nervous system tells them to do so. Muscles may be receiving signals to contract to play an instrument, to tighten in response to a threat, or to relax after a calming meditation session. Understanding the structure of the nervous system can give us perspective as to which movements we have control over and which ones happen automatically.

Nervous System

The nervous system transfers information from the brain and spinal cord to the periphery and vice versa via electrochemical nerve impulses carried by neurons. You can see a simplified flowchart of the nervous system in Figure 3.3. The brain and spinal cord make up the central nervous system (CNS), whose neurons are called upper motor neurons. The peripheral nervous system (PNS) consists of the somatic nervous system and the autonomic nervous system. The PNS is made up of motor and sensory nerves. Lower motor neurons connect the spinal cord to the muscles. Neurons release chemicals that cause muscle contraction, which in turn causes a feedback loop sent back to the brain through sensory neurons. The somatic nervous system is responsible for voluntary muscle actions, such as those necessary to move fingers and limbs, and the autonomic nervous system is responsible for involuntary muscle actions, such as the heartbeat. The autonomic nervous system consists of two further systems: the parasympathetic nervous system and the sympathetic nervous system. These systems

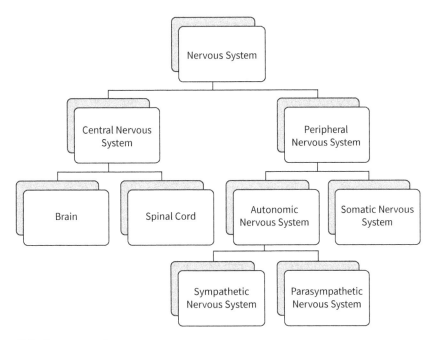

Figure 3.3. Nervous system.

have received the most attention in musicians' research, as they are respectively responsible for the stress and relaxation responses. The sympathetic nervous system activates the fight-flight-freeze response, triggering the body's alarm system when we are in situations we perceive as dangerous. This complex alarm system triggers the release of stress hormones, which essentially prepares the body to respond to the situation by increasing the heart rate and sending an oxygen supply to the muscles by increasing blood flow. The parasympathetic nervous system complements the sympathetic nervous system by activating a relaxation response, which, among other calming effects, slows down the heart rate, contracts the pupils, and promotes digestion.

Chronic activation of the fight or flight reaction results in an ongoing state of heightened stress. When muscles are contracted for long periods of time, fatigue and pain set in. Tapping into the body's internal calming mechanism through practices such as breathing and yoga enables musicians to restore equilibrium. Next, we will examine in more detail the causes of the most common types of injuries, as well as typical treatment procedures.

Musculoskeletal Injuries: Causes, Types, and Treatment

It is no secret that injuries are rampant among musicians. Study after study demonstrates the high percentage of professional and student musicians who experience pain on an ongoing basis or have experienced pain in the past.[1] In a study by Ackermann et al., nineteen out of twenty collegiate flute players reported dealing with a performance-related musculoskeletal disorder.[2] An international survey of 2,212 orchestral musicians conducted by Fishbeing et al. found that, at the time of the survey or in the past, 76 percent of musicians had a medical problem so severe that it affected their playing.[3] Another study of approximately 100 Swedish musicians showed that musculoskeletal pain in the neck and shoulders was the most common problem.[4] A more recent national survey of 1,000 college students and faculty conducted by Stanek et al. showed that 67 percent of musicians experienced performance-related pain, with the highest prevalence in woodwinds (83 percent) and the most common areas being the upper back, lower back, and fingers of the right hand.[5] Out of the 218 vocalists who participated in this study, about 50 percent reported experiencing pain, with the throat being the most common location, followed by the lower back. Although other studies have found that pianists and string players have the highest injury prevalence, the takeaway from all the studies is the importance of educating our students about biomechanics and providing them with preventive tools as early in their careers as possible.

Overview of Causes

Musculoskeletal injuries is a broad term used to define injuries that affect such structures of the musculoskeletal system as muscles, joints, ligaments, tendons, and nerves. The term *overuse injuries* is used to describe injuries related to repeated loading of the musculoskeletal system. Other terms commonly used are *cumulative trauma disorders* and *repetitive strain injuries. Misuse* is another term used to refer to injuries caused by movements of the body that go against its natural biomechanical tendencies and that result in poor technique or alignment. All these terms refer to a negative symptom that may be impacting the effective function of a specific area. In the field of performing arts medicine, the commonly used term that encompasses musicians' injuries is *playing-related musculoskeletal disorders* (PRMDs).

As you can imagine, there is a long list of factors that place musicians at risk for developing an injury. These include ineffective technique, a sudden increase in practice time (usually at the beginning of the school year after a summer break), moving in joints' extreme range of motion, attempting more challenging repertoire than is physically possible, adjusting technique to a new instrument, an intense performance schedule, a lack of strength and flexibility in the body to support musical activities, and genetic factors such as the size of the hand and hypermobility.[6] Injuries may also be caused by non-musical activities such as exercise, carrying heavy loads, use of electronic devices, or accidents.

Performance anxiety and other psychological factors also play a role in developing an injury and in the perception of pain. A competitive atmosphere in the studio or the school may lead to more tension when playing and contribute to longer practice hours without breaks. It is important to note that, generally, an injury occurs when there are multiple factors present, not just one. Therefore, a holistic approach to prevention that fully addresses multiple risk factors is more advantageous. Most injuries are preventable, which means that through injury-prevention education, we can support our students' pursuit of long and healthy careers in the arts. We can't prevent injuries, however, unless we are aware of the different types, causes, and treatments.

Types of Injuries

Acute versus Chronic Injuries

Acute injuries have a sudden onset and may be defined by a specific incident, for example a fall, or lifting a heavy object. A student who comes back after a summer of light practicing and dives into four to five hours of daily practice on new and difficult repertoire may be at risk for an acute injury. If he comes to you and says, "I suddenly felt pain after my first week back," that could be an indication of an acute injury. Chronic injuries are present for prolonged periods of time (typically three months or more) and are more likely to reoccur. Mild expressions of chronic pain such as neck and shoulder tightness are common among musicians. Other chronic injuries such as tendonitis may go away for some time but may reappear if one is not diligent about preventive or maintenance practices.

Muscle Strain

A muscle strain is the breakdown of muscle tissue and can occur to varying degrees, ranging from a micro-tear to a full muscle tear. Usually, strains are caused by repetitive use or over-stretching. Factors that may be putting a musician at risk for a muscle strain include tightness in the muscles, poor technique, overuse, lack of recovery time, or practicing without warming up the muscles first. Common areas of muscle strain are the lower back, neck, and shoulders. Symptoms include soreness, stiffness, and sudden onset of pain. Rest, light movement, ice, and anti-inflammatory medication can help treat a muscle strain.

Myofascial Injuries

Myofascial pain can interfere with a musician's ability to practice and perform. It can have many causes, including trigger points in the muscle fibers. Myofascial trigger points, tightly contracted muscle spots, can limit range of motion, inhibit normal muscle contractility, and cause localized or referred pain (pain in adjacent areas of the body). Myofascial injuries can appear along with tendinitis because they are both overuse injuries. However, they can also appear independently.

Tendinopathies

There seems to be a great deal of bewilderment surrounding the terms *tendinopathy*, *tendinosis*, *tenosynovitis*, and *tendinitis*, leading to a non-medical condition known as tendino-confusion! I reached out to my colleague Dr. Jeremy Stanek, a physiatrist at Stanford University's School of Medicine, to help me understand the terminology. Here is a breakdown of all the tendon-related terminology.

Tendinopathy
Tendinopathy is an umbrella term for any injury to the tendon. If you call any of the following injuries tendinopathies, you will be correct, as they all fall under this category.

Tendinosis
Tendinosis is caused by tiny tears in the tendons that are extremely difficult to heal. The most common cause is chronic overuse. Tendinosis is often misdiagnosed as tendinitis. A main difference between the two conditions is that tendinitis is an injury of the tendon accompanied by inflammation, whereas tendinosis is degeneration or injury of the tendon without an inflammatory component. Frequently, an injury starts as tendinitis and then progresses to tendinosis as inflammation dissipates. A common location for tendinosis to occur is the tendon on the outside of the elbow. Recovery time for tendinosis is significantly longer than for tendinitis. Treatment includes physical therapy, exercises, injection, and, in some cases, surgery.

Tenosynovitis
This injury is commonly caused by repetitive motion that leads to swelling of the protective tendon sheaths, and sometimes swelling of the tendons themselves. It could be caused by an inflammation of the tendon or the muscle. Immediate treatment involves rest and applying ice to the affected region. Muscle strengthening and stretching are two strategies that can prevent tenosynovitis.

DeQuervain's tenosynovitis is an example of tenosynovitis that musicians often experience. This condition affects the tendons on the thumb side of the wrist. The tendon sheath that wraps around the two tendons connecting the thumb and the wrist becomes thick and swollen. A visible swelling in the base of the thumb may be present. It is a painful condition that is aggravated by grasping motions of the palm. DeQuervain's tenosynovitis has been linked to chronic overuse of the wrist, repetitive lifting of a baby, and inflammatory conditions such as rheumatoid arthritis. Ice, anti-inflammatory medication, and splints may be used to help reduce inflammation and relieve pain. Frequently, however, an injection with a steroid is required for definitive resolution.

Tendinitis

Tendinitis is caused by inflammation of the tendon that connects muscle to bone. Tendons have lower blood supply than muscles, which means they are more susceptible to injury and can take longer to heal. Common areas in musicians that are affected by tendinitis are the elbow, wrist, and thumbs. Irritation of the tendon at the elbow is called medial or lateral epicondylitis (also known as golfer's elbow or tennis elbow). The sensation that arises as a result of these conditions is sensitivity to the touch and soreness. In lateral epicondylitis, discomfort may be felt on the outside of the forearm when the wrist is extended. In medial epicondylitis, pain is experienced when the wrist and fingers move to type, text, play an instrument, or grip.

Tendinitis that affects the wrist can be flexor or extensor tendinitis. These long tendons connect the muscles of the forearm (which are responsible for finger movement) to the bones in the fingers and thumb. The tendons on the back of the hand are called extensors, and they are responsible for straightening the fingers. The tendons in the palm side of the hand are called flexors, and they flex (or bend) the fingers. Several of the flexor tendons go through the carpal tunnel in the wrist and are protected by tendon sheaths and a ligament known as the flexor retinaculum that keep them in place.

Flexor tendinitis, which affects the flexor tendon, causes pain when the fingers are bent, difficulty in bending fingers, numbness in the fingertips, and tenderness. Extensor tendonitis affects the extensor tendon and may cause symptoms such as swelling, discomfort, and stiffness. Physical therapy is generally recommended for recovery from tendonitis, in addition to home remedies such as icing, heating, taking anti-inflammatory medication, and following home exercise programs as part of physical therapy treatment.

Trigger Finger

Trigger finger is caused by repetitive motion that results in thickening of the flexor tendon, most commonly affecting the ring finger. The symptoms are decreased range of motion in the finger and a clicking or popping (triggering) sensation. Treatment includes rest and stretching. A doctor may recommend using a splint and taking anti-inflammatory medications if swelling is present. In severe cases, a steroid injection or surgery may be needed.

Nerve Entrapments

Often caused by poor posture, nerve entrapments are common among musicians and can occur anywhere from the neck to the wrist. Commonly, nerve entrapments occur due to swelling of the surrounding structures in a tunnel. A tunnel is a small structure through which muscles, ligaments, blood vessels, and nerves travel. The compression of the nerve may not only affect the point of compression but also distribute discomfort to other areas of the body. For example, a compressed nerve in the shoulder may cause numbness and tingling sensations in the fingers.

The injuries that many musicians fear the most are *carpal tunnel syndrome* (median mononeuropathy) and *cubital tunnel syndrome* (ulnar mononeuropathy). While they pose real threats to the instrumentalist because of the delicate anatomical structures, the good news is that they are preventable and treatable. The cubital tunnel is located in the inside part of the elbow where the "funny bone" is located. The sensation of pain experienced with cubital tunnel syndrome is similar to hitting the funny bone. The main cause is bending the elbow past 90 degrees frequently. Instrumentalists, such as string players, are prone to developing cubital tunnel syndrome because the position at the instrument requires keeping the elbow bent for long stretches of time. Symptoms include numbness in the hand, particularly in the ring finger and pinky, hand pain, and pain on the inside of the elbow.

Cubital tunnel syndrome is diagnosed by a physical examination conducted by a healthcare professional, followed by an electromyogram, a nerve conduction test, X-rays, an ultrasound, or magnetic resonance imaging (MRI) scans, if needed. Treatment may consist of a combination of rest, wearing a splint, nerve gliding exercises, and anti-inflammatory medication. Sometimes, a steroid injection or surgery is required. Preventive strategies for both cubital tunnel and carpal tunnel syndrome include warming up, maintaining flexibility in the upper body, and proper body positioning.

The carpal tunnel is a tiny tunnel, about an inch wide, located on the palm side of the wrist. The median nerve goes through this tunnel, along with nine tendons that attach to the fingers. Carpal tunnel syndrome occurs when the nerve is compressed. It's much like when one encounters road construction on a highway. When too many cars try to fit through at the same time, it's inevitable that there's going to be a traffic jam! Sensations that accompany carpal tunnel syndrome include numbness, tingling, pain, or burning in the thumb, index, middle, and ring fingers. Symptoms are often worse at night, when bending the wrist, or during gripping activities such as typing. The onset of the condition is usually gradual, which means that early prevention is possible. Early treatment includes bracing (to keep the wrist in a neutral position), nonsteroidal anti-inflammatory medication (to reduce swelling and relieve pain), nerve gliding exercises, and steroid injections. Depending on the severity of the syndrome, for example, if motor function is impaired, surgery (called carpal tunnel release) may be recommended by a doctor to relieve pressure on the nerve.

Thoracic outlet syndrome is another type of nerve compression that occurs between the collarbone and the first rib (where the thoracic outlet is located). Symptoms include tingling, numbness, swelling, and pain in the shoulder, neck, or hands. Common causes of thoracic outlet are poor posture and repetitive use.

Focal Dystonia

Focal dystonia is perhaps more feared than the aforementioned injuries because it can be a devastating, career-ending disorder that only few musicians fully recover from. The main symptom is a loss of voluntary motor control in either the ring and pinky fingers, or the facial muscles affecting coordination of the embouchure (in brass and wind players). Symptoms appear early as "sticky" fingers, involuntary flexion of fingers, and momentary loss of coordination of the fingers or embouchure in certain passages. These symptoms are generally not accompanied by pain. Dystonias affect approximately 1 percent of musicians, most often men, and unlike other disorders, in mid-career rather than earlier.

Although other disorders have much clearer causes and a pathophysiological explanation, that is not the case with dystonias. Dystonia is caused by an abnormality of the sensorimotor cortex in the brain. The brain fires for extended periods of time, causing co-contraction in the flexor and extensor muscles in the forearms and the activation of unnecessary muscles. The representation of the fingers or lips in the brain appears to be impaired in patients with focal dystonia.[7] In the fingers, dystonia appears as an involuntary curling. Musicians whose instruments require high-level fine-motor skills are at a higher risk for developing dystonia, as are those who are prone to perfectionist tendencies and experience more anxiety.[8] Repetitive use has been identified as a risk factor as well. There may also be a genetic predisposition; however, that has not yet been fully investigated.

Treatment depends on the type of dystonia and ideally involves a team of medical professionals. An effective combination of treatments includes oral medication, somatosensory retraining, instrument adjustments, retraining at the instrument, botulinum toxin injections, and constraint-induced movement therapy. Prevention is even more crucial in the case of dystonia, as the path to treatment is not as clear as with other playing-related injuries. Addressing the known causes, such as perfectionism, anxiety, and overuse, by establishing a supportive atmosphere, discussing practice routines, preventing overuse, and promoting healthy practice behaviors are some of the ways the instructor can support the student.

Skin

Contact dermatitis is a common skin irritation that occurs among instrumentalists. It appears as swelling of the skin or eczema. The irritation may also lead to calluses, as are common in the violinist's proximal interphalangeal joints.[9] Fiddler's neck, which is characterized by thickening and discoloration of the skin on the side of the neck where the violin or viola rests, is also common among upper string instrumentalists. There are several reasons for these conditions, such as cysts in the salivary glands, allergic reaction to rosin or a type of wood, and the pressure of the instrument or strings on the skin. Prevention of skin conditions involves good hygiene with the points of contact with the instrument and using a cloth over the chin rest. Cheilitis, the swelling and flaking of the skin around the mouth, is another condition that affects brass players. It is caused by the contact of certain types of metal with wet skin. An example of a common culprit is nickel, which is used as part of alloys in mouthpieces. Prevention may be achieved by replacing the mouthpiece with one that has a thin silver or gold lining.[10]

∗∗

We now have a clearer understanding of basic body structures, common injuries, and their causes. Even though as teachers we are not equipped to offer treatment, we can certainly educate our students about preventive steps, guide them toward seeking appropriate help, and be on the lookout for warning signs. While we cannot replace the treatment of a medical professional, there may be circumstances where the student needs immediate care before they can see a doctor. Knowing the basics of injury first aid may prove critical in those situations.

Injury First Aid

Treating an acute musculoskeletal injury is often best approached as described by the acronym RICE:

Rest
Ice
Compression
Elevation.

This approach should be taken within the first twenty-four to forty-eight hours of the injury until proper treatment can be received. By applying RICE, injury recovery time may be reduced. Resting means minimizing weight-bearing activities (depending on the location of the injury) and reducing movement. This allows the tissue to heal and prevents any re-rupturing that may occur when the muscle has to exert force again. Rest should be relative to the person and the location of the injury. Resting for too long should be avoided, as other issues of muscle atrophy could arise.

Ice reduces swelling and inflammation of the muscle by constricting blood flow. Ideally, ice should be applied for approximately ten minutes, followed by ten minutes of no ice, and should not be applied for more than twenty minutes at a time. A thin towel between the skin and the ice pack helps to protect the skin from ice burn. Applying an elastic bandage to the location of the injury provides compression, which also helps to minimize swelling by reducing blood flow to the tissue. Elevation of the injured area above heart level also helps reduce swelling.

Common over-the-counter medications such as nonsteroidal anti-inflammatories (e.g., ibuprofen or naproxen) may also be used to alleviate pain. The recommendation for ibuprofen is a maximum dosage of 2,400 mg per day for approximately one week, and for naproxen, it is 1,000 mg per day for three to five days. Anti-inflammatory medication should always be taken with food to avoid an upset stomach. People with renal dysfunction or stomach ulcers should avoid taking anti-inflammatories, as they can have a negative impact on their conditions. An option for a naturally derived anti-inflammatory is turmeric, which should be taken as a capsule. Studies have shown it takes at least 1,500 mg per day of turmeric to get a true anti-inflammatory benefit. Aspirin also has some anti-inflammatory benefits; however, it should not be taken by those who have a bleeding disorder.

Heat provides pain relief and helps relieve tightness in the muscles and joints. It should be applied as a treatment for chronic injuries, but usually not for acute injuries. Alternating heat and ice is another effective method for treating chronic conditions. If a student is experiencing mild muscular discomfort, you might suggest starting a practice session by applying heat to the affected area, followed by self-massage, a gentle warm-up, and starting with the easiest repertoire or technique. It would be a good idea to end the practice session with applying ice (in addition to gentle cooldown exercises) to reduce any swelling that might have occurred while practicing.

Seeking Help

When a music student is experiencing pain, a million different thoughts race through his mind. I can all but guarantee that those thoughts are negative. "What could be causing the pain? Is there something wrong with me? Will I have to stop playing? What will my teacher think of me? Am I weaker than the rest of the students in my studio? Will I have to postpone my recital? My teacher will definitely think I am a failure and a disappointment. If it doesn't get any better soon, I may never be able to play again and will have wasted all this money and time in getting this degree." This type of catastrophizing is not uncommon in people who tend to have a perfectionistic attitude toward their craft and fear that a small setback will have a negative long-term impact on their lives. We will discuss perfectionism in greater detail in Chapter 7.

By maintaining an open channel of communication with regard to a healthy physical approach to playing, the instructor can signal to the student that she is willing to help him should any issues arise. Instructors hold the power to support a change in perception of injuries by creating an environment where injuries are accepted not as a personality fault, but as a physical challenge that is common among musicians and that, most of the time, can be overcome with proper treatment and help. Creating such an environment means not shying away from conversations about injuries, asking questions related to any discomfort you might be perceiving in your students' playing, and actively encouraging preventive strategies.

Applied faculty are generally the first line of defense when it comes to reporting pain. In fact, 49.5 percent of injured undergraduates and 34.1 percent of injured graduate students in the aforementioned study by Stanek et al. sought help from their primary instructor.[11] In addition to support from the instructor, students tend to seek care from other sources outside of the medical field. Ackermann et al. noted that none of the students in their study who were injured consulted a medical doctor. Instead, most of them sought Alexander technique lessons.[12] Students look to their teachers for guidance, for emotional support through the injury, and, most importantly, for musical rehabilitation, as they often have to rework their technique or posture to overcome the injury. Being armed with information and resources about the effectiveness of medical and nonmedical treatments will allow you to support your students in the best possible way.

At the first sign of pain, the student must stop playing until she can talk to her teacher or a medical professional about the issue. If the pain is minor and most likely caused by faulty technique or posture that can be corrected in the lesson, the resolution should be relatively quick. If, however, the diagnosis of a medical professional must be sought, then the recommendations will likely vary depending on the condition, the individual, and the severity of the problem. Recommendations by a healthcare professional may include some rest time, modification of practice intensity and duration, medication to reduce inflammation, and use of splints or braces. Braces and splints immobilize the body part, assisting in the reduction of inflammation and pain caused by movement. These must be used mindfully and not for long periods of time, as they may have adverse effects, such as joint stiffness and muscle weakness.

When seeking medical treatment, usually the point of entry within the medical system would be the primary care physician, or, where available, a doctor who specializes in performing arts medicine. If there isn't a specialist in the performing arts locally, then a doctor who specializes in musculoskeletal injuries, such an osteopath or a rehabilitation or sports medicine doctor, can be very helpful. If a visit with a specialist or a primary care physician through the local medical system is not available through insurance coverage, the campus healthcare center would be the place to go. During the first visit, the physician will ask about the patient's history and perform a physical exam. Whenever possible, the student should bring his instrument along for an evaluation with the instrument. If this is not possible, bringing a video recording of the student playing would be a helpful alternative. When hand or arm injuries are suspected, the doctor may run tests by palpating, tapping on nerves, or asking the patient to perform motions to determine if there are any tingling sensations or a limited range of motion. Injuries can be complex, and it's possible one is incurring more than one injury at a time; therefore, the doctor may need to verify the diagnosis through X-ray, ultrasound, electromyography (EMG), or MRI. Once the diagnosis has been verified, treatment or rehabilitation would be the next step.

For treatment to be most effective, medical professionals need to work together with the instructor and the patient as a team to ensure complete rehabilitation and avoid relapse. The two-step process to recovering from an injury and returning to performance involves healing the injury (through recommendations set forth by the team of medical professionals overseeing the patient) and retraining the body to function in a more efficient way in performance (with the support and advice of the applied instructor). A comprehensive team could include a physical therapist, a hand therapist, the music instructor, and a psychological counselor.

Steroid injections may be recommended by a doctor to provide pain relief for conditions such as tendinopathies. Steroids act on the white blood cells that help reduce the inflammatory chemical mediators from the area, thereby reducing inflammation, swelling, and pain. A common misconception is that steroid injections provide immediate relief. The fact is that steroids are often accompanied by numbing medicine. The immediate pain relief is a result of the pain-numbing medication, not the steroid. It can take approximately two to seven days for the steroid to start working, and its effects can last for up to three months.

There are several precautions to take into consideration before a steroid injection. Inserting a needle into the skin always runs the risk of injuring a nearby tendon or nerve, or causing an infection. Steroid injections cause an increase in blood pressure and blood sugar, which means that diabetic patients should be monitoring their insulin intake carefully in the days that follow. Facial flushing and pain flare-ups are also possible risks that may appear within forty-eight hours. Frequent injections are contraindicated, as they weaken the tendon and the body's ability to regenerate cartilage and may cause thinning of the bones, leading to osteopenia and osteoporosis.

While medical treatments are necessary, they can be even more effective when used in conjunction with nonmedical treatments that can aid in improving posture, strengthening the body, and deepening the mind–body connection. Such activities include the Alexander technique, Feldenkrais, Pilates, Rolfing, and myofascial release. Frequent massages can serve as both a preventive mechanism and a recovery tool by releasing muscle tension.

When playing or singing becomes impossible because of an injury, the musician may be required to take some time off. The consequences of taking time off can be devastating. For those students who rely on their performance for their income, that means having to find a sub and forgoing their income for the duration of their injury. Depending on the job and the amount of time needed off, a replacement may end up taking their position permanently. The social stress of having to explain to peers and professors why they are not performing in choir or orchestra, or why they are wearing a splint, adds another dimension of pressure that could lead to them feeling isolated and withdrawing from social life. The emotional stress of not knowing when they'll be able to return to playing may cause anxiety, feelings of inadequacy, and dissatisfaction with life. Taking time off should only be encouraged in consultation with a medical professional. But even then, a doctor may not be aware of the full extent of the implications. The stress of taking time off can be alleviated with early detection and, even better, with prevention. Absent these steps, one can easily slip into habits that slowly build toward moments of heightened stress, leading to physical breakdowns without obvious warning signs.

Warning Signs

The most common and obvious sign that something is wrong with one's musculoskeletal health is pain (except in the case of focal dystonia). Pain may arise before, during, or after playing. Depending on the cause and the person, the physical sensations will vary. There may be swelling, tightness, stiffness, lack of mobility, tingling, or numbness accompanying the pain. Feeling physically, mentally, or emotionally exhausted may also be a sign that the body needs recovery time.

The earlier an injury can be recognized and treated, the better the outcomes for the student. Even though most music instructors are not certified medical professionals, this does not mean that they cannot be on the lookout for signs of potential injury and discuss these issues with their students in a productive way. A few signs an instructor might notice in his student that may signal discomfort include

- Rubbing the arms, neck, or shoulders after playing
- Needing to stretch right after playing
- Fidgeting
- Showing visible signs of discomfort in facial expressions
- Playing in an unusually tight manner
- Shaking hands after playing
- Fatigue, both physical and emotional.

If the student recognizes that she may have an injury, a grading system for the severity of the pain may be used to identify what needs to be done. Although it is somewhat generalized, the following rubric has positive implications because it helps us quickly identify the severity of the potential injury and objectively discuss an appropriate course of action.

> Grade 1: Pain while playing or for a short time directly afterward. Changes in technique may resolve the issue. Posture may be addressed as well.
> Grade 2: Pain lasting for hours after playing. Changes in technique and cutting practice time in half can help.
> Grade 3: Pain worsens while practicing, requiring shortened practice sessions; pain resolves between sessions. Again, decrease practice time.
> Grade 4: Pain worsens while playing and does not resolve completely between sessions. Begin relative rest and seek medical attention.
> Grade 5: Constant pain that interferes with or prevents playing. Seek medical attention as soon as possible.[13]

While playing-related musculoskeletal injuries are extremely common, they are not the only physical ailment musicians face. Vocal injuries, which we will explore next, can affect both voice students and the occupational user, such as a student teacher in a classroom environment.

Vocal Health

Basics of the Vocal Mechanism

Vocal health depends on multiple factors, such as a healthy alignment, proper care of the vocal instrument, appropriate singing and speaking technique, correct breathing, and constant guarding against pathogens. The vocal mechanism, as shown in Figure 3.4, consists of three subsystems: (1) The respiratory system or power source (the lungs and upper airway); (2) the phonatory system or sound source (the larynx); and (3) the resonator (the implied space reaching from the top of the vocal folds up to the lips, also called the supraglottic vocal tract). The structures responsible for articulating speech and singing are the teeth, tongue, lower jaw, lips, soft palate, hard palate, and the alveolar ridge. The production of voice begins and ends with the breath. Upon exhalation, the air is channeled up to the larynx and forced through the space between the vocal folds, called the glottis. Once air from the lungs reaches the glottis, it sets off the Bernoulli effect, which is an aerodynamic principle that—along with the mechanical approximation of the vocal

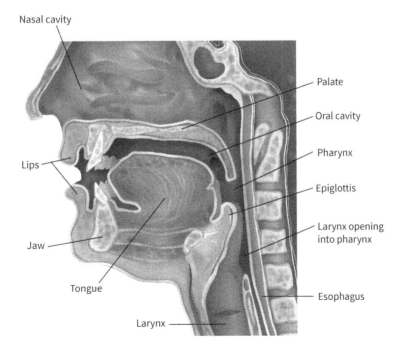

Figure 3.4. Vocal mechanism.
Figure by Amber Huo.

folds by muscles, joints, and cartilage that bring the vocal folds together, and the biomechanical pliability and elasticity of the vocal folds themselves—contributes to the sustained vibration of the vocal folds. The vocal folds are specialized muscles that have a skin-like epithelial layer on top. The gelatinous substance between the skin layer and the muscle allows the epithelium to vibrate and slide over the muscle. This phenomenon is called the mucosal wave, and this is what ultimately creates the sound wave that becomes the voice. The sound waves produced by the vocal folds travel up through the vocal tract, where they are shaped and amplified by the resonator and articulator subsystems.

Common Injuries to the Voice

You might think that the most common cause of injuries in singers would be the act of singing! I was surprised to learn that in his clinic, Sataloff, author of *Professional Voice: The Science and Art of Clinical Care*, found that most of the singers he treats suffer from problems unrelated to performance, such as infection, hormonal problems, and reflux laryngitis. In my interview with Elizabeth Ford Baldner, a speech-language pathologist at the University of Michigan's Vocal Health Center, I learned that the most common problems she encounters in both professional and occupational voice users are with muscle tension dysphonia, nodules, and hemorrhages. Other problems that affect performance include laryngitis, heartburn, trauma to the vocal folds, polyps, and cysts. We'll now learn about the causes, risk factors, treatment, and prevention of the most common voice disorders.

Muscle Tension Dysphonia
Muscle tension dysphonia (MTD) is caused by an imbalance of the laryngeal and paralaryngeal muscles, deviations in the head and neck posture, a high-positioned larynx, and tension in the associated musculature. These imbalanced vocal mechanics may be present due to a recent illness, or because the singer may be pushing her voice beyond its limits, perhaps when singing in an unsuitable style or due to prolonged voice use. This can lead to feeling a lump in the throat, or may even cause pain with speaking or singing. The voice sounds hoarse and strained and is easily fatigued. Ultimately, MTD may be present in the absence of any identifiable pathology, or it can co-occur with other voice disorders, such as nodules, polyps, or vocal fold paralysis, due to overcompensation of the vocal instrument.

Laryngitis
Inflammation of the larynx, called laryngitis, is one of the most common voice disorders. It is caused by an infection, allergies, or gastroesophageal reflux disease (GERD) and/or laryngopharyngeal reflux (LPR). GERD and LPR, which may be felt as heartburn or burning in the throat, are the reflux of stomach acid beyond the protective wall of the stomach itself. It can cause irritation in the lining of the

esophagus and all the way up to the larynx and pharynx. Vocal fold problems may be caused by GERD/LPR, such as edema and granulomas, which are swellings filled with white blood cells, which remove infection in the affected area.[14] Left untreated, GERD/LPR may cause chronic hoarseness and even difficulty swallowing. Fluid retention (edema) in the larynx occurs when there is inflammation as part of the body's natural response to infection. With laryngitis, it is critical to rest the voice from both speaking and singing, as muscle tension and/or other injury to the delicate layers of the vocal folds may occur and cause long-term damage. Anesthetic sprays that cause numbness should be avoided to prevent creating a false sense of recovery.

Phonotrauma

Phonotrauma is defined as "the result of a vocal behavior, either volitional or involuntary, impacting vocal fold vibration in a manner that compromises vocal fold integrity."[15] Phonotraumatic behaviors are categorized as non-phonatory behaviors (such as coughing, grunting, throat clearing) and phonatory behaviors (such as using the voice in a loud, pressed manner, as when yelling or shouting). When a patient is seen for phonotrauma, both non-phonatory and phonatory behaviors are assessed in the initial appointment to better understand what the behavioral causes might be. In consultation with a speech-language pathologist, the patient will be able to identify behaviors he can reduce or improve upon. A baseline assessment of the vocal fold condition can determine a singer's risk of developing phonotrauma. The effect of phonotrauma on the vocal folds ranges from minor irritation and swelling to more severe laryngeal pathology, such as polyps or vocal fold hemorrhages, depending on the frequency and intensity of the phonotraumatic behaviors and the number of vocal fold layers that are affected by lesions.[16]

Vocal Fold Lesions

Vocal fold lesions include polyps, nodules, and cysts, as well as resultant vocal fold scars. Vocal fold nodules are callus-like growths that appear on the surface of the epithelium. They generally occur bilaterally at the midpoint of the folds, also known as the "striking zone," where the vocal folds sustain maximal impact force during vibration. Polyps generally appear on only one vocal fold, may be larger and more defined than nodules, and may appear as a result of hemorrhage from a small blood vessel. Nodules and polyps are associated with phonotrauma. Vocal fold cysts are less common and may or may not be associated with phonotrauma. These growths consist of a sac surrounding retained fluid, typically in the deeper layers of the vocal folds. A vocal fold scar can result from the healing process of any vocal fold lesion and occurs when the epithelial layer becomes adhered to the underlying muscle. All of these lesions prevent the vocal folds from vibrating properly, resulting in hoarseness, difficulty with pitch and loudness, and possibly also compensatory strain, such as muscle tension dysphonia. The commonality among the disorders mentioned here is that the causes are, to a great degree, caused by behaviors: posture, singing outside of the comfortable range, or pushing the voice beyond its comfort levels. Understanding habits that put one at risk is key to prevention.

Risk Factors

Warning signs for an injury to the voice range from a change in the tone of the voice (becoming more hoarse or raspy), difficulty with singing softly in the higher range, voice breaks or trembling, coughing, pain in the larynx or associated muscles, or loss of voice. Factors that place the singer at risk for developing a voice disorder are as follows:[17]

- Drying medication
- Exposure to irritants such as cigarette and marijuana smoke and alcohol
- Excessive use of the voice
- Talking or singing loudly
- Habitually clearing the throat
- Excessive caffeine intake
- Straining to compensate for vocal fatigue
- Eating foods that may cause acid reflux (spicy foods, highly acidic foods, carbonated drinks)
- Singing without warming up first.

Modification of these behaviors contributes to prevention; however, it's not a 100-percent foolproof method. There are several factors involved in an injury, and there are situations where, in spite of our best efforts, we still get injured. In those situations, it's helpful to have a plan of immediate action before a doctor can be seen.

Treatment

Immediate home treatment usually involves vocal rest and increasing hydration. When the singer is experiencing discomfort and a worrisome change in voice, it is wise to limit speaking and singing until a comprehensive voice evaluation can occur.

When a concern arises, the singer should seek the advice of an otolaryngologist (also known as an ear, nose, and throat doctor, or ENT), or a laryngologist, who has more extensive training and specialization in managing voice disorders. An injury to the voice may be caused by multiple factors and will also require a comprehensive approach to rehabilitation. When seeking a healthcare professional, I suggest researching providers in your area to find out if there is someone who routinely works with singers and is familiar with the specific challenges professional singers deal with.

A complete voice evaluation will consist of collecting the patient's medical history and history of the voice problem; head and neck examination; laryngeal imaging (through videostroboscopy, which is considered the golden standard in laryngeal imaging); perceptual, acoustic, and aerodynamic evaluation of the speaking and singing voice; and therapeutic probing for voice therapy's appropriateness.[18]

Ideally, a team approach will be taken toward evaluation and recovery. The team may include the laryngologist or otolaryngologist, a speech language pathologist, the applied instructor, and a psychological counselor. A comprehensive care plan may include behavioral intervention (e.g., hydration and reduction of phonotraumatic behaviors) and direct voice therapy with the speech-language pathologist. A speech-language pathologist will assist the rehabilitation of the voice through indirect and direct approaches. Indirect approaches involve counseling the patient about vocal hygiene and conservation. Direct approaches might include voice therapy, myofascial release therapy, circumlaryngeal massages, body stretches, and postural adjustments.[19] The instructor plays an important role in the entire process, as, often, she will be the first person to suspect a vocal injury and make recommendations for medical treatment. During the recovery process, the instructor should work closely with the rest of the voice care team to retrain the student in tandem with the medical professional's work, or to incorporate the work done with the medical care team into the lesson. The instructor may be invited to attend therapy sessions so she can provide her insight into the recovery process. Medication may also be prescribed to reduce swelling, manage reflux, or fight off an infection. Surgery should be treated as a last resort for singers, as there may be adverse risks involved, such as permanent scarring of the vocal folds. Considering the risks involved in the recovery process, improving behaviors that could potentially be damaging can save a lot of trouble!

Prevention

Preventing injury to the voice involves awareness of both vocal and non-vocal behaviors that could potentially be harmful. Those of you who are voice instructors are certainly intimately familiar with ways to prevent damage to the voice. However, there may be readers who are not voice students or instructors who use their voice to teach or to present who would also benefit from knowing the basics of protecting their voice. Here are some guidelines applicable to both singers and occupational voice users:

- Stay hydrated throughout the day with beverages such as water, herbal tea, or warm water with honey and lemon.
- Use a humidifier when needed.
- Speak in your vocal range and avoid straining. Avoid whispering and speaking at a high volume.
- Use amplification when speaking to a group or in a classroom.

- Avoid smoky environments.
- Give your voice time to recover after singing or speaking for long periods of time.
- Eat well ahead of bedtime to avoid reflux.
- Sanitize and wash hands frequently to prevent transmission of infections.
- Use saline sprays with a mixture of water, salt, and baking soda to keep the mucosa hydrated and to reduce any inflammation.
- Avoid using aspirin products, as they can cause vocal fold hemorrhage.
- Speak to your doctor about ways to treat allergies and avoid taking dehydrating allergy medication.

Now that we have learned more about the voice, let us turn our attention to the protection of hearing health against hearing loss—a sinister type of injury that may be hard to detect.

Hearing Health

Basic Anatomy of the Ear

The ear, as shown in Figure 3.5, consists of the outer, middle, and inner ear. The pinna and external ear canal comprise the outer ear and serve to collect and direct sound to the eardrum, located in the middle ear. The eardrum continues to transmit vibrations onward to the middle and inner ear. The three very small bones (called auditory ossicles) located in the middle ear (the malleus, incus, and stapes) are connected to the eardrum and mechanically transmit the vibrations to the inner ear, where they are converted into nerve impulses in the cochlea. The cochlea, a fluid-filled snail-shaped structure, is lined with microscopically fine hair cells. It is organized in such a way that different pitches are supported by different areas. The high-pitch sounds are supported in the basal area of the cochlea, progressively moving toward low-pitch receptors in the cochlea's apex. Damage to these hair cells causes hearing loss that is, unfortunately, permanent. Protection against overexposure is the best way to prevent the most common hearing disorder: noise-induced hearing loss.

Noise-Induced Hearing Loss

Nationwide studies by the Centers for Disease Control (CDC) have shown that about 15 percent of adults in the United States (37.5 million) report trouble hearing, and one in eight people in the United States (30 million) over the age of twelve have hearing loss in both ears.[20] Noise-induced hearing loss (NIHL) can be caused by exposure to an extremely loud sound such as an explosion, or by exposure to loud

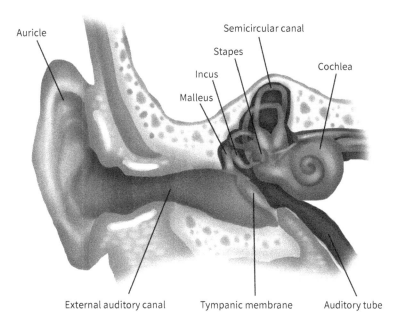

Figure 3.5. Ear anatomy.
Figure by Amber Huo.

sounds over long periods of time. Importantly, NIHL cannot be well predicted. That is, individuals have different tolerances to noise exposure. When noise exposure occurs over a long period of time, NIHL may not be discernible until hearing loss becomes more obvious. Symptoms of NIHL include tinnitus (ringing or buzzing in the ear), a temporary feeling of fullness in the ear, or temporary hearing loss, which could become permanent with repeated exposure to very loud sound. Tinnitus has an impact on the individual's quality of life. It is minimally distracting during daily tasks. When louder and/or continuously present, tinnitus can also cause feelings of anxiety and depression.[21]

Temporary threshold shift (TTS) is a temporary change to the auditory system that occurs after being exposed to loud sounds for a shorter period of time. If you've ever attended a rock concert or club where you were exposed to loud sounds for a period of time, you probably noticed muffled hearing or tinnitus afterward. These effects are usually temporary; however, they can become impactful and long-lasting with repeated exposure.

Sound exposure can also cause hyperacusis or diplacusis. Hyperacusis is defined as hypersensitivity to normally occurring sounds. Sound that is normal for other people (for example, regular conversation) is painful for someone with hyperacusis. Methods of desensitization can be used for treatment. Diplacusis is defined as the distortion of sound, wherein a single sound is perceived as two or more separate, distorted sounds. Although these conditions are cause for concern, particularly where the damage is permanent, the good news is that, to a great degree, they are preventable. Understanding the causes of hearing damage and the limits of duration and exposure are critical to hearing conservation.

Causes

The main risk factors for hearing loss are the volume of the sound and the length of the exposure. The standards for exposure to various levels of sound have been set by the National Institute for Occupational Safety and Health (NIOSH). There are no music-specific standards, so we have to adapt the data from NIOSH to our settings. Typically, sounds below eighty decibels (dB) measured in sound pressure levels (SPL) are less likely to cause any damage to hearing or to cause tinnitus, hyperacusis, or diplacusis. As sound level is calculated as a logarithmic function, with every increase of 3 dB, perceived loudness of sound doubles, and so the total amount of exposure time is reduced by half. See Table 3.1 for a summary of dB volumes and exposure times.

Dr. Marshall Chasin, director of research and chief audiologist for the Musicians' Clinics of Canada, has a helpful table in his article on hearing aids for musicians that includes decibel measurement ranges for instruments and singers.[22] Sound measures were taken at a distance of three meters. See Table 3.2 for a breakdown of the ranges. In addition to risk associated with instrument volume, listening to music through earbuds or headphones is another potentially harmful source of exposure. At their highest volumes, earbuds and headphones can deliver more than 100 dB which is only safe for about fifteen minutes of listening time over a total period of twenty-four hours, in the absence of additional exposures. Again, each person's susceptibility to temporary or permanent effects of noise exposure varies, so caution is advised.

Table 3.1 Allowable Daily Sound Dose According to NIOSH

Time to Reach 100% Maximum Allowable Daily Dose	dBA
Unlimited	0–80
8 hours (NIOSH recommended exposure limit)	85
4 hours	88
2 hours	91
60 minutes	94
30 minutes	97
15 minutes	100

Source: US Department of Health and Human Services, Public Health Service, Centers for Disease Control and Prevention, National Institute for Occupational Safety and Health, *Criteria for a Recommended Standard: Occupational Noise Exposure*, Cincinnati, OH: DHHS (NIOSH) Publication 98–126 (June 1998): 2.

Table 3.2 Musical Instrument Sound Measurements

Musical Instrument (3 Meter Measurement)	dBA
Normal piano practice	80–90
Loud piano	70–105
Vocalist	70–85
Chamber music (classical)	70–92
Violin/viola	80–90
Cello	80–104
Clarinet	68–82
Oboe	74–102
Saxophone	75–110
Flute	98–114
Piccolo	96–112
French horn	92–104
Trombone	90–106
Trumpet	88–108
Timpani and bass drum	74–94
Percussion (near left ear)	68–94
Symphonic music	86–102

Source: Marshall Chasin. "Hearing Aids for Musicians: Understanding and Managing the Four Key Physical Differences between Music and Speech." *The Hearing Review* (March 2006): 24.

Warning Signs

Hearing concerns generally go unreported because their onset is not as obvious as the onset of a musculoskeletal injury. Given this challenge of accurately tracking hearing disorders, you may be wondering how common, then, they are among musicians. I took a look at some of the data to better understand the answer to that question. A study from 1987 indicated an incidence of 52 percent of NIHL among professional orchestral musicians.[23] More recently, researchers at the University of North Carolina–Greensboro examined the occurrence of NIHL in student musicians and found that the overall prevalence of NIHL among a population of 329 students aged eighteen to twenty-five years was 45 percent.[24] Another multiyear study at the same institution investigated hearing loss among freshmen, sophomores, and juniors, with some repeat testing of the same students over the years. The researchers found that over half of the student musicians tested were at risk for NIHL, presumably due to a combination of increased exposure to loud sounds and genetic predisposition to noise-induced hearing loss.[25]

While it's impossible to arrive at a firm number of hearing loss incidence, based on the data, it's not far-fetched to assume that approximately half of musicians may be exhibiting some symptoms of NIHL. Common warning signs of NIHL include tinnitus, ear fullness, hypersensitivity, asking others to repeat themselves frequently, ability to hear better through one ear when speaking on the phone, and speaking louder than other people. In a lesson, you might observe the following symptoms:

- Frequent requests to repeat yourself
- Maintaining a loud volume of playing or singing even though the student is capable of playing softer
- Exhibiting hypersensitivity to loud conversation
- Consistently turning the same ear toward the person speaking in order to hear more clearly.

When you notice any of these signs, consider encouraging your student to visit an audiologist for a hearing assessment.

Preventive Measures

Hearing loss is preventable with education on hearing conservation. A complete preventive program for musicians, as recommended by NIOSH, includes the following[26]:

- Educating musicians about risks to their hearing health.
- Offering annual audiological testing (hearing screening and complete clinical hearing assessments).
- Frequent assessments of sound levels in rehearsal and practice rooms.
- Frequent breaks in quiet areas (as applicable to the sound levels of the rehearsal).
- Identifying solutions for each individual's situation.

Two areas related to prevention in which the instructor can provide guidance are modifications to the environment and protecting the ear from the entry of sound vibrations. Practicing in a small room can mean being exposed to both the sound production of the instrument or voice and the rebound caused by hard walls, floors, and ceiling. Practicing in a larger space or one that has absorbing materials such as rugs or foam can help alleviate this issue. When performing in a large ensemble, it is best to position the brass section on risers so their sound travels over the musicians seated in front of them. Sound shields may offer effective protection when placed within seven inches of a musician's ear; however, they may increase the potential risk for hearing loss in the musicians who are on the receiving end of the sound rebounding off the shields.

Custom-made and non-custom earplugs can be effective methods for protecting one's hearing health, although they should be used with caution and awareness of any negative impact they might have. Research by Chesky et al. examined the perception and ability of college students to communicate and play music with earplugs as well as their comfort over time.[27] Approximately half of the study participants were music majors, and the other half were enrolled in an occupational health course. The music majors appeared to be more sensitive to sound exposure, indicating that they would be more likely to protect themselves from such high volumes. Music students who used the non-custom earplugs for practice also indicated that the earplugs made it harder for them to play, citing difficulty hearing themselves and others, as well as communicating musically. Even though the students identified the most obvious disadvantages of using earplugs, they still believed that, in spite of those issues, earplugs were an effective method for protecting their hearing health. Indeed, earplugs are beneficial in reducing hearing damage but should be used in a manner appropriate to each student's circumstances.

The primary factors to consider when selecting earplugs are their attenuation effectiveness, comfort, and cost. The two main types of earplugs are premade and custom-mold. Premade earplugs come in two varieties: foam and flanged. With either type, earplugs must be correctly placed by the user for a full acoustic shield and for attenuation to be effective. Custom-mold earplugs allow for a choice in attenuation levels and can be especially useful when one is in an environment where one wants to both play music and also listen to conversation. These can initially be fitted by an audiologist to ensure an appropriate fit. Filters are available for both custom-mold and non-custom types. The advantage of a filter is better sound quality while providing adequate protection against loud sound. The cost is dramatically different between the two types: premade earplugs cost approximately $20–50, whereas custom-made ones can range from $150 to $300 or more.

Other steps may be taken that might minimize individual costs while maximizing impact. One example is the use of a sound level meter, which measures sound intensity in decibels, in ensemble rehearsals. Using a sound level meter with an LCD display can effectively check the average and maximum sound levels produced by the ensemble and can also serve as a reminder to be mindful of the time spent rehearsing the loudest sections.

There are also several sound level meter apps that are helpful tools for increasing awareness of the sound we are exposed to. There are free ones available on that market that are accurate enough for raising awareness. NIOSH also has its own sound level meter app, which claims accuracy within ±2 dBA.

Other methods for reducing sound exposure include practicing at lower volumes, alternating practicing soft and loud passages, keeping the volume low when listening to music, and, when possible, simply walking away from a loud noise source. Additionally, extracurricular exposures to loud sound must be accounted for and controlled by the musician.

Supporting Rehabilitation

As experts in their performance medium, instructors can play a crucial role in the process of rehabilitation. Technique and alignment will almost always need to be addressed when there is a musculoskeletal injury or injury to the voice. Instructors can help identify potential faulty techniques or misalignments and address them in the lesson. Here are a few questions you might ask your student to help you understand more about her injury:

- Has anything changed in your practice routine this past week?
- Have you experienced this type of pain in the past? If so, what worked before?
- What did you do as soon as you realized you were experiencing pain?
- How would you describe the pain?
- When was the first time you felt the pain?
- Does it hurt while you are practicing? After? Before?
- Is there a specific piece or technique you are working on that worsens the pain?

Depending on the responses, you can suggest an appropriate course of action (refer to the pain grading system for more information). Through the motivational interviewing techniques outlined in Chapter 2, you can facilitate a conversation in which the student can feel empowered to pursue appropriate treatment. In the process of the recovery, the mentorship relationship becomes a source of support and much-needed validation at a time when the student may be experiencing feelings of guilt and helplessness.

Recovering from an injury is both an emotionally and a physically challenging experience. In addition to reworking technique and identifying areas for improvement, the instructor must be mindful of the emotional impact an injury has on the student. Even though the student is receiving proper treatment and support, that doesn't mean that his mind is not racing with catastrophic scenarios of long-term inability to recover and concerns over what his teacher and peers think of him. The following guidelines may be helpful as you support your students in this process:

Provide unconditional support. Remain positive, even when there are setbacks along the way. Considering that music students often view the teacher in a parental role, it is important that they feel supported through this process and know that their teacher understands what they are going through.

Select appropriate repertoire. Consider what caused their injury in the first place and proceed with caution. Select repertoire that is at a lower technical level, which will allow them to work on rebuilding technique gradually.

Avoid setting deadlines. End-of-semester performance exams can be difficult to work around and may be causing a great deal of stress to injured students. If possible, leave the performance exam date open-ended, instead of setting a deadline, which could potentially lead to tense practicing and reinjury.

Allow ample time for recovery and retraining. Be mindful of how long it takes for an injury to heal and for technique to be retrained. Slow practice allows the brain and body to integrate and reinforce new information.

Encourage physical awareness. Ask questions that facilitate tuning in to the body and noticing how it's adapting to recovery and retraining. There may be low-grade pain lingering in the shoulder, for example, or other compensations that occur. By remaining tuned in to the body's messages, one ensures the pacing of one's recovery and the prevention of any reinjury. Another way to increase physical awareness is through somatic education. You might encourage your student to participate in an Alexander technique, Feldenkrais, or body mapping class.

Focus on other areas of musical development. No doubt the student will feel frustrated if she cannot perform the repertoire she previously was able to execute, or at the level that was expected. This might be a good time to focus on other areas of musical development by assigning other projects. Examples of such projects are:

- Listening: comparing recordings of the same repertoire by different performers.
- Analysis: comparing editions; analyzing a piece the student is learning.
- Mental practice: memorizing away from the instrument through analysis, imagining physical movements mentally, and making musical decisions.
- Writing: researching and writing program notes for pieces the student enjoys listening to; responding to a piece of music by writing a poem.
- Concert attendance: attending concerts within and outside of the student's discipline. A concert reflection may be assigned as well.
- Creative projects: creating arrangements, exploring composition, curating a concert, etc.

Such projects are critical for continued musical growth and intellectual fulfillment. Even though the applied instructor may be encouraging these complementary activities, there may be other academic areas affected by the injury as well. However, the student may not be comfortable sharing information about her injury with other instructors, so she may not be getting the advice needed to protect her physical health when it comes to schoolwork outside of lessons. Where appropriate, you may offer advice such as:

- Investing in speech recognition software to avoid typing, in cases of an upper extremity injury.
- Requesting permission to contribute to class discussion in a written format before or after class, if vocal rest has been recommended.

***

Supporting our students' physical health is a responsibility not to be underestimated. This endeavor requires education and an understanding of how the body functions optimally in practice and performance. We can support prevention by sharing key principles such as warming up, cooling down, exercising, and using appropriate methods for hearing conservation and vocal maintenance. When pain or injury arises, we can ask questions to help understand the type and degree of the injury and encourage the student to contact a medical professional to receive an accurate diagnosis. Even when students are in good hands with their medical team, the teacher continues to play a vital role in retraining technique, selecting appropriate repertoire, and keeping students engaged musically through the process. Most importantly, we can influence our students' attitude toward their injury by maintaining positivity and providing ongoing support and encouragement through the stressful period of recovery. Addressing physical health generally can pay dividends in terms of fostering an equally important, directly related wellness principle—physical alignment—which is the subject of our next chapter.

4

Stacking the Joints

Physical Alignment

Optimal alignment looks slightly different for each individual, dependent upon their physical structure. Before alignment at the instrument can be addressed, one must have an awareness of one's own neutral alignment in a seated or standing position. This is essential in order to find and maintain an adjusted posture with the instrument. Teaching basic seated and standing alignment to students is the first step toward establishing a solid physical foundation for movement. From there, the dance of shifting one's weight and moving in and out of balance begins. In this chapter, I aim to move away from the common notion of posture as a purely external image and toward unlocking proper alignment. We will explore this through an approach rooted in kinesthetic awareness training, grounded on biomechanical facts about joint alignment and the breathing mechanism.

Standard phrases aimed at guiding students toward their best alignment, such as "stand up straight," "lift your head up," and "push your chest out," only succeed in promoting rigidity in alignment and tightness in the muscles. The word *posture* (derived from *positura*, which means "position" and from *ponere*, "to place") is arguably the most common word used to refer to physical alignment. Using this word comes with the implication that alignment is static when, in fact, it is not. Even in stillness, we activate subtle movement as a result of breathing. "Posture" also fails to encompass the need to address alignment during movement. For these reasons, I prefer to use the terms "optimal alignment" or "dynamic alignment," as opposed to "posture." The word "dynamic" suggests an interplay of the internal sensations and external bodily motions as we continually adjust to the technical demands of the instrument and the expressive quality of the music.

Common Misalignments

Misalignments can and do occur at any of the joints, regardless of whether those joints are acting as stabilizers or actively moving to support performance. When one body part is out of alignment, the rest of the body will be affected. Think about riding a bike, for example. It is not possible for one spoke of the wheel to be bent and the bike to continue to function properly.

Teaching the Whole Musician. Paola Savvidou, Oxford University Press (2021). © Oxford University Press.
DOI: 10.1093/oso/9780190868796.003.0004

Here is an example of this ripple effect at work: One of the most common faulty alignments is the head protruding forward. With the head weighing approximately ten to eleven pounds, the upper body will have to make adjustments to keep us from toppling over. The shoulders often round forward, and the hips tilt toward the back, creating a C-curve in the upper body. In this scenario, the quads may be working harder than they need to in order to keep us upright, and the feet may be in an unbalanced position. This wave-like effect on the rest of the body does not even begin to address the muscular overexertion that will occur once we start playing or singing.

A study by Blanco-Piñeiro et al. compared posture among conservatory students by their instrument families.[1] The three components of ideal posture, as identified by the authors, were alignment of the spine and the head, freedom in the arms, and grounding through the legs. It is not surprising that postural defects related to the position of the pelvis, head alignment, and curving of the back were consistent among musicians specializing in specific instrument families. In vocalists and standing players of both string and wind instruments, the pelvis tended to be tilted forward. Percussionists, on the other hand, tended to tilt the pelvis backward. Most pianists tended to have a slouched position, while most seated string players were rigid. Seated vocalists, however, were split between rigid and slouched postures. Despite these variances, it is clear that musicians need to be mindful about their posture and its impact on their comfort.

Neck–shoulder pain is one of the most common grievances among musicians due to both alignment and movement issues, as well as psychological factors. Playing in an elevated arm position increases the muscle activity and restricts blood flow to the neck and shoulder region.[2] Nyman et al.'s analysis of the correlation between playing with an elevated arm position, the duration of playing, and neck–shoulder pain among orchestral musicians indicated that those musicians who play with an elevated arm position (e.g., flutists, violinists, violists, and trumpet players) had a higher prevalence of neck–shoulder pain as compared with those who play in a more neutral position.[3] The amount of time spent playing in a neutral position did not affect the prevalence of neck–shoulder pain, but a higher number of hours playing with elevated arm positions did lead to a significant increase in neck–shoulder pain prevalence. Even though Nyman et al. demonstrated that musicians with an elevated arm position experience more neck–shoulder pain, it is a mistake to assume that other musicians with more symmetrical instruments (such as pianists and singers) experience less pain, as research has shown that they, too, are "vulnerable to performance-related problems."[4]

As part of our Wellness Initiative at the University of Michigan, we have been offering musculoskeletal assessments for our incoming freshman music students. Co-led with my colleague Kristen Schuyten, physical therapist and champion of musicians' physical health, these assessments are conducted by athletic trainers and physical therapists in order to identify postural misalignments and test range of motion and strength. The data provided here, derived from over one hundred postural assessments of music students, have been analyzed to determine whether or not particular areas of misalignment and weakness are common among musicians. We have found that the most common postural misalignments are rounded shoulders, forward head, and, at equal levels, hyperextended and flat lower back. In the upper body, myofascial restrictions were found in the upper trapezius, rhomboids, anterior middle scalenes, and levator scapulae. In the lower body, myofascial restrictions were found in the hip flexors, quadriceps, and hamstrings. These areas of tightness are not surprising given the static, seated postures many of the students assume for hours every day, whether they are practicing, working at the computer, or attending class. Our team's primary recommendation is to pay particular attention to those areas when warming up and stretching. Students receive individualized home programs with strengthening and stretching exercises specific to the results of their assessment.

Unbalanced positions, compounded by long practice hours, reinforce poor habits. A basic anatomical knowledge and a willingness to make adjustments mindfully are powerful tools for improving alignment.

Principles of Optimal Alignment

The first step toward finding optimal alignment is becoming aware of inefficiencies and resolvable tensions in the body. It is important to guide one's student to feel the sensation of proper balance so that the student can be sensitive to any compensatory adjustments he may unknowingly be making. When altering joint positions to find balance, movement may feel unnatural. The body is used to moving in a certain way, efficient or not. There are times when this automatic physical response keeps us from harm. The body instantly reacts to a stimulus that may be dangerous. However, automatic or habitual responses are not necessarily based on alignment or correct biomechanics. Retraining the body involves "tuning in" to our kinesthetic sense by slowing down our movements, noticing the habitual motions of the body, and developing a more efficient approach. Put simply, training the body to move in a different way requires patience and slow, mindful movements.

When helping our students retrain their alignment, we must balance giving them biomechanical information and external visual feedback (i.e., how the body looks, using mirrors or video recordings) while providing opportunities for them to enhance their kinesthetic awareness. Kinesthetic awareness is commonly referred to as our "sixth sense." Through the proprioceptive system, we know about the condition of our body without having to rely on any of our other senses. An overly simplified explanation of how this works is that information about position, direction, and speed of movement is picked up by sensory neurons located in the muscles, tendons, and ligaments, as well as the inner ear, and sent to the brain. The brain then sends information back through the motor neurons. This process happens almost instantaneously. An example of kinesthetic awareness at work is to close the eyes and lift your arms up and down. You know exactly how your arms moved without having to look at them because your kinesthetic awareness allows you to be in tune with your body internally, without having to use other senses.

Part of the reason finding ideal alignment is so challenging is because we are continuously working against gravity to stay upright. If our muscles are not strong enough to maintain a sense of elongation in the body, we will start to slouch and settle into less than optimal positions. Another reason is the way in which we interact with our environment. Many of us spend hours on a daily basis using computers, tablets, and phones. Using technology often puts us in positions with the head protruding forward, rounded shoulders, and overactive thumbs.

Shoebridge et al. identified a major challenge for musicians developing an understanding of correct posture. In their study, they found that musicians consult with various sources on posture, namely Alexander technique teachers, applied music instructors, and physical therapists. However, it is not clear whether these professionals share an understanding of optimal alignment or whether their posture goals are aligned with performance goals.[5] Their team conducted semi-structured interviews of practitioners of the Alexander technique, physical therapists, and university instrumental department heads, with the goal of developing an interdisciplinary theory of musicians' posture. The theory that arose through the study was "Minding the Body." Within this theory, several "subprocesses" were identified: finding balance within oneself and with one's instrument, playing with minimal effort, challenging poor habits, expanding traditional understanding to improve performance, and examining barriers to improving posture. All the participants interviewed agreed that for the musician, posture is "multidimensional," encompassing cognitive, emotional, physical, and situation-specific aspects. The music professionals interviewed also pointed to the assertion that physical posture is fundamental to producing beautiful sound.[6]

I couldn't agree more with Shoebridge et al.'s theory that optimal posture comes through mind–body integration. The authors suggest several strategies that I consider to be foundational to retraining alignment. Here is a list, adapted for the studio teacher:

Invite Awareness from Day One

Ask questions regarding alignment, starting from the first lesson, in order to raise physical awareness. Without awareness, we risk superficial postural corrections. Some questions you might ask are: How does your neck feel when you play that difficult passage? How would you describe the sound quality in that legato passage? Where was your best breath in this section? Which part felt the most comfortable to play? Can you describe the quality of your movements that made that section feel so comfortable?

Use Imagery

Imagery is a powerful tool when used thoughtfully: for example, imagining one's head as a helium balloon floating on top of the spine. This image can elicit release in the neck muscles and lengthening of the spine. I frequently borrow the yoga image of the feet growing roots into the ground. This allows the lower half of the body to actively plant into the ground, activate its muscles, and facilitate lengthening in the upper half.

Slow Down and Guide

When repatterning alignment and movement, it is important to slow down and notice sensations that arise. This is very much like relearning fingering for a passage, an endeavor that requires the player to slow down in order to gain comfort with the new fingering. When guiding the student toward a new position, try the principle of whole-part-whole (borrowed from the process of learning a new piece of music). Invite the student to notice the alignment of the entire body. Then, isolate body parts that may be tight or out of alignment. Guide the student to notice the positioning of various body parts that may appear or feel misaligned. Invite gentle adjustments through breathing and encourage releasing any unnecessary muscular tension. Finally, revisit alignment of the whole body with awareness of how small adjustments might have impacted overall comfort.

Prioritize Ease

When the body is in optimal alignment, movements should not feel forced or painful. Again, it is normal that a new and improved pattern will feel slightly uncomfortable at first because the body is not used to moving in that way. It takes time and repetition to settle into an improved way of moving, sitting, or standing. Before aligning with the instrument, start by finding the ideal standing or sitting alignment. The body should feel centered and balanced with minimum muscular effort. Movements such as picking up the instrument should be examined closely. Often, tension and misalignment arise even before the instrument is picked up.

Use a Variety of Mind–Body Practices

I wish there were a quick fix for improving alignment and one method that worked for everyone! That would make this process much simpler. In the absence of such a one-size-fits-all method, though, the work of the instructor becomes more complicated. I recommend exploring various somatic practices and borrowing components that the student responds well to. Experiencing these practices (such as Feldenkrais, Alexander technique, or yoga) for yourself, in combination with reading books and research on these topics, is obviously ideal before incorporating some of their elements into your teaching. Even if you don't have formal certifications, this should not prevent you from recommending that students explore these practices as a means to improve their ease and comfort, or from drawing on their principles in your teaching. The more informed you are, both in the reading you do and in the experiences you have, the more effectively you can utilize these concepts.

Match Movement to Inner Intent

Technique does not exist in a vacuum; it is inherently connected with expression. This is because our body does not function independently of our mind or emotions. Accordingly, a disconnect or lack of clarity between our intention and our outward expression can cause unnecessary tension in the body. We can help our students develop effective movements in performance by helping them clarify their aural image. This process involves experimenting, making mistakes, receiving feedback, and trying again. The clearer the inner image of the musical expression, the more effective the outward expression will be (see Chapter 6 for an exploration of the expressive component of musical performance).

Consider Language

Use language that invites effective use of body weight. Avoid using words such as "relax," which could indicate collapsing the body rather than balancing it. Opt for words such as "balance," "align," "release," "support," "lengthen," and "elongate."

Use Principles of Body Mapping

Body mapping was founded by Bill and Barbara Conable on the principle that accurate mental representation of the body's structure and function improves its movement efficiency and coordination. A body map is the mental interpretation of "our body's size, structure, and function."[7] In my experience, the most common mapping error that musicians have is an incomplete picture of the arm. When musicians play their instrument, they focus intensely on the movements of the fingers and wrist without a clear concept of how they are affected and supported by the upper arm, shoulder blade, clavicle, and sternum. Another common mis-mapping issue is of the head/neck joint, which leads to neck and shoulder pain. Body mapping invites the performer to notice their internal perception of the structure and function of a specific body part. It involves learning information about accurate mappings of joints and body parts and moving in a way that aligns with appropriate function of the body. Looking at anatomical images and even recreating them via drawing are helpful tools for sharpening the internal image. In the next section, I explore guidelines from body mapping to discuss points of balance and present movement experiences, where applicable.

Alignment Basics

Alignment seems like a simple concept, but actually it functions much like a complex, invisible game of Jenga. When all the blocks are in place, the tower is sturdy and secure. As blocks are removed, the support starts to wobble until the tower collapses. If we can imagine the human body in that scenario, instead of falling on the floor and collapsing, the muscles will compensate for the weight shifts. Such compensations may include non-weight-bearing muscle groups being called upon to support more weight (this often happens with the neck muscles supporting the weight of the head). For alignment to work optimally, six key joints must be aligned: head and neck, shoulder, lumbar spine, hip, knee, and ankle. The straight line in Figure 4.1 shows an approximation of how the joints should stack up. Obviously our bodies are not built on straight lines, so this image serves more as a frame of reference for how to balance and organize movement around those joints. Now we will learn more about each of these structures. A basic anatomical understanding is key to mapping alignment correctly.

Head/Neck

When I ask students to point to their head/neck joint, I'm always surprised that they point to the back of their neck when, in fact, the joint is located higher and more forward than that. A quick way to envision the location of the joint is to point the index fingers toward each other through the ear canal and imagine a line connecting the two. The atlanto-occipital joint is located at the point where the two imaginary lines would meet in the middle of the skull. Notice that about half of the head is in front of the joint and the other half behind the joint. Nod "yes" and "no" from this position to feel the difference between engaging the neck muscles and moving the head independently of the neck. Another effective technique for finding the head alignment is the "chin tuck": gently press the chin backward with your fingers and feel the back of your head moving back and up. When the head is aligned with the cervical spine, the muscles of the neck are working minimally to maintain that alignment.

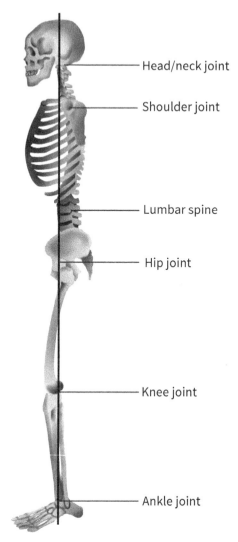

Figure 4.1. The six points of standing alignment.
Figure by Amber Huo.

Shoulders

Mapping the shoulder complex accurately allows for ease of movement and less muscular effort. The shoulders should ideally be at 90 degrees, with the arms hanging freely to the sides. Most of us hold our shoulders forward, resulting in shortening of the chest muscles and lengthening of the back muscles.

The shoulder complex consists of three structures (clavicle, scapula, and humerus) and four joints (glenohumeral, acromioclavicular, sternoclavicular, and scapulothoracic), which you can see in Figure 4.2. The glenohumeral joint is a ball-and-socket joint that attaches the humerus to the scapula. This joint is very flexible

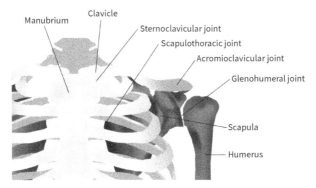

Figure 4.2. Shoulder complex.
Figure by Amber Huo.

and is susceptible to injury because of its lack of stability. The acromioclavicular joint functions differently: it is a gliding joint that connects the scapula to the clavicle and allows for scapular rotation.

The sternoclavicular joint connects the clavicle to the manubrium of the sternum, allowing for rotation in the vertical, horizontal, and sagittal planes. It is a saddle joint, allowing for axial rotation, elevation and depression, and protraction and retraction. However, the sternoclavicular joint does not function entirely independently, as movement in the scapulothoracic joint, which attaches the scapula to the thorax, affects movement in it as well. These joints work together in coordination to ensure smooth movements of the arm. Visit the companion website for a shoulder joint exploration (Movement Exploration 4.1 ▶).

Scapulohumeral rhythm refers to the ratio of the arm lift and shoulder blade rotation to accommodate that lift. For every two degrees of humeral elevation, there is one degree of shoulder blade rotation. Repeating these exploratory movements on the other side may also reveal differences in mobility between the two sides. Scapular dyskinesia occurs when the shoulder blade is not moving as it should (i.e., there is asymmetric movement between the two scapulae during movement) and may be caused by tightness in the surrounding muscles.

In order to counter the constant muscular pull from the front of the chest, think about the shoulder blades moving toward the opposite "back pocket." Additional imagery for expanding the shoulders is to envision the tips of the shoulders moving to opposite sides of the room, opening up the chest.

Arms

When the arms are allowed to hang freely to the sides, there is a slight bend in the elbows, the wrists are aligned, and the fingers exhibit a C-curve. The elbow joint is a hinge joint that also allows for rotation in the ulna and radius. Hold your elbows next to your body and bend your forearms up with your palms facing each other. In this position, the ulna and radius are parallel. Now, rotate your palms toward the floor. For this rotation to occur, the radius crosses over the ulna. This motion is critical to support movements of the hand more generally.

Hands

Ideally, we want the wrist and fingers to maintain their neutral position for as much playing time as possible. However, since instruments were not designed with ergonomics in mind, the position of the wrist often has to be compromised to fit the instrument. Accordingly, ergonomic options for aligning the wrist(s) should be explored wherever possible.

The wrist is located between the radius and ulna of the forearm (distal radioulnar joint) and the metacarpal bones of the fingers (as you can see in Figure 4.3). It consists of eight carpal bones, roughly arranged in two rows: the proximal carpals (closer to the forearm) and the distal carpals (farther from the forearm). The metacarpal bones attach to the distal carpals. The joints that articulate within the carpal

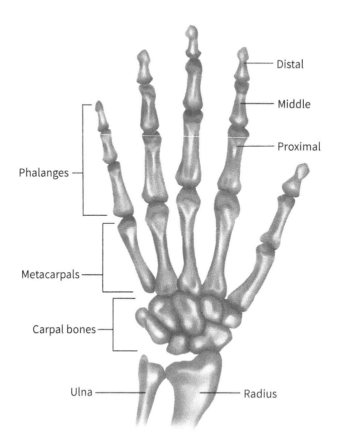

Figure 4.3. Wrist and hand.
Figure by Amber Huo.

bones and between the carpal bones and the forearm bones allow for the wrist's flexibility and range of motion. Each of the fingers (except for the thumb) has three bones: the proximal phalanx (closest to the palm), the middle phalanx, and the distal phalanx. The three joints of the fingers in order from the metacarpal bones to the nails are: the metacarpophalangeal joint, the proximal interphalangeal joint, and the distal interphalangeal joint.

It is important to continue to debunk the myth that there are muscles in the fingers and thus avoid technical exercises that claim to "strengthen the fingers." The fingers move as a result of the flexors and extensors in the forearm that move the tendons in the hand and fingers. The hand warmup glide exercises provided on the companion website can serve as an exploration of the movement possible in each of the hand joints (Exercise 5.7 ⊙). In order to find the neutral position of the wrists and hands, drop the arms to your sides and let them hang. Notice the natural curve of the hand and the aligned wrist. Maintain that rounded shape as you align yourself with your instrument. Despite our efforts on a micro-level to support a rounded hand position, there are larger issues afoot. If the hand is not supported by infrastructure that connects it to the spine, misalignment becomes inevitable.

Spine

There are two common misconceptions about the spine that I frequently encounter in my students: the first one is that an aligned spine is a straight spine; the second one is that the vertebrae are the superficial protrusions on the back. The fact is that the spine cannot support the weight of the body while still allowing for full breathing to occur if it is in a stiff, straight position. The vertebrae are much farther into the center of the body than most of us perceive in our body map. The bones we feel when we run our fingers along the spine are the spinal processes that extend behind the vertebrae and provide the point of attachment for muscles and ligaments.

The cervical spine comprises the seven vertebrae of the neck. Below these are twelve thoracic vertebrae located behind the chest. The five lumbar vertebrae are underneath the thoracic spine and are also the thickest in diameter. The S-design of the spine creates space for the lungs and the heart (the thoracic vertebrae curve outward), while providing support in the core of the body (the lumbar vertebrae are thick and curve inward). The lower part of the spine consists of the sacrum, which are five vertebrae fused together connected to the pelvis, and the coccyx, a non-weight-bearing structure also known as the tailbone. Figure 4.4 shows the different parts of the spine.

In an aligned neutral position, the weight of the upper body transfers through the thicker lower vertebrae and into the sit bones (or the feet when standing). The spine maintains its alignment without strain on the three natural curves. When the muscles are functioning with minimum effort, the spine can then rotate, lengthen, curve, and bend sideways with ease. Visit the companion website for an exercise that

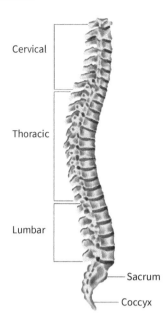

Figure 4.4. Spine.
Figure by Amber Huo.

explores movements of the spine (Movement Exploration 4.2 ▶). As you explore these movements, you will notice that the capitulation of the spine extends into the pelvis.

Pelvis

The pelvis plays an important role in aligning the spine and transferring weight to the chair or the floor. The bony structure of the pelvis consists of the sacrum, the coccyx, and the hip bones on either side, as you can see in Figure 4.5. A pelvis that is tipped forward or backward not only pushes the spine out of alignment but also affects the position of the head. The pelvis protects some of the most sensitive organs in the body. Its shape is not only protective by nature (enclosing the guts and reproductive system in a bowl shape) but also wide to allow for the transfer of weight from the upper body to the lower body. The upper ridges of the pelvis (iliac crests) are easily palpated by following the edge of the bones around the sides and the front of the body. The hip bones attach to the sacrum via connective tissue and to the femur bones at the hip joints. A common mis-mapping of the hip joint is placing it at the waist (by the iliac crests). A quick way to find the hip joint is to bend the leg, or sit down, and notice the crease between the leg and the pelvis. The hip joint is located in that crease. On the companion website, you will find an exercise that assists with balancing the upper body on the sit bones (Movement Exploration 4.3 ▶).

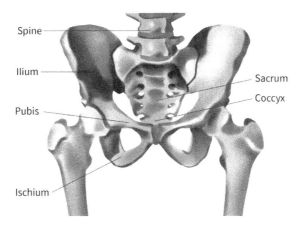

Figure 4.5. Pelvis.
Figure by Amber Huo.

Knees

When standing, the knees should remain unlocked. I think about the knees as "soft" but not overly bent. When seated, the knees should be at 90 degrees. It is important to correctly map the knee joint as located behind and below the patella (see Figure 4.6).

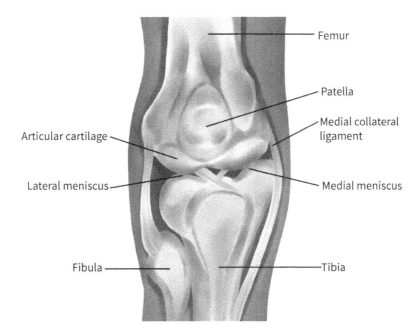

Figure 4.6. Knee.
Figure by Amber Huo.

Ankles and Feet

The feet play a crucial role in finding balance; however, if the aforementioned points of balance are ineffectively aligned, then weight will not be distributed properly through the feet. A closer look reveals a highly complex structure that is able to both stabilize the body and move it through space. Each foot consists of twenty-six bones and thirty-three joints and is organized into three sections, as shown in Figure 4.7: the hindfoot (ankle bone and heel bone), the midfoot (five tarsal bones), and the forefoot (phalanges and metatarsal bones). Because of the complexity of its structure, the foot is able to perform movements in several planes: point and flex, turn inward and outward, bend and flex the toes, and spread the toes and bring them together. Of particular interest to proper body mapping is an awareness of the ankle, where the tibia and fibula join together on either side of the ankle bone.

On the companion website, you will find an activity on weight transfer which helps activate the bottom of the feet to find balance (Movement Exploration 4.4 ⊙).

Returning to neutral alignment of these joints frequently throughout the course of the day or during practice allows us to "check in" to make sure we are not holding unnecessary tension and plays an important role in the prevention of injury.

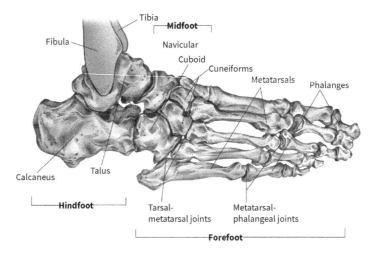

Figure 4.7. Foot and ankle.
Figure by Amber Huo.

Aligning with the Instrument

The tendency to "reach toward" the instrument, instead of bringing the instrument to us creates inefficient positions, which in turn affect breathing, embouchure, and finger positions.[8] Certain instruments, such as the violin and flute, are more conducive to asymmetrical positions. Extra care must be taken to guide the student through proper alignment using the least muscular effort possible.

More often than not, the design of an instrument does not match its performers' anatomical measurements. The piano keys may be too wide for a small-handed pianist, the violin height too shallow for a violinist with a long neck, and a flute's keys too far apart for a young flutist. These mismatches between performer and instrument cause strain in the playing mechanism of the musician. Ergonomic modifications to instruments, which the instructor is no doubt familiar with, may be necessary to relieve additional pressure in muscle groups that are already overworked.

No discussion about optimal alignment is complete without the breathing mechanism, which in many ways serves as the engine of our dynamic alignment. An incomplete or inaccurate understanding of the breathing mechanism leads to inefficient breathing and misconceptions of how the breath functions. If we incorrectly assume that we actively draw air in while inhaling, instead of expanding the ribs to allow air to rush in, this will result in forced inhalation and tightening of the muscles associated with breathing. We can actively counter this misconception, and others, by combining cognitive understanding of the breathing mechanism with embodied knowledge. This is best accomplished with a variety of interactive activities.

A Closer Look at the Breathing Mechanism

Singers and wind instrument players tend to be more familiar with the breathing mechanism out of necessity because without air flow, there is no sound. For instrumentalists who don't rely on the breath to produce sound, this element of alignment can slip under their radar. But all musicians, no matter their medium, can benefit from deepening their understanding of the relationship between their breath and music-making.

In essence, breathing is the exchange of air that occurs in the lungs: we inhale oxygen and exhale carbon dioxide. This gaseous exchange occurs as a result of our chest cavity changing in size. The resulting imbalance of air pressure between the lungs and the outside air is what causes air to move in and out. In this section we will increase our technical understanding of this mechanism. Although memorizing all the muscles involved is not necessary, understanding the complexity of the process and all its moving parts is crucial to ensure unencumbered breathing.

Lungs, Diaphragm, and Intercostals

Breathing is facilitated by the movement of the diaphragm, a dome-shaped muscle with fibrous tissue that attaches to the lower ribs and the front of the lumbar spine via the central tendon, as you can see in Figure 4.8. It separates the thoracic cavity from the abdominal cavity; the viscera are located right underneath its dome shape,

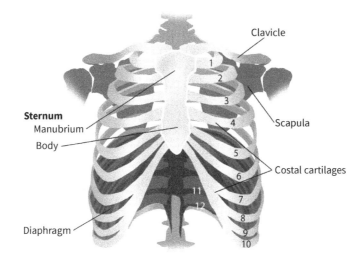

Figure 4.8. Ribs and diaphragm.
Figure by Amber Huo.

and the lungs sit on top of it. The diaphragm has three openings, which allow the esophagus and the vagus nerve (both of which control digestion), the aorta (the main artery that transports oxygen-filled blood from the heart to the lower body) and thoracic duct (a key vessel of the lymphatic system), and the inferior vena cava (an artery that transports deoxygenated blood to the heart) to pass through. The range of motion of the diaphragm is approximately 1.5 cm at rest and 6–10 cm during vigorous exercise.

The intercostal muscles are located between the ribs and consist of the external intercostals (located on the outside) and the internal intercostals (positioned on the inside). They facilitate expansion and contraction of the ribs during inhalation and exhalation, respectively.

The lungs are sponge-like structures filled with air that are located on each side of the trachea. They are surrounded by the pleurae, a pair of thin membranes that lubricate the area around the lungs and allow for their smooth movement. Air travels from the mouth or nose through the trachea and into the lungs through the bronchi. The bronchi divide into smaller branches called the bronchioles, which are then divided into microscopic sections called the alveoli. The exchange of oxygen and carbon dioxide occurs in the alveolar sacs.

Inhalation and Exhalation

During inhalation, the diaphragm contracts, pushing down on the viscera and the pelvic muscles. This movement of the belly moving outward is often called *diaphragmatic* or *belly breathing*, even though we are not actually inhaling from our belly. Air does not travel below the diaphragm, which means that where the ribs end, so does the air. Since the diaphragm is attached to the bottom ribs, as it contracts, it pushes out on those ribs, causing the ribcage to lift and expand. The lungs are attached to the thoracic cavity causing them to expand horizontally, vertically, and sagittally (i.e., front and back) as the ribcage lifts. As more space is created by the movement of the ribs and the diaphragm, air pressure decreases, causing air from the outside to rush in and equalize the pressure. Air enters the body through either the mouth or the nose and travels down to the lungs via the trachea and bronchial tubes. The volume of air that enters the body is dependent upon the motion of the diaphragm and ribs, as well as the resulting outward movement of the abdominal cavity.

After inhalation, elastic rebound (defined as the ease with which the lungs return to their original position) encourages expiration, aided by upward pressure on the diaphragm by the pelvic floor muscles and the viscera. Simultaneously, air flows out of the lungs to equalize pressure as the diaphragm returns to its dome shape. During deep breathing, the diaphragm massages the heart and viscera, improving their function.

Ribs and Spine

The spine and ribs are the bony parts of the breathing mechanism. The thoracic spine, which consists of twelve vertebrae, has an outward curve designed to make room for the heart and lungs. There are twelve ribs on each side of the body, attached to the thoracic vertebrae with the costovertebral joint. As the ribs curve around the front of the body, they become cartilage and connect with the sternum. The two lower ribs on either side do not curve all the way around and do not join with the sternum. These ribs are known as *free-floating ribs*, and they are easy to find if you place your hands at the bottom part of your ribcage and walk your fingers from the back to the front. The ribs are progressively longer moving from top to bottom. If you trace your hand along the side of the ribs, starting from the armpit moving down toward the bottom of the ribs, you will notice that the ribs form a steep curve downward and then inward at the bottom. It is important to correctly map the shape of the ribs so that when we are deepening our awareness of our breath, we are not working counterproductively to their shape and natural motion (see the shape of the ribs in Figure 4.8). Visit the companion website for a body mapping activity exploring the ribs (Movement Exploration activity 4.5 ⊙).

Mapping the Arm and Rib Motion

A common mapping error is associating movement of our ribs with movement of our shoulders. I notice this especially with students at the pre-collegiate level, who may not have a clear map of their breathing mechanism yet. When I ask them to take a deep breath, inevitably they will lift their chest up and raise their shoulders up to their ears. A good way to feel the independence of the arm structure from movement of the ribs is to place one hand on the collarbone and the other on the ribcage below it. Take a breath and shrug the shoulders. Drop and shrug the shoulders a few times, noting how the ribs don't move along with the shoulder motion. Unnecessary tightening of the shoulders while breathing can inhibit the free and full motion of the ribs and thus negatively impact alignment.

Accessory Muscles

Several muscles are involved in the breathing mechanism, as shown in Figure 4.9. An accurate map of where these are located and an understanding of their function allow the ribs to move more freely and fully. Central to achieving this goal are the levatores costarum muscles, twelve muscles on either side of the vertebrae, running from the seventh cervical vertebra to the eleventh thoracic vertebra and connecting to the ribs below the vertebrae from which they originate. During inhalation, the levatores costarum assist with lifting the ribs. The serratus posterior superior muscles also assist with the process of inhalation by elevating the second to fifth ribs. These muscles originate from the seventh

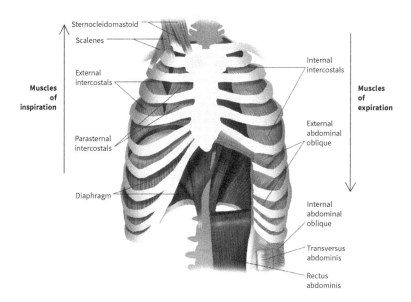

Figure 4.9. Muscles involved in breathing.
Figure by Amber Huo.

cervical vertebra through the third thoracic vertebra and connect to the ribs they elevate. Additional muscles that assist and support the breathing mechanism are the pectoralis group. The pectoralis major is primarily responsible for flexion, adduction, and medial rotation of the arm. This muscle covers the area of the upper chest from the shoulder to the sternum, attaching to the clavicle, sternum, and top six ribs. The pectoralis minor is located underneath the pectoralis major and connects the third, fourth, and fifth ribs to the scapula. This muscle group assists by helping to raise the ribs during inhalation. Continuing, the serratus anterior connects the front part of the shoulder blade to the first through eighth or ninth ribs. Its primary function is to pull the shoulder blade forward and around the ribs. When the shoulder blade is at rest, it assists with raising the ribs during inhalation. The scalene muscles connect the second to sixth cervical vertebrae with the top two ribs. These three muscles (the scalenus anterior, scalenus medius, and scalenus posterior) primarily allow for flexion and rotation of the neck. They also lift the first two ribs but should not be actively involved during the respiration process.

The four muscles of the abdominal wall (external obliques, internal obliques, transversus abdominis, and rectus abdominis) support voluntary expiration. These muscles are superimposed on one another, creating a three-layer structure, and they run along the front and sides of the body. The external obliques, as their name suggests, comprise the outermost layer of the abdominal wall. They are located on the side of the abdomen and run between the pelvis and the lowest ribs. The internal obliques form two layers and run between the lumbar spine and the top of the pelvis around the front of the body to the pubic crest and lower ribs. In contrast, the rectus abdominis runs vertically in the front of the body, crossing the two layers of the internal obliques for part of the way. It connects the pubic bone in the pelvis with the fifth through seventh ribs. The rectus abdominis are the group of muscles we commonly call a *six-pack*. Behind this muscle group is the transversus abdominis, which forms the deepest layer of the abdominal wall. Because of its position deep within the body, it is attached to several structures as it wraps around the sides of the body to the back (the diaphragm, the lower six ribs, the spine, the hip bone, and the pubic symphysis), thus affecting both posture and breathing. During inhalation, the diaphragm presses against the abdominal muscles, which in turn relax, allowing the viscera to move out. If these muscles are toned, they will quickly spring back to their shape. However, if the abdominal muscles are tense, the breath is restricted.

The muscles of the pelvic floor also contribute to the process of breathing in a subtler way, contracting to protect the organs of the pelvis during breathing. These muscles do not contract on their own, but work together with the abdominal muscles and the diaphragm to relax during inhalation and contract during exhalation, increasing pressure on the diaphragm as it moves up.[9]

Breath–Alignment Relationship

> ### Alignment and Breath
>
> There is no doubt that physical alignment affects our breathing. Take a moment and move into a slouched position. Hold it there for a second and try to take a deep breath. You will notice that your chest and ribs will feel compressed. The breath will feel forced and tight. Then move into your best alignment, one in which your spine is tall, the head floats above it, and the chest is wide. Take a breath here. Notice how much easier it is to breathe when the ribs have room to expand and the muscles can function optimally.

In order to consistently maintain a tall alignment that facilitates optimal breathing, we must train the deep postural muscles that help us do so. Recent research has demonstrated that training these deep postural muscles does indeed have a positive effect on "postural control and quality of breathing movements."[10] Szczygieł et al. recruited eighteen volunteers, who were asked to complete a training program designed to activate deep postural muscles. At the end of the study, they found that the trained participants had significantly improved their posture and breath control. The musicians among us who tend to avoid strengthening exercises (myself included!), citing a busy schedule, may want to reconsider finding time to strengthen those muscles considering the benefits this might have on performance, not to mention overall wellness.

There are two layers of deep postural muscles in the spine that keep our body erect and allow for optimal breathing.[11] The deepest layer consists of small muscles attached to the vertebrae that support the spine and keep it long. The sacrospinalis muscles form the second layer that runs up and down the spine and attaches to the ribs. When these muscles are tight, the ribs do not move as freely, therefore restricting the breath. The sternocleidomastoid muscle also supports our posture. You can feel this muscle's insertion if you palpate the back of the bottom of the skull and around the side of the neck. This muscle attaches to the clavicle and sternum. The serratus posterior superior muscles also support our upright posture and, as described earlier, play an important role in allowing the free widening and narrowing motion of the ribs.

Another set of muscles in the back that assists with the proper movement of the ribs consists of the muscles attached to the scapula (the levator scapulae, rhomboid major, and rhomboid minor). These elevate and stabilize the scapula when the arm moves. Their proper functioning enables the ribs to widen during breathing.

The trapezius and latissimus dorsi comprise the outermost layer of the muscles of the back. The trapezius muscles cover most of the area over the neck, shoulders, and thoracic spine. This muscle group assists with pinching the shoulder blades together and supports the arm. The latissimus dorsi, as its Latin name suggests, is the broadest muscle of the back, covering its lower half. It inserts at the lower part of the spine (sacral, lumbar, and lower thoracic vertebrae) and attaches to the upper arm. The latissimus dorsi assists with flexion and extension of the arm and trunk, rotation of the trunk, and scapular movements. Because of the size of this muscle, it plays a crucial role in breathing and the action of the ribs.

Even with a strong understanding of these muscular relationships, we must apply them to basic decisions of how we manage our physical body on a day-to-day basis. Those include important decisions about when to practice standing or sitting, when given the choice.

Sitting or Standing?

Considering the complex relationship between physical alignment and the breath, one cannot help but question how seated or standing positions impact breathing. What should musicians be aware of, especially those who have the choice between the two?

The research shows that standing promotes higher abdominal muscle activation, thereby assisting the process of breathing and the control of expiration, which can be significant in wind instruments. A study by Ackerman, Dwyer, and Halaki examined the impact of playing postures on muscle activity in controlling expiration into an instrument.[12] Musicians performed five excerpts in one of four positions: standing, sitting flat, sitting inclined forward, and sitting inclined backward. The results showed greater chest expansion and almost doubled abdominal activation in the standing position, which could lead to better breath control, as compared to the sitting positions. The musicians indicated a strong preference for the standing position, perhaps due to the fact that it was easier to breathe more fully.

For many musicians, especially those who perform in ensembles, standing is not an option. The issue that arises from playing an instrument in a seated position is not so much that the muscular activation is not as effective, but the fact that this position works against the breath by maintaining less than optimal alignment. The importance of maintaining an aligned seated position, as opposed to a slouched posture, for optimal breathing is further supported by research conducted by Albarrati et al.[13] They investigated the effects of the slouched versus tall postures on respiratory muscle strength in healthy young males by measuring sniff nasal inspiratory pressure (a test that measures the muscular strength of inspiration). The results showed significant score differences between the slouched position and the upright position. A slouched position may cause less action in the diaphragm and movement of the ribs, as opposed to an upright position, which allows for more diaphragmatic action and more movement. Maintaining a tall alignment allows us to breathe more fully and avoid any potential breathing disorders caused by prolonged slouched positions.[14]

Now, the question becomes, what type of chair should be used for seated practicing and performance? For brass players, the common recommendation is to use a downward-sloping chair (from back to front) because it allows the lumbar curve to maintain a posture that is closer to that of standing. Price et al. examined the effect of posture on breathing in brass players by comparing breathing while standing and seated in various erect postures that are typical for brass players (flat, downward- or upward-sloping, or reclining seat).[15] The researchers found that the type of chair used affects breathing, but their findings don't necessarily fully support the exclusive use of a downward-sloping chair. The tension in the abdominal wall when sitting on such a chair was not high enough to be comparable with standing. Sitting on a chair that had a sloping back or an upward-sloping seat produced negative effects on breathing. A great degree of reclining produced the highest vital capacity in breathing but proved to be uncomfortable for the musicians. Based on this study, the researchers recommend that musicians alternate between seated on sloping seats and standing postures in their practice so they are better prepared for both performance situations.

When practicing while seated, ergonomic chairs may be helpful to promote lengthening of the spine and to facilitate alignment of its natural curves. Ohlendorf et al. investigated the effects of the construction and surface quality of six ergonomic musicians' chairs on musicians of different playing levels.[16] Pressure changes were

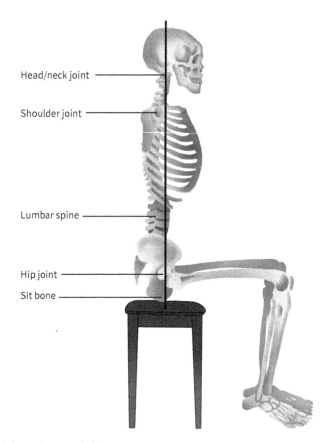

Figure 4.10. Balance in seated alignment.
Figure by Amber Huo.

noted between the different chairs (cushioned and non-cushioned; wide and narrow) and between the playing conditions (with and without instrument). Cushioned and wide chairs had a 25-percent reduction of load, which may be helpful for people who have skin conditions, since there is less weight placed on the skin. Takeaways from this study include the considerations that must come into play when selecting an ergonomic chair: width, cushioning, resulting posture, pressure on the chair, and comfort.

When ergonomic chairs are not available, there are several ergonomic modifications that can be used to improve alignment and breathing. A curved foam cushion or a wedge pad can provide back pain relief. A wobble cushion or balance disc trainer also activates the core, providing exercise at the same time. Figure 4.10 shows how the points of balance should be stacked in a seated position. Ergonomic modifications can help with more comfortably aligning these joints.

Practicing in a seated position for extended periods of time, especially for those musicians who need significant abdominal strength for sound production, may indeed lower abdominal strength and thus make the practice of demanding repertoire more challenging and tiring. It also increases the risk of slouching, which causes inefficient engagement of the muscles needed for breathing. For these reasons, when the option is available, students may choose to combine seated and standing practice in order to fully engage the breathing muscles.

∗∗∗

Optimal alignment is fundamental to the development of effective technique for any instrumentalist or singer. Teaching these principles is best done through a multifaceted approach that is based on breath, kinesthetic awareness, correct mapping, and stacking of the joints. In retraining alignment, use language that promotes comfort and gentle exploration of the body, rather than a forced positioning. Remember that alignment looks different from person to person and even from day to day, depending on various other factors such as mood or fatigue. Revisiting neutral alignment frequently throughout the day is a way to check in with the body and release any unnecessary tension. This ability to release tension, the result of maintaining a balanced body position, is critical beyond the development of a robust technique. It may also help prevent physical injuries of various types, which we will explore in the next chapter.

5

Protecting the Body

Injury Prevention

Prevention education should start from the very first lesson, irrespective of the student's age. The old adage of "if it ain't broke, don't fix it" should not be a guiding principle when it comes to injuries. Even students with what we would consider "good technique" may be vulnerable to injury because they may not be taking care of their bodies by warming up and cooling down before and after practicing. It is my contention that all students, regardless of their level of playing and musicianship, must be familiar with prevention strategies and should be actively encouraged by their instructor to apply them in their daily practice routine. These active steps, as we will explore in this chapter, involve performing warm-up and cool-down exercises, developing positive practice habits to safeguard the body against injury, and becoming familiar with mind–body practices as well as other preventive and treatment modalities.

In addition to the recommendations in this chapter, I suggest sharing information about injury prevention with students early in the semester or study period. The PAMA/NASM advisory documents on musculoskeletal, hearing, and vocal health are helpful resources that summarize useful information (visit the companion website for direct links ⊙).[1] These electronic documents exist in formats that can be shared verbally as part of a student orientation or via a handout.

Guidelines for Injury-Prevention

There is a wealth of resources available offering in-depth guidance on practicing, and undoubtedly, conversations on practice tools are commonplace in lessons. The advice given in this section applies more to the habits surrounding practicing than to the actual learning of the repertoire itself. I drew information here from useful guidelines that many researchers, teachers, and healthcare professionals agree upon.[2] You can find a handout with these guidelines on the companion website that you can print and give to students [Worksheet 5.1 ⊙].

- Increase practice time gradually after a long break. Overexerting muscles that have potentially weakened will cause undue stress and may increase the potential for injury.

Teaching the Whole Musician. Paola Savvidou, Oxford University Press (2021). © Oxford University Press.
DOI: 10.1093/oso/9780190868796.003.0005

- Practice for about twenty-five minutes and take a break for five. Use different movements during your break than you were using while practicing. For example, if you are practicing piano, avoid using the computer or your phone during your break, as those activities use the same muscles as playing the piano. Here are some ideas for what you might do during a break: hydrate, take a walk, stretch, meditate, chat with a supportive friend or family member, lie down in a constructive rest pose (Figure 5.1).
- Alternate between less and more technically demanding repertoire with breaks in between.
- Set an alarm on your phone to check in with your physical alignment and breath every few minutes. Take five or six seconds to notice any unnecessary tension that may have crept in.
- Develop a habit of warming up before practicing and cooling down after (for more information, see the Injury-Prevention Toolkit section at the end of the chapter).
- Maintain a neutral position in the joints as much as possible when practicing (and during other activities such as typing and texting).
- Notice sensations that arise in your body while you are practicing. If you are noticing discomfort, try to identify what might be causing it.
- Slow down and notice when a passage is not working. Analyze your movements to see where there might be tension or spots where coordination of the movement can be improved upon (consult Chapter 6 for a model you can use to analyze movement).
- Minimize muscular effort where you can.
- Pay attention to the quality of the movements you are using to produce the desired sound.
- Schedule practice sessions during times of day when you are alert and focused.

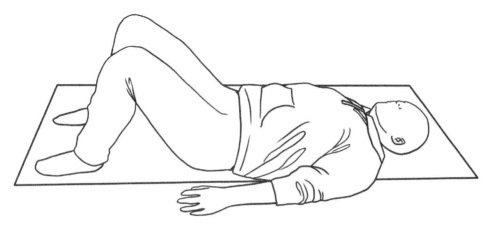

Figure 5.1. Constructive rest pose.
Figure by Amber Huo.

Physical Warm-Up

A typical first question I ask my students about physical warm-ups is: "How many of you warm up before you practice?" You'd be pleased to know that most hands usually go up. And then the follow-up question comes: "What do you do for your warm-up?" That's where we typically get stuck. The responses are usually a variation on "ten minutes of scales." Pretty quickly, we dive into the conversation about the differences between a whole-body warm-up and technical exercises. There is merit to both, but they have to be done in the right order. A whole-body physical warm-up should precede technical exercises or repertoire practice.

The ideal type of warm-up is one that students can easily fit into their daily routine. Time is of the essence in every music student's busy schedule; therefore, I recommend between five and ten minutes of aerobic movement before practicing. Warming up the body means elevating the heart rate up to 110 beats per minute and increasing blood flow to the muscles and tendons. A warmed-up muscle is less likely to get injured. A simple warm-up, such as walking briskly in the practice room area or going up and down the stairs, can easily accomplish this elevation in heart rate. If a student is able to dedicate a full ten minutes to warming up, I recommend spending the first five elevating the heart rate and the last five in dynamic stretching, focused on muscles that will be heavily used during the practice.

After a whole-body warm-up, singers should follow their usual routine of warming up the voice through humming, lip trills, and vowel glides. Instrumentalists should ease into playing by playing through easier repertoire or technical exercises before moving on to more challenging technical requirements. While warming up is critical to setting up practice sessions in a healthy manner, the ways in which we take care of ourselves afterward are just as important. The most critical immediate concern after practicing is to return the muscles to an elongated state through stretching.

Stretching

For many of us, stretching happens intuitively. Our body knows we need a stretch after sitting for long periods of time, when we wake up in the morning, when we yawn, or need to energize ourselves. Stretching allows the muscles to return to their original length and helps us maintain our range of motion. When the antagonist muscle is stretched, the agonist muscle can return to its original, relaxed position more quickly.

Although general stretches that apply to all musicians are recommended in the following section, it is best to remain mindful of each individual's particular needs. Someone who is experiencing particular tightness in the forearm may need to focus on that area and include more forearm stretches as part of the daily routine. As a basic guideline for stretches, think about the position you are in when practicing and the main muscle groups at work in that scenario. Then, stretch those muscles in the opposite direction. It is important that opposite groups of muscles have equal strength and flexibility. This prevents one muscle group from overexerting and increases the efficiency of the movement.

Skipping the stretching portion of the practice routine means the muscles do not lengthen to their original position and mobility is reduced. When mobility is reduced, muscles must work harder to accomplish the desired movement. Chronically shortened muscles get tight and may eventually lead to pain and injury. A common misconception is that deep stretching should happen before practice; however, that approach could cause serious damage to cold muscles. Students must be made aware of the difference between dynamic and static stretching and when to use which to avoid harm.

Dynamic versus Static Stretching

Static stretching occurs when we stretch for an adequate amount of time to allow the muscle to lengthen. The recommended amount of time for holding a static stretch is thirty seconds. Static stretching should never occur when the muscles are cold, as they are more likely to get injured. It is best to do static stretches during a break or at the end of a practice session when the muscles are already warmed up. Dynamic stretching should occur when the muscles need to warm up, such as at the beginning of a practice session. Dynamic stretching differs from static stretching in that the positions are not held. Instead, the motion into and out of a stretch is repeated a few times before moving on to the next stretch. Moving through the positions increases blood flow and warms up the muscles, preparing them for activity. See the Injury-Prevention Toolkit section at the end of the chapter for more information on warm-ups and cool-downs.

Tips for Stretching

- Encourage students to take a few minutes before playing to warm up and a few minutes after playing to cool down.
- Perform dynamic stretches before playing.
- After playing, engage in a series of static stretches, holding each for thirty seconds.
- A stretch should be felt in the muscle belly, not in or near the joint, to avoid causing any damage to the tendon or the ligament.
- Never push the body farther than what feels comfortable.
- Breathe steadily through the exercises.
- Deepen a static stretch slightly on the exhale.

Physical Exercise

Dr. Richard Norris, specialist in Physical Medicine and Rehabilitation and founding member of PAMA, suggests that musicians have to take care of their bodies through a comprehensive exercise program in order to maintain a healthy approach to their instrument. He suggests a combination of cardiovascular fitness, flexibility, and strength training. Benefits of exercise include mental clarity, reduced weight gain, lower risk of cardiovascular disease and diabetes, reduced risk of anxiety and depression, improved sleep, and an overall sense of well-being.[3]

Aerobic activity is defined by the intensity, frequency, and duration of the exercise. The US Department of Health and Human Services' physical activity guidelines suggest that adults should do at least two and a half hours of moderate-intensity or 75 to 150 minutes of vigorous-intensity aerobic exercise per week. Ideally, the total amount of time would be spread over the week. Examples of moderate-intensity activities include brisk walking, yoga (e.g., Vinyasa), and exercise classes. Vigorous-intensity activities include running, tennis, swimming, interval training, and exercise classes with vigorous motions. Muscle strengthening should ideally occur twice per week and include all the major muscle groups.

Interestingly, the previously mentioned study on flute students by Ackerman et al. showed that even though some of the students participated in exercise such as tennis, swimming, and Pilates, it was not enough to safeguard them against performance-related injuries.[4] This demonstrates that musician-specific exercises may be more beneficial. I suggest that in addition to the preceding recommendations for exercise, students also focus on stretching and strengthening muscles specific to their instrument. See the companion website for core and back strengthening exercises that are beneficial for musicians (Exercise 5.1 ▶).

Choosing the Right Type of Exercise

The word "workout" is often used to describe exercise. No wonder many of us are averse to the idea of exercising: precisely because it feels like "work" instead of an enjoyable way to find release from mental and physical tension and to stay healthy. Exercising should be an activity that feels good to the body and the mind alike. I suggest trying different types of activities before selecting a favorite one to do on a frequent basis.

Another challenge with exercising on a regular basis is the time it takes away from practicing, studying, working, and otherwise fulfilling our day-to-day responsibilities. If we break down the barrier that exercise only happens at the gym, we are more likely to find time to fit it into our routine. For example, physical activity can be accomplished during an extended practice break (e.g., taking a long walk, going up and down stairs), or by pursuing activities that are more physically demanding, such as housework or yardwork. Here is a list of practice break ideas, that may include exercising, to share with your students (Worksheet 5.2 ▶).

Ideas for Practice Breaks

- Hydrate.
- Eat a healthy snack (list your favorite nutritious snacks):
    - _____
    - _____
    - _____
- Walk around the building.
- Walk outside.
- Stretch (list your favorite stretches):
    - _____
    - _____
    - _____
- Meditate for two minutes.
- Say a mantra to yourself for a full minute (list your favorite mantras):
    - _____
    - _____
    - _____
- List other practice break ideas here:
    - _____
    - _____
    - _____

Another activity you can do in your studio to facilitate physical exercise is to have your students create their own video of their favorite exercises. Each student can contribute one dynamic and one static stretch. The exercises can be easily compiled into one video that can be shared with the entire studio. Another way to incorporate the students' ideas on taking care of their physical health is to have them contribute their favorite three- to five-minute stretching YouTube videos to a playlist maintained by you. All the students could then have access to the playlist, which would contain several short videos they can use. If your students enjoy running or walking, you might suggest they form a walking or running group to support each other and develop camaraderie in the studio.

Dr. Jeremy Stanek, who was cited in Chapter 3 in our discussion on pain experienced among musicians, boils down key injury-prevention practices to the following five tips:

1. Perform a proper warm-up every day before you practice.
2. Take frequent breaks from practicing.

3. Listen to your body.
4. Exercise to balance your body.
5. Seek help when and if you think something is wrong.

These simple, straightforward suggestions summarize the fundamental information our students should know to protect themselves against injuries.

Mind–Body Practices

Research indicates that, when injured, musicians are more likely to seek mind–body practices than visit a physician.[5] According to Stanek, mind–body practices are extremely advantageous in the process of recovery, but even more so when the injured musician is under the care of a physician who can monitor progress and make appropriate recommendations. Mind–body practices seek to improve the efficiency of the neuromuscular system while integrating the person as a whole. A foundational principle permeating these practices is that the mind, body, and spirit function optimally when they are integrated and treated as part of the same system. In this section we will explore some of the most common techniques that musicians pursue for both prevention and recovery.

Alexander Technique

Developed by Frederick Matthias Alexander (1869–1955), the Alexander technique (AT) does not require an extensive introduction, as it has become widely popular among musicians in the past fifty years for improving alignment and efficiency. The technique is offered in both group and private lesson formats. The premise of AT is that excess muscular effort and postural misalignments are habits that do not serve the performer well and can be changed through psychophysical re-education. Use of the body becomes more efficient through the process of improving the relationship of the head and neck (referred to as the *primary control*), inhibiting movements that are inefficient or potentially harmful, and replacing them with more efficient patterns.

The effects of the AT have been researched in the past thirty years, with outcomes indicating effectiveness in terms of managing chronic pain, improving movement coordination and posture, deepening body awareness, and introducing injury-prevention tools. A study by Janet Davies investigated the self-reported effects of a musician-focused AT course on music students' playing-related pain, risk factors for pain, and any perceived changes in the quality of their playing.[6] All participants indicated receiving some benefit from the AT classes with regard to their pain level, technique, posture, and stress.

Feldenkrais Method

Mosché Feldenkrais (1904–1984) was the creator of this method, which is founded on the idea of improving the efficiency of movement by increasing self-awareness through slow, exploratory movements. The method can be taught one of two ways: (1) with an instructor in a class setting (this format is called Awareness Through Movement, or ATM) or (2) with an instructor in a one-on-one setting (known as Functional Integration). In an ATM session, the instructor typically guides the students through the movement experiences verbally. Ample time for rest is provided during the lesson, inviting the body and mind to integrate new-found awareness and movement patterns. The movements are often subtle, slow, and gentle, allowing one to notice how body parts work together and in isolation. In a Functional Integration appointment, the practitioner uses a hands-on approach to physically manipulate the student's body.

There are five principles that form the foundation of the Feldenkrais method: the learning process, posture, tonic state, variation and repetition, and visualization.[7] The learning process refers to the idea that we are constantly evolving throughout our lives and discovering previously unnoticed connections in our bodies. In the Feldenkrais approach, posture is not static, but in constant motion, adjusting to our needs and environment. A basic seated alignment is described as centering the upper body over the hip joints and sit bones, maintaining a relaxed back, and having flexibility in the legs for movement.[8] The tonic state refers to the baseline muscular activity that is present at all times. Feldenkrais explained this state as one in which the body is at ease and ready for action. From this state, an activity can be maintained for long periods of time without fatigue.

ATM lessons are designed to provide ample opportunities for variation and repetition. Through these movement experiences, students return to movement that is based on the developmental progression (e.g., rolling, crawling). Lessons generally progress from simple to complex and then back to simple again. This process allows the students to notice their habitual patterns and build new ones through deep awareness and gentle movement. Visualization echoes a similar process to body mapping. Students in ATM classes are invited to visualize how a body part moves before moving it physically. Visualizing brings awareness to body parts that may have been difficult to access previously and improves coordination of movement.

Yoga

Yoga, an ancient Eastern philosophical system that has become popularized in the Western world in the past few decades, is based on the idea of integrating mind, body, and spirit through the practice of breathing (called *pranayama* in Sanskrit), poses, and meditation. Practicing yoga restores the balance of energy. For the beginning yogi, the variety of yoga types can be overwhelming and confusing. And to make matters even more confusing, teachers often blend different types of yoga, or combine yoga with other practices such as Pilates (Yogalates). Here is a breakdown of the most common yoga practices:

Hatha yoga is the umbrella term that refers to any type of yoga that includes poses as part of the practice. In the West, these classes generally provide a gentle and accessible introduction to poses.

Bikram yoga is a type of "hot yoga," known for the hot room where it is practiced. The room is maintained at 105 degrees Fahrenheit and 40 percent humidity, so this kind of yoga tends to appeal to individuals who don't mind breaking a sweat! Bikram consists of a fixed sequence of twenty-six poses, and classes generally run for ninety minutes.

Iyengar, developed by B. K. S. Iyengar, is known for its highly specific instructions, focus on the detail in the form, and use of props to assist in the process. In an Iyengar class, poses are maintained for extended periods.

Restorative yoga consists of gentle poses supported by props such as bolsters, blankets, and straps. Gravity is used to elongate muscles and release tension, leading to a calmer state of mind.

Vinyasa consists of a sequence of poses practiced without a break. The flow requires intense physical engagement, and the poses vary from class to class. There is a focus on connecting the movement with the breath to find ease in the poses and transitions.

Ashtanga is similar to Vinyasa, only the sequence of poses is the same for each class. It is physically demanding, and one can expect a vigorous workout.

Kundalini yoga is based on the idea that kundalini energy is trapped in the lower spine. The poses focus on releasing that energy through working out the core, breathing exercises, chanting, and meditation.

Kripalu yoga combines poses, breath practice, and meditation in a way that is accessible to people of all ages, fitness levels, and body types. Kripalu classes consist of three stages:

- Willful Practice: combining body and breath through poses and building the flow of *prana* (which translates from Sanskrit as "breath" or "life force").
- Holding the Posture: longer poses and meditation with the goal of restoring mental balance.
- Meditation in Motion: deep relaxation.

Several universities now offer Yoga for Musicians classes, and students are enjoying the benefits of the integration of the mind, body, and spirit. A study on the effects of nine weeks of yoga practice in undergraduate and graduate conservatory students found that there were large decreases in both music performance anxiety and trait anxiety after the completion of the series. The positive effects continued for several months after the intervention.[9] Another study by Khalsa et al. recruited young adult professional musicians to participate in a two-month yoga and meditation program.[10] Self-reported questionnaires were collected on performance anxiety, mood, sleep, performance-related musculoskeletal disorders, stress, and sleep quality. The group that participated in the yoga and meditation program showed reduced performance anxiety, stress, anxiety, depression, and anger compared to the control group. These results demonstrate that musicians benefit holistically through the practice of yoga, with a particularly positive impact on the reduction of performance anxiety.

A concern that may come up with students when suggesting yoga practice is its religious association. Although it does have its roots in the sacred Vedic texts, classes in the West do not generally emphasize this component. Yoga can be practiced in a secular way and can be incorporated into lessons without the concern of religious discrimination. Considering the many benefits that yoga offers, simple poses and breathing exercises can be easily introduced to the student during the lesson. If you are unfamiliar with yoga, I would suggest taking a few classes yourself before introducing any of these to your students. Visit the companion website for some simple, accessible poses you can safely teach your students (Exercises 5.2–5.4 ▶).

Pilates

Pilates is commonly practiced among singers, especially to develop their core strength. It was developed by Joseph Hubertus Pilates (1883–1967), whose goal was to restore people's health, not just to design exercises for strengthening. Pilates is rooted in an understanding of human anatomy, exercise methods, and Greek and Eastern philosophies. As such, the method combines exercises in a rigorous classroom setting that promotes full mental and physical involvement. The Pilates approach has gradually evolved over time, and one could argue that (as with yoga), not all classes are true to their roots. The classical version of Pilates is on the floor using a mat. Props such as the TheraBand™ and OverBall are often used to assist with any limitations. Standing Pilates was developed by Joan Breibart with the goal of maximum transfer of the exercises to daily life. Other popular Pilates approaches include equipment such as the reformer and the tower.

The six principles of Pilates are concentration, control, precision, centering, breathing, and flow. Pilates instruction is highly detailed, requiring intense concentration. Focusing on the verbal instruction allows one to observe one's movements in more detail, revealing how body parts work together. Attention to detail results in maximal control of movement. A focus on precision in this state of awareness helps the practitioner minimize unnecessary and potentially tension-inducing movements.

Studies on Pilates have demonstrated effectiveness in alleviating chronic low back pain, chronic neck pain, postural alignment, and flexibility.[11] One of the main tenets of Pilates is to strengthen the abdomen, shoulder girdle, back, hips, and buttocks.[12] The purpose behind strengthening this "powerhouse" is to improve posture and to stabilize the trunk and shoulders. Breathing permeates all the principles of Pilates. Coordinating breath with movement improves the quality of the movement and activates the core. Flow refers to finding continuity in the movement and getting into a state in which one is fully immersed in the activity. Visit the companion website for one of the fundamental exercises in Pilates, called Pilates 100, which builds strength by activating the core muscles (Exercise 5.5 ⏵).

This overview covers the most common practices musicians have adopted. There are certainly several more that resonate with individuals, including Body Mapping, which is covered in more detail in Chapter 4. Whereas these methods require physical engagement by the recipient, the treatment modalities presented in the following section involve more passive means of participation. In these techniques, the practitioner uses pressure and various types of physical manipulation to relieve muscular tension.

Other Treatment Modalities

Rolfing

Driven by her own physical challenges, biochemist Ida Rolf (1896–1979) developed her ten-session series of structural integration as a way to optimize physical performance. In a Rolfing session, the practitioner uses hands-on manipulation to release myofascial restrictions and improve alignment. Rolfing differs from a massage in that its end goal is not relaxation, but deep restructuring of the fascia. It can be painful depending on an individual's condition and trigger points.

Acupuncture

Chinese medicine is based on the philosophy that to treat a physical ailment, patients must be viewed from a holistic perspective in terms of their physical, mental, emotional, and spiritual states, as well as their environment. Acupuncture is commonly used to treat musculoskeletal disorders and has been proven effective in the treatment of tennis elbow, shoulder pain, low back pain, and neck disorders.[13] In Chinese medicine, energy is considered to flow through twelve meridians (or pathways) in the body. Inserting thin needles in selected spots aims to balance the flow of energy throughout the body. Needles are placed on points near and distal to the pain site, as well as on Ashi points, which are similar to trigger points.

Osteopathic Manipulative Treatment

The training of osteopathic physicians (DOs) is heavily focused on the musculoskeletal system and how imbalances in one system can affect overall health. DOs use hands-on osteopathic manipulative treatment (OMT) primarily to evaluate and treat problems related to muscular pain. The treatment includes applying gentle pressure, stretching, and resistance to improve the range of motion in the joints. OMT is recommended by the American College of Physicians for those patients who are experiencing acute, subacute, or chronic low back pain.

Chiropractic Care

Chiropractic treatment is used as an alternative way to relieve pain caused by either a traumatic event or repetitive stress. A chiropractor performs manual adjustments to manipulate the joints. The motions are usually quick and forceful. The results are increased range of motion and pain relief. Chiropractic treatment is usually done in conjunction with other medical modalities in order to treat patients and has proven effective especially in treating spinal pain.

Myofascial Trigger Point Therapy

Trigger points are tightly contracted muscles that feel like knots. These occur halfway through the muscle fiber. Blood flow to the area is restricted because of the contraction. Over time, the muscle becomes weak and more easily fatigued. Nerve entrapment may also occur as a result of chronically tight muscles.[14] Common muscle groups that develop trigger points are those of the neck, shoulders, upper arms, forearms, and hands. Usually, intense pain is experienced when pressing into a trigger point. Massaging and releasing the muscle provides relief and improves blood flow and mobility. Another method of releasing the trigger points is using a lacrosse ball, tennis ball, or ping-pong ball to apply pressure to trigger points and encourage release.

The techniques presented here are but a few of the many treatment modalities available. Even with an awareness of these effective practices, prevention is the best medicine. So far we have discussed several preventive measures—from warm-ups to stretching, and mind–body practices—but in order to cover all our bases we must also consider some practical tools that will help our students effectively integrate prevention techniques within their day-to-day musical activities.

Injury-Prevention Toolkit

In this section, you will find activities you can use with your students to help build awareness around their practice habits and take steps toward incorporating sound injury-prevention strategies. Worksheets and videos of warm-up and cool-down sequences are available on the companion website ⏵.

Practice Habits Student Questionnaire

The beginning of the semester is a good time to reboot practice habits with returning students and to learn more about new students' practice habits. The following questionnaire may be distributed during studio class as a way to give the teacher information about areas that can be improved and education that needs to happen to improve injury-prevention habits (Worksheet 5.3 ▶).

1. How many days do you practice per week?
   1–2   3–4   5–6   6–7
2. On a typical day, how many hours do you practice?
   1–2   2–3   3–4   4–5   more than 5
3. On a typical day, how many hours do you spend in rehearsal?
   1–2   2–3   3–4   4–5   more than 5
4. Do you warm up and/or cool down before and after practice?
   a. I only warm up.
   b. I only cool down.
   c. I warm up and cool down.
   d. I neither warm up nor cool down.
5. How many minutes do you spend warming up?
   0   1–3   4–6   7–9   10–12   13–15   more than 15
6. What is your favorite way of warming up?

7. How many minutes do you spend cooling down?
   0   1–3   4–6   7–9   10–12   13–15   more than 15
8. What is your favorite way of cooling down?

9. How many breaks do you take during practice?
   None   one   two   three   more than three

10. How long is each break usually (in minutes)?
    0   1–3   4–6   7–9   10–12   13–15   more than 15
11. What do you do during your break?

12. How would you describe your state of mind when you are practicing?

13. What do you do when you get distracted?

14. What are some strategies you can think of to improve your practicing habits?

Daily Practice Journal

Keeping a daily practice journal can serve as a tool for reflecting on practice habits, celebrating positive behaviors, and encouraging ongoing improvement. The following prompts are merely suggestions for what could be included in a practice journal. The instructor can tailor, add to, or remove from the following prompts to meet their studio's needs (Worksheet 5.4 ▶).

Today I used the following tools in my practice:

Hydration

Warm-up

Cool-down

Rejuvenating break

Hearing protection

Healthy snack during my break

My state of mind during my practice session was: _____

I took a total of _____ breaks. During my break, I _____

My physical state felt _____

I am pleased with how _____

Tomorrow, I will _____

Warm-Up and Cool-Down Sequences

Warming up and cooling down will vary for individuals and their instrumental or vocal needs. On the companion website, you will find a dynamic whole-body warm-up sequence, exercises for warming up the hands, and whole-body static stretching cool-down sequences (Exercises 5.6–5.8 ▶).

After warming up the whole body, singers should ready their vocal fold muscles for practice. Professor Freda Herseth at the University of Michigan recommends a combination of humming, lip or tongue trills, glides on favorite vowels, vocal function exercises, and vocalises. In addition to a whole body stretch, the same series of exercises done softly and gradually can be used as a cool-down at the end of the session to protect the voice.

***

In this chapter, we explored the importance of proper alignment as the foundation for injury prevention. Movement experiences selected from Body Mapping, yoga, and several other mind–body practices can serve as useful tools for developing alignment that integrates the person as a whole. Guiding our students through proper warm-up and cool-down routines, as well as informing them about injury-prevention habits and practices, can protect them from harm. There isn't a single technique that works best, as so much of it depends on the individuals and their genetics, needs, environment, instrument, and habits. Students should be encouraged to explore tools that resonate with them. If they find enjoyment in their exercise plan, warm-ups and cool-downs, and practice breaks, they are more likely to practice those routines on a daily basis.

6

Expressive Performance

Laban Movement Analysis

A performer's movements play a crucial role in helping audiences understand and connect more deeply with the music. Training our students to become effective communicators in performance requires that we understand how physical movements affect the audience's perception and facilitate exercises for our students to develop their kinesthetic awareness and expand their movement vocabulary. Such communicative and embodied performances contribute to the performer's sense of musical ownership and enjoyment, thus positively contributing to her overall wellness. In addition, clarified and coordinated movement reduces the risk of injury and heightens expressive intent. In this chapter, we will take a deep dive into how Laban Movement Analysis (LMA), a method primarily used in dance for analyzing human movement and preserving choreography, can be used effectively as a tool for improving kinesthetic awareness and heightening the expressivity of a musical performance. Before we delve into the details of this system and specific exercises you can incorporate in your lessons, let's first explore physical movement as an integral component of performance.

Movement in Performance

The importance of body language in understanding another person's intent has been acknowledged and researched in the fields of psychology, speech therapy, theater, dance, and, more recently, music. Several studies have dealt with examining the importance of the visual element of a performance and have discussed how a performer's movements affect the audience's overall perception.[1] In a study conducted by Jane Davidson, a group of violinists were instructed to play the same excerpt of music in three different ways: (1) deadpan (without expression), (2) projected (with normal expression), and (3) exaggerated (with exaggerated expression).[2] A group of subjects, consisting of both musicians and non-musicians, was asked to only watch, only listen, or both watch and listen to the performances and to rate them from "inexpressive" to "highly expressive." Interestingly, musically untrained subjects were more successful than musically trained subjects in identifying the expressive intent when they were only watching the performance. This indicates that audience members rely heavily on watching the performer's movements to understand the musical gestures that are being expressed. Another study by Broughton

Teaching the Whole Musician. Paola Savvidou, Oxford University Press (2021). © Oxford University Press.
DOI: 10.1093/oso/9780190868796.003.0006

and Stevens compared the audience's experiences between listening-only and listening and seeing the performers' movements.[3] Being able to see the performer, as opposed to only listening to the performance, increased the differentiation between intentionally expressive and inexpressive performances.

Further evidence of the correlation of sound and movement appears in a study by Dahl and Friberg, who examined whether specific emotional intent could be identified in performers by observing only body movements, without sound.[4] A marimba player was asked to perform the same piece of music with four different emotions: fear, anger, happiness, and sadness. Recordings were edited to show the player in four different conditions: full body, no hands, torso, and head only. Subjects were asked to rate the emotional content of the performance on a scale from 0 (nothing) to 6 (very much) of four emotions. The results showed that it is possible to communicate emotion through movements only, without sound: sadness, happiness, and anger were more successfully communicated, though fear was not. Different body parts communicated certain emotions more effectively, although the overall emotion was identified successfully regardless of the body part being viewed. For example, the head was important in communicating sadness. The research outlined here provides evidence that physical expression heightens musical expressivity, increasing its communicative power for the audience.

Medical research supports the notion that the visual aspect of a performance is responsible for arousing an emotional response in the audience. This response is ascribed to mirror neurons. Research by a team of neuroscientists led by Giuseppe di Pellegrino in Italy discovered that neurons fire not only when we perform a movement ourselves, but also when we observe a movement in someone else.[5] For example, neurons will fire when we pick up a glass of water just as when we observe someone else pick up a glass of water.

Mirror neurons not only imitate the action, they also help us understand actions and emotions. We are able to decipher facial expressions and body language because we have the capacity to recreate those expressions ourselves. As these movements are a physical manifestation of emotions, our mirror neurons fire instantly, helping us identify emotions such as anger, boredom, or happiness.[6] Thus, coupled with the visual comprehension of emotion, we are also able to perceive expressive intention through our own kinesthetic experience. We perceive that someone is exuberant because of their upright posture, the smile on their face, the openness in their chest, and their exaggerated gestures. Similarly, we make assumptions about performers' personality and attitude by the way they carry themselves on stage. We begin to evaluate a performance the moment the performer walks on stage. Anthony Tommasini's review of two pianists is a clear example of the strong effect a performer's attitude has on our perception of the performance.[7] He describes the first performer as performing with "prodigious technique, myriad shadings and scrupulous accuracy." However, when the audience applauded his playing, he "appeared to be miserable." The second performer, although he "lacked in virtuosic dazzle and sonic power," appeared to perform with much more enthusiasm, "musical authority and pianistic flair." This account shows how audience response is affected by the way performers carry themselves on stage, how they move and communicate.

Expression and Technique

Based on the aforementioned research, we can see that observing movements in a performance is crucial to understanding the expressive and emotional intent within that performance. The types of movements that contribute to this understanding are both technical and expressive. Technical movements are required for sound production. Through honing technique, we develop accuracy, expand our repertoire, and develop a more refined sound. Our neuromuscular system responds to our mental state, which means that we move not only to execute technical actions but also to express emotions.[8] Expressive movements, although not always necessary components of sound production, complement technique. Movements that are expressive in nature can further be analyzed into movements that are (1) communicative, (2) sound-facilitating, or (3) sound-accompanying.[9] Communicative gestures may consist of facial expressions or tilting of the head to show emotion. Sound-facilitating movements are preparatory movements that precede sound production. Follow-through gestures usually accompany the sound post production. The ability to communicate a variety of emotions through movement and sound means that one must develop a wide palette of movement vocabulary.

Improving communication in performance is often associated with purely perfecting mechanical dexterity. Although there is merit to isolating technique on occasion, a failure to train expression as a synergistic component to technique can potentially be detrimental to one's physical health. This overemphasis on technique may be due to the high level of technical achievement expected within our competitive profession, or perhaps due to a lack of common vocabulary among musicians to talk about movement.

The interconnectedness of technical and expressive movements in musical performance calls for using kinesthetic training that improves alignment and functionality, expands the range of expressive movement, and provides appropriate vocabulary for describing movement in a concrete manner. Such an approach presents the performer with a wider range of sound color and touches, more tools with which to express her musical choices, more efficient use of the body (thus reducing the risk of injury), and improved communication with the audience. LMA is a system that can be applied toward these goals. Working toward improved coordination between physical movements and expression has the potential to positively affect our students' physical, mental/emotional, and intellectual wellness. LMA is a unique tool in the way that it synthesizes several aspects of wellness through a performance lens. As you read through the next sections, which detail the background and components of LMA, I encourage you to pause between sections and go through the movement experiences to extract a richer experience of this complex system (demonstrations are available on the companion website ▶).

Laban Movement Analysis

LMA is a system developed by Rudolf von Laban[10] in the twentieth century with the purpose of analyzing human movement and preserving choreography through notation, much like musical notation. During his extensive process of creating this system, what has become known as Labanotation, Laban developed four interrelated categories that are used as the basis for LMA analysis:

1. Body: the changing relationship of body parts when moving
2. Effort qualities: inner intent and resulting quality of movement
3. Shape: changes of body position in relation to itself
4. Space harmony: change of body position in relation to its surrounding space.

While in England, he worked with employees at factories who, because of the nature of their work, were used to executing repetitive movement patterns. He developed ways of relieving excess tension, improving efficiency, and developing more easeful movements. Laban is credited as the first person to present dance as a means for self-expression to a wider public. He also helped establish movement education as a curricular component in schools.

Irmgard Bartenieff, a student of Laban's, further developed Laban's ideas under the Body category. As a physical therapist, she had a thorough knowledge of the functions of the human body. She used movements in Effort, Shape, and Space to re-pattern neuromuscular connections. Bartenieff's understanding of the psychological implications of movement led her to pursue dance therapy. She founded the American Dance Therapy Association and worked at the Albert Einstein Hospital in New York. Her work was based on movement observation and re-patterning through exploratory movements. This resulted in the subsystem of LMA known as Bartenieff Fundamentals: movement experiences sequentially designed to revisit and reset the neuromuscular connections established during childhood. The neuromuscular patterning follows the sequence from when a child first connects her breath to her limbs, through creeping, crawling, and eventually walking.

The applications of LMA within music remain fairly unexplored at this time. Some of the research utilizing LMA within music has focused on using the Effort and Shape categories for analysis in an effort to establish a reliable system for analyzing performers' expressive movements.[11] Other researchers have used the system as a way of training conductors to improve communication with their ensemble, improving bow movement in string players, and teaching music to younger children, as incorporated within Edwin Gordon's Music Learning Theory.[12] Applying

LMA to kinesthetically train musicians, particularly as it relates to improving overall well-being, is a new endeavor, but one that holds promise.

LMA provides the means to reconnect the body with the breath and has the potential to allow us to experience music with the fullness of body movement. As such, the work presented in this chapter builds upon the foundation of physical alignment discussed in previous chapters, while integrating the mental-emotional-intellectual component that goes into performance. Although the LMA system is complex, some of its fundamental aspects can easily be applied in the private lesson as a means to objectively analyze movement, train kinesthetic awareness, and heighten musical expression. For the purposes of this chapter, I have chosen to include what I consider to be key components of the system that I have found to be effective in my own teaching and performing.

In the next section, you will find scripts for movement explorations and scripts for applying those experiences to music-making. You can also visit the companion website for demonstrations of the movements ⏵. You may like to use a yoga mat or a towel for the floor. Even though LMA is closely associated with dance, be sure not to place any visual expectations on the movement. Each body has its own way of moving and expressing. The goal is to expand the range of movement in ways that best communicate the musical intent (which is why these are called movement experiences, not exercises). Try to keep an open mind, explore, listen to your body, and notice how expression might start to take different shapes. Feel free to adjust the movement experiences for your students. They might even be done as a group, with opportunity for reflection afterward. The system is quite complex, and to fully experience it would require taking classes and even pursuing a movement analyst certification.

Body: Bartenieff Fundamentals

Peggy Hackney, a student of Bartenieff, gives the following description of Bartenieff Fundamentals: "[It] is an approach to basic body training that deals with patterning connections in the body according to principles of efficient movement functioning within a context which encourages personal expression and full psychophysical involvement."[13] Irmgard Bartenieff, during the process of developing her Fundamentals in the 1960s, noticed that the most prominent body areas lacking connectivity were the upper and lower halves, with the division occurring at the pelvis. The reasons for this lay in societal norms, a culture based on achievement, success, and individualism which necessitated overidentification with the upper body and a disassociation with the lower body.[14] One of the most obvious ways of identifying missing body patterns is to watch someone walk and notice which parts of the body carry more weight and which parts tend to lead the body in forward movement. For example, a person walking with an overarched back and the head tilted upward or the head tilted forward and the back slumped (as indicated in Figure 6.1) shows that he is not using the pelvis as a source for carrying weight.

Musicians, especially ones who perform while seated, are often disconnected from their pelvis, and, consequently, the lower half of their body. This may have roots in earlier education, as beginning method books often fail to address grounding through the feet. The still pictures commonly provided in the first few pages of methods books and the general minimal attention toward large-scale movement in the field often leads musicians to create fixed, stiff positions. What we fail to understand is that posture is ever changing. As we move, we constantly change the relationships between our body parts and also with the space around us. Movement choices are available to us when we move in and out of our neutral alignment. Such choices are limited unless we develop a kinesthetic sense and connection with our core.

The principles of Bartenieff Fundamentals are based on the concept that all neuromuscular connections develop sequentially during the first few years of our lives, from the time we are in the womb through the gradual development into fully mobile and communicating children. Patterns are based on primitive reflexes, righting reactions, and equilibrium responses.[15] We are already wired with these reflex

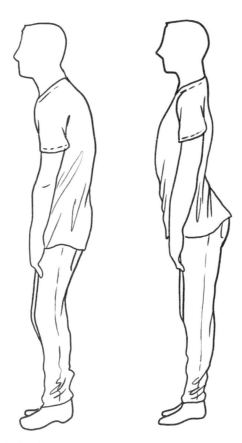

Figure 6.1. Head-tail relationship.
Figure by Amber Huo.

reactions from birth. These reflexes establish the basis for body function and start the process of developing neuromuscular connections as we begin to learn how to creep, crawl, and eventually walk.

As we grow into adulthood, our movement vocabulary is often limited and repetitive. This is a result of social circumstances, imitation of parents' habits, and the nature of our professions. Revisiting the initial patterning we went through in the process of developing our movement patterns is essential in reconnecting and further developing them. It is also important in increasing clarity of expression and in facilitating technique. The ultimate goal of Bartenieff Fundamentals is to enhance a lively interplay between inner connectivity and outer expressivity.[16] This goal speaks to addressing wellness holistically, as it contributes to training students to healthily express their intentions through efficient and expressive movement.

Connectivity does not refer to how bones are joined together, but rather to how different parts of the body are activated together to allow a free flow of movement to travel without unnecessary tension.[17] The fundamental patterns for doing so, as coined by Bartenieff and developed by her student Peggy Hackney, are:

1. Breath
2. Core–distal connectivity
3. Head–tail connectivity
4. Upper–lower connectivity
5. Body-half connectivity
6. Cross-lateral connectivity.

In the descriptions that follow, I have included short movement experiences aimed at highlighting these neuromuscular patterns. You will find traditional Bartenieff floor activities and explorations of how they can be applied in the practice setting. Moving the body in these various ways may not only improve awareness, but also spark curiosity to explore what movements are possible and how efficiency can be improved.

Breath

Breath creates unity between us and the outer world. This incredible process occurs automatically, and represents the most fundamental, essential movement of being alive. However involuntary it may be, though, breath can still be influenced by both internal and external factors such as negative thoughts or a threatening situation. Breath awareness is at the heart of many Eastern practices (such as yoga and t'ai chi). Many of the twentieth-century somatic practices (Feldenkrais, body–mind centering, etc.) agree that awareness of breath should be the starting point of any kinesthetic exploration, since it determines the flow of energy through the body. After working with breath patterning, one of the students in my class (who is a singer) offered the following reflection in her journal: "Another thing I've found helpful is breath patterning. So, by breathing into all parts of my body, I find that it helps me relieve all types of tension so as to free up my sound. It's hard to focus on that while performing, but I employ it more in the practice room so I can relieve tension before I perform."

The pressure of learning music quickly and producing high-quality performances is a heavy burden for musicians that often results in shallow breathing patterns. Since the different layers of our body (muscles, organs, bones) are interconnected and affect each other in major ways, constricted breathing patterns cause disconnectedness between different parts of the body and result in inefficient movement patterns. Working with the breath provides immediate access to the state of the body and recognition of any tension (for a discussion of the breathing mechanism, see Chapter 4; for breathing exercises, see Chapter 8).

Core–Distal Connectivity

Core–distal connectivity refers to the connectedness of our core to our limbs. This is based on the principle that when a change occurs in one part of our body, it is inevitable that a change will also occur in another.[18] Movements initiating from the core and radiating out to the periphery establish the connectedness of the core to the limbs. Instrumentalists may often feel that their arms are disconnected from their core. Likewise, singers might feel that their head is disconnected from the rest of their body. One of the reasons for this disconnectedness is that we tend to rely mostly on the muscles that are required to execute sound production and as a result lose the power and freedom that can be gained when using the core and the feet for support. When core–distal connectivity is re-established, movements of the limbs may become more coordinated and supported from the breath and the core.

Movement Exploration: Core–Distal Connectivity

(Movement Exploration 6.1 ▶)

Lie on the floor in an X position with your arms and legs pointing diagonally away from the body. Take a few deep breaths. Imagine there is a ball of your favorite color in your belly. With each exhale, you are sending some of that color to your pelvis, your head, your right arm, your left arm, your right leg, and your left leg. Gradually, you "paint" yourself in your favorite color.

On the next exhale, extend the right leg and the right arm even farther away from the body and bring the left arm and left leg closer together. Repeat on the other side. The next time the right arm and leg extend, reach a little farther, drawing an imaginary arc overhead and to the left side with the right arm. Allow that movement to lead into rolling over to the left side and exhale into fetal position, drawing all your limbs in to the core. With the next inhale, extend all your limbs away from your body, and with the exhale, pull your limbs back toward your center. Inhale deeply again and allow your pelvis to roll off the side and onto its back, bringing the rest of the body into the X position. Repeat on the other side.

Movement Exploration: Core–Distal Connectivity in Performance

Start by finding a comfortable position with your instrument (or standing if you are a singer). Take a few deep breaths, noticing how the body adjusts to the rising and the falling of the breath. With each exhale imagine that you are sending breath into each limb, one at a time. Now move slowly and select a phrase or a scale to play/sing. As you play or sing, first focus on leading with your breath, then choose a limb to lead the sound production with. Try your upper limbs first, then your lower limbs. How does it feel when you lead with your left leg as opposed to when you lead with your tail, or your head? Can you lead with all six limbs at the same time?

Head–Tail Connectivity

Head–tail connectivity is the pattern most readily associated with identifying people's personalities and sense of self-esteem. Both ends of the spine are important in recognizing habits and attitude toward life. If one carries her head forward and has a slumped back, we often assume that she is depressed or bored. If one has a hyperextended lower back with the pelvis tilted forward, we might read that as tightness. The most common issue that exists in these spinal movements is when the head becomes disconnected from the spine. A student responding to the head–tail connectivity work noticed that a lack of awareness of the lower back and pelvis makes it difficult to perform. She said the following in her journal: "One thing I have been neglecting is my head/tail patterning. I have a tendency to not focus any support toward my lower back, and that makes it hard for me to feel grounded while performing. By focusing on the connection between head and tail, I have found it easier to feel supported while singing and performing."

Disconnectedness of the head from the bottom part of the spine results in pain in the shoulders and lower back. Part of the issue arises from extending the head forward in order to read the score and tilting the head forward to look at an instrument. We forget that our eyes are capable of moving up and down without the head actually having to move with them! Head–tail connectivity is crucial not only in negotiating technical movements at our instrument, but also in maintaining alignment in any situation when not much movement is required.

Through this patterning sequence, we are reacquainting the head with the pelvis and the spine. In a body that is patterned properly, a change in the tail should result in a change or readjustment of the head.

Movement Exploration: Head–Tail Connectivity

(Movement Exploration 6.2 ⏵.)

Move into a yoga "table pose," on all fours. The shoulders should be above the wrists, with the fingers spread wide and the hips above the knees. The neck is long, and the head is facing toward the floor. Slowly and mindfully start curving your pelvis toward the core. Allow that motion to sequence through the spine. Notice how one vertebra after the other moves, like a domino effect. Allow the movement to continue through the head, noticing how it responds. Then slowly initiate a movement sequence by lifting your head away from the core and looking upward. Allow that pattern to continue downward along your spine. Repeat this sequencing and experiment with other movements of the spine.

Movement Experience: Head–Tail Connectivity in Performance

Find your neutral position with your instrument (where applicable). Hold a long tone and make small movements with your pelvis. How do those movements affect your breath, the sound, or the muscular tension in your upper body? Hold another long tone and make small movements with your head. How does that feel?

Select a phrase to play or sing, and as you go through it, deliberately move the spine gently. Notice where the movement tends to initiate from (head, tail, or a part of the spine) and how it sequences through the rest of the spine.

Upper–Lower Connectivity

Upper–lower connectivity refers to connecting the function of the upper body with the functions of the lower body so that they work together as a coordinated whole. The developmental stage in which this pattern develops takes place before a baby learns to crawl. At this stage, the baby can yield and push, in response to a threatening situation, or reach and pull, as a result of a wish to reach a goal, such as a colorful toy. Both patterns should develop equally to allow for healthy building of self-esteem (i.e., the ability to reach goals). Adults tend to deaden the central part of their weight support located in the pelvis, which results in disconnected upper and lower halves, a misaligned body, and a disconnected head–pelvis spinal relationship. The iliopsoas muscle, which runs deep in the center, tends to be underdeveloped and underutilized. It is very easy for musicians who perform seated to ignore the lower half of their body and to inadvertently deactivate their pelvis. If the pelvis is tilted too far forward, the muscles in the lower back must overcompensate by tightening excessively for support.

Most vital and sensory organs are located in the upper half. This means that incomplete connectivity patterns may lead to inefficient functioning of any of these organs. Tightness may occur at different parts of the upper body. In developing a connected upper body the aforementioned patterns of breath, core–distal, and head–tail connectivity must be in place. The shoulder, elbow, and wrist joints must be free and their connectedness to each other fully realized.

Movement Exploration: Upper–Lower Half Connectivity

(Movement Exploration 6.3 ▶.)

Lie on your back with your arms by your side. Imagine a tiny hole in the soles of your feet. Imagine inhaling from there. The breath travels all the way through your body and exhales from a tiny hole at the top of your skull. Breathe a few times with this imagery. Keeping your feet slightly flexed, start to rock your feet forward and backward. Imagine that movement as initiating a little wave. Allow the wave to grow bigger and cause a movement in your pelvis (without actively moving your pelvis). Then allow the wave to get even bigger to where your head is also responding to the motion by moving up and down. Then gradually quiet down the rocking. Notice how the body feels when the energy flows freely between the two halves.

Movement Experience: Upper–Lower Half Connectivity in Performance

---

Find your neutral playing or singing position. Firmly ground your lower half through the feet into the floor without allowing it to move. Try playing just while moving your upper half. Then switch, making your upper half solid and inflexible while allowing for movement in the lower half. Use minimal movements in the upper body while allowing the lower half to move or even walk around if your instrument allows. Now try playing again, but this time allow the two halves to communicate with one another. When you need more power, use your feet against the ground to generate more momentum. When you need lightness, allow the entire body to participate.

Body-Half Connectivity

Body-half connectivity refers to stabilizing one half of the body while moving the other, with an imaginary separation line vertically cutting through the body. Exploring the movement potential of each body half allows for more choices in stability and mobility, as well as clarity in decision-making.[19] In instrumental performance, the hands are almost always executing different actions. In some cases, one side acts as a stabilizer while the other half is mobile. Actively addressing body-half connectivity can clarify the patterns of stability and mobility of each half and help with coordination.

Movement Exploration: Body-Half Connectivity

(Movement Exploration 6.4 ▶.)

   Lie on your belly, with your palms flat on the floor near your shoulders, and your elbows near your body. Imagine a line separating your body down the middle (from the head down to your pelvis). Imagine a darker color and a lighter color filling up each side. Press into the ground with the darker side. Simultaneously lift the other side, extending the arm forward and reaching the leg behind you. Bend the extended knee and the elbow, bringing them toward each other. Return to the starting position. Now switch sides.

Movement Exploration: Body-Half Connectivity in Performance

Find your neutral playing or singing position. Deactivate one half while activating the other half through gentle movements (to the extent that it's possible). Play a phrase and notice how that perhaps gives you better control over the moving half but disables you in other ways. Switch sides. Do you notice any differences between the two sides? How can you perform in such a way that the two sides are working together effectively?

Cross-Lateral Connectivity

Cross-lateral connectivity is the final step in synthesizing all of the previous patterns to realize complex movements such as walking. Moving with opposing sets of limbs while transferring weight and employing the whole body is the most complex set of movements we learn in our early years of development, and one that we can keep improving on. Even if we are limited to sitting or standing in place when we are performing, we still use our whole body in complex movement patterns that cross the midline of the body. Such movements include torso twists and arm crossings.

Movement Exploration: Cross-Lateral Connectivity

(Movement Exploration 6.5 ▶.)

   Start in a yoga "table pose," on all fours. Feel supported through all four limbs. On an exhale, extend your right arm forward and your left leg backward. Bring your knee and the elbow to the center, extend again, and return to table. Repeat on the other side. Allow this motion to transition into the act of crawling. Notice how the opposite limbs work together to move you forward.

Movement Exploration: Cross-Lateral Connectivity in Performance

Find your neutral playing or singing position. Choose a phrase to experiment with. As you play, subtly move your right arm toward your left leg, then your left shoulder toward your right leg. Use your breath to feel the connectivity between opposites. What do you notice about your movement quality as you explore cross-lateral connectivity?

Fully embodied movement not only is more enjoyable to perform, but also enables the brain and the body to function at their best. I would agree with Peggy Hackney's view that "these cross-connections enable our brains to play effectively between right and left brain functioning, connecting the symbolic and the analytic, allowing a beginning connection between feeling and form, while also connecting 'grounding' with 'reach into the world.' "[20] Clarity of intent in the mind results in more precise and embodied movements and expressivity, both in musical performance and in daily life.

Space Harmony

The Space Harmony category of the LMA system identifies the space in which we move, in terms of how that relates to our own body. It includes both how we move to get from point A to point B (for example, do we walk in a straight line from the hallway to the fridge, or do we follow a zig-zag pattern?) and how we move *through* the space in that process (are we taking big steps, or crawling on the floor?). Since most musicians don't move across the stage when they perform, in this section we will focus on how the body moves through space while in a stationary position, introducing some descriptive terms for these different physical possibilities that may be useful in our teaching practice.

Physical and Psychological Kinesphere

The Physical Kinesphere refers to the three-dimensional space around us in direct proximity to the body: (1) the immediate physical space closest to our body (short-reach kinesphere), (2) the space we can comfortably reach when we extend our arms and legs (mid-reach), and (3) the area just outside our comfortable range of movement that we have to extend, without walking, to get to (far-reach). See Figure 6.2 for an illustration of this spatial relationship.

The Psychological Kinesphere (also separated into short-, mid-, and far-reach) refers to our outward attitude toward the space we inhabit, which is a critical consideration in refining the way we project on stage. In the short-reach psychological kinesphere, we project only to our immediate space that surrounds us. Such a state can exist when we are having an intimate conversation with a friend. In the mid-reach kinesphere, we project to a classroom, or perhaps the closest rows in a performance hall. In the far-reach kinesphere, we are connecting with as big a space as an entire city, state, or even country. This is not to say that we could actually have the capacity to physically project to such a big space, but psychologically, our awareness is much bigger.

Observing how we inhabit the space around us in our daily lives gives us an insight into how we communicate. More introverted personalities tend to use the short-reach kinesphere, whereas more extroverted people tend to use the entire range of their kinesphere. How, then, do these movements translate into the musical performance? We sometimes see extroverted people play with a timid use of space. In other words, an extroverted personality does not automatically translate to a performer with a big sound in a huge venue. Learning how to utilize our space for maximum expressivity is yet another area that requires training.

The space available to us is in some ways predetermined by the size and shape of our instrument. The movements available need to be explored and decided upon based on parameters such as the build of the performer, the instrument, the repertoire, and the performance venue.

Envisioning the venue and an appropriately sized kinesphere may help the student prepare better for a more convincing and space-appropriate performance. I often utilize these concepts in my teaching and watch the student's gradual transformation from a timid interpretation to an open and confident performance. I start by asking students to perform for themselves, then for me, then for a friend who lives nearby, and finally for a friend or family member who lives far away. This explores the idea

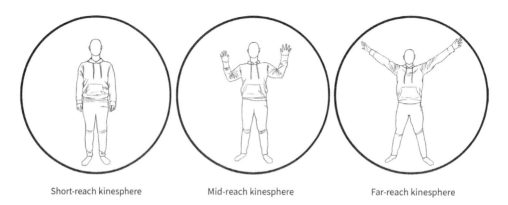

Short-reach kinesphere   Mid-reach kinesphere   Far-reach kinesphere

Figure 6.2. The physical kinesphere.
Figure by Amber Huo.

of expanding one's psychological kinesphere. If the friend who is too far away to hear had the ability to somehow see the student perform in my studio, the student would have to make all the gestures very big and try to show the music physically too. The use of this type of imagery explores both the physical kinesphere and the psychological kinesphere, expanding both mental awareness and physical gestures.

Cross of Axes

Axes, as shown in Figure 6.3, are imaginary lines that go through our center and form the foundation of movement analysis in terms of the Space category. We can move our body along the vertical axis (downward gravitational pull and upward body pull), the horizontal axis (side to side), or the sagittal axis (forward and backward). Each of these axes consists of one pull in each direction. These axes are perpendicular to one another. The point at which they intersect coincides with the center of gravity.

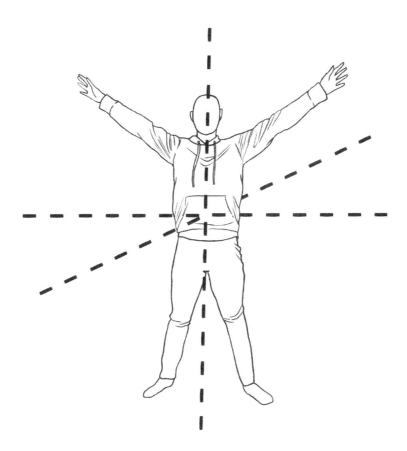

Figure 6.3. Axes.
Figure by Amber Huo.

The Cross of Axes is an LMA movement sequence that presents all the possibilities of direction and movement in the axes. This is much like playing a scale for musicians. It can be used as a similar type of warmup that prepares a musician for the instrumental topography when playing a piece in that particular key. Just as minor scales have a different affect than major scales, each direction in the cross of axes carries with it a different expressive intent. The directional paths along with their intents are:

High (rising/lightness)
Low (sinking/strength)
Left (narrowing/directness)
Right (widening/indirectness)
Front (advancing/sustainment).
Back (retreating/quickness)

I think about these affinities of movement quality and direction much like shaping in music. Although it is not a hard and fast rule, when a melodic line moves up, we often choose to shape it with a crescendo, and when it moves down, we get softer. Similarly, when we move down toward the earth's gravitational pull, we tend to do so with strength; when we lift up on our toes, we do it with lightness. This is not to say that we always perform movements in this way; however, they provide a frame of reference for how movements in different directions can be combined with expressive qualities. Moving through the cross of axes scale helps us embody these qualities so that we may more easily access them in musical performance.

Movement Exploration: Cross of Axes

(Movement Exploration 6.6 ▶.)

Begin standing with neutral alignment. Lift your arm and reach toward the ceiling. Leading with the right arm, reach down toward the side of your right foot, traveling along the vertical plane. Bring your right arm across your body, reaching toward the left and crossing the right foot over the left (traveling along the horizontal plane). Open up the right arm and take a step to the right with your right foot. Reach forward with your right arm, taking a step forward with your right foot. Take a step back behind you with your right foot and swing the right arm backward (traveling along the sagittal plane). Return to center and repeat with the opposite side, leading with the left arm.

Planes

Combining two-dimensional pulls between two of these axes creates planes. For example, a pull downward and another pull toward the right side, acting

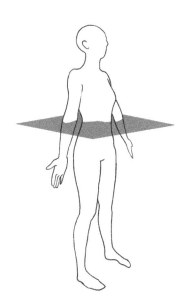

Figure 6.4. Planes.
Figure by Amber Huo.

on a person, result in the person moving in the right–low diagonal. The planes created as a result of two-dimensional pulls are the vertical plane (or door plane), horizontal plane (or table plane), and sagittal plane (or wheel plane). Pianists and percussionists' arm movements mostly occur along the horizontal and sagittal planes, with the upper torso moving along the vertical and sagittal planes. Clarinetists move mostly in the sagittal plane, with some movement in the vertical plane.

The planes are illustrated in Figure 6.4 (from left to right: sagittal, vertical, and horizontal). When combining three-dimensional pulls, we have the full space around us, in the shape of a cube, available for three-dimensional movement. This provides the largest space for more complex movement.

Movement Exploration: Space in Performance

Find your neutral playing or singing position. Find your largest movement possible and the smallest movement possible. Pick a musical phrase from your repertoire or a scale to experiment with. Play your selection with the most use of space and with the least use of space. Experiment with the range of space between these extremes until you find what feels comfortable and matches the music. Play the same phrase or scale, imagining that you are sending sound only to the first row, then to the very back row, then to the entire building, and the entire city. How does each intent affect your approach? Notice which plane you are most comfortable moving in. Try moving through different planes as well and pay attention to how that affects your balance and communication.

Shape

Shape refers to the way the body is shaped in relation to itself and the environment (or other people). Shape Flow Support, a subcategory of shape, refers to the opening and closing of the torso, led by the breath. Movements included in shape flow support are:

1. Lengthening or shortening in the vertical plane
2. Widening or narrowing in the horizontal plane
3. Bulging or hollowing in the sagittal plane.

These are demonstrated on the companion website (Movement Exploration 6.7 ⊙).

When preparing to play any instrument or to sing, it is best to start from a position of length and openness, rather than a contracted, hollow shape, to allow for the breath to flow freely and move the body efficiently and effectively. During performance, the upper torso will shift and adjust itself, depending on the technical demands of the music and its expressive intent. Establishing an open shape as the neutral starting shape and returning to that position during the performance allows the performer to momentarily realign and prevents awkward shapes from lingering for too long.

Movement Exploration: Cross of Axes with Shape

(Movement Exploration 6.8 ⊙.)

Repeat the Cross of Axes exercise, this time adding the matching torso movements. As you lift up, lengthen the torso. Shorten as you reach toward the ground. Narrow as you reach across the body and widen as you reach out to the side of the body. Bulge as you move forward and hollow as you move backward.

Movement Exploration: Shape in Performance

Find your neutral playing or singing position. As you play/sing through your selected repertoire, experiment with the shape of your torso. Explore all six shapes available to you: long, narrow, short, wide, bulging, and hollow. How does each shape affect your performance? Which shapes does your body instinctively favor?

Effort

Effort refers to the quality of movement. This quality is analyzed based on four factors: space, weight, time, and flow. Effort factors are not only visual descriptors of movement, but also a reflection of inner thoughts and states of mind, therefore providing a means of defining inner expression and outer movement.[21] The extremes of Effort range from indulging (less muscular resistance) to condensing (more muscular resistance). See Table 6.1 for the resulting Effort qualities with each combination, and Movement Exploration 6.9 on the companion website for a demonstration ⏵.

Flow

When movement contains Free Flow, it exhibits a free, unrestrained outpouring of energy. When movement is directed by Bound Flow, it is restrained and held back. Free Flow can easily be seen in a child's movements when running toward her mother. Bound Flow can be observed when picking up a delicate object or when stretching after exercising.

Time

We obviously do not have control over the natural progression of time as we know it, but we do have control over our attitude toward it. In movement with sudden time, there exists a sense of urgency, as when one is late for an important meeting. When movement takes place with sustained time, there is a sense of lingering and taking time, as when one is taking a leisurely walk.

Table 6.1 Effort Qualities

Effort Factors	Indulging (Less Resistance)	Condensing (More Resistance)
Flow	Free	Bound
Time	Sustained	Sudden
Weight	Light	Strong
Space	Indirect	Direct

Weight

Weight Effort does not refer to the actual mass of a person, but rather to the person's attitude toward his weight. When the body is neutral or passive, there is no attention to weight, only an exertion of either muscular control or giving in to gravity.[22] I often show my students a video of a traditional Maori war dance to demonstrate Strong Weight, using muscular effort to activate the weight of the body. The opposite end of the weight spectrum, Light Weight, can be observed in certain Japanese Kabuki dances.

Space

Direct attention to space is required when walking on a ledge. One has to carefully carve through the space, calculating one's body movements carefully so as not to fall. Indirect attention to space is illustrated by gesticulations during conversation.

Action Drives

Effort elements usually appear in combinations of two, three, or, very rarely, four. The combination of efforts creates action drives (eight possible combinations of space, weight, and time). Refer to Table 6.2 and Movement Exploration 6.10 for a demonstration ⊙. Action drives are usually easy to relate to physically and are also readily discernible in a musical performance. The descriptive words are reflective of both what the movement looks like and how it feels kinesthetically.[23]

Students in my wellness class have been finding creative ways to incorporate effort and action drives into their practicing and rehearsing. One student talked about communication in a chamber group through clarifying the movements for cuing and conducting: "The LMA concepts have been helpful in my chamber groups, as

Table 6.2 Action Drives

Action Drive	Space	Weight	Time
Float	Indirect	Light	Sustained
Punch	Direct	Strong	Sudden
Glide	Direct	Light	Sustained
Slash	Indirect	Strong	Sudden
Dab	Direct	Light	Sudden
Wring	Indirect	Strong	Sustained
Flick	Indirect	Light	Sudden
Press	Direct	Strong	Sustained

I am always thinking of the best movements to cue the ensemble without being confusing. Dabbing is effective for downbeats. Gliding is good for conducting beats. I've also been expanding my kinesphere to be able to show more style and phrasing to lead the quartet." This exemplifies how LMA can be a productive way to give students specific vocabulary and movements for improving their craft, while reducing frustrations that may arise from communication issues in an ensemble.

Movement Exploration: Effort and Action Drives

Select an everyday movement to act out (e.g., brushing your teeth, eating, walking). First, act out the movement as you normally would. Then, repeat the movement, varying the effort quality. Try to find the extremes of each quality. Notice which qualities you are most and least comfortable with. Choose a different movement to act out. Repeat the movement using all the different action drives in a sequence. How does communication of the movement change through the usage of each action drive?

Movement Exploration: Effort in Performance

Find your neutral playing or singing position. As you play through your selected repertoire, use the table of effort qualities to experiment with what it would feel like to change the quality of the movement. Try to embody each effort quality in its extremes and then see if you can develop a range of movement from one extreme to the next. Exaggerating the gesture helps strengthen neuromuscular connections and also helps clarify the expression. Which effort seems to fit the music best? How does that change as the expressive qualities of the music change?

   You may already have a habit of assigning words that signify the emotion or character of a particular phrase. Another way to connect with the music is to explore how Effort or Action-Drive terminology might be used in specific spots either to add emphasis to the expression or to help with a difficult technical passage. Much like deciding on the expression of the piece, you might make decisions on movements as well by using these tools as the foundation for those choices.

Movement Observation Toolkit

Observing one's own performance through the lens of LMA is a powerful tool for identifying the movements that are present, noticing the effectiveness of the visual communication, and coming up with ideas for exploring how movement can be altered or clarified to heighten expressivity. One of the singers in my class was surprised to notice that every time she hit a high note, she also lifted her right arm slightly in the vertical plane using light weight and sustained time. It was an unintentional movement that didn't serve an expressive purpose. A cellist was alarmed to find out that he wasn't activating his lower half to support movements of the upper body, resulting in a hollowed upper body shape and shallow breathing. With this newfound awareness, students were able to make conscious adjustments to their movements and felt more confident about their performances.

A helpful sequence for honing one's analytical skills is to start by analyzing performances by others (both professional musicians and peers), then practice observing together with the instructor, and then move on to an independent self-evaluation. This progression is reflected in the following sequence of exercises.

It's important to view these exercises objectively and to remember that they are simply tools that assist in the process of developing kinesthetic awareness. In other words, encourage your student to avoid an overly critical eye, but rather, inasmuch as possible, to maintain an objective perspective.

Movement Observation Exercise

The complexity of movement in a musical performance can be overwhelming, especially when setting out to label movements. As the eye becomes more trained and the vocabulary more comfortable, the analysis will also be easier and quicker. Observing someone else is often easier, as the eye may be too self-critical when observing oneself. The following exercise may be assigned to students as a first step in honing their movement analysis skills (Worksheet 6.1 ▶).

Instructions: Choose approximately one minute of a high-quality video-recorded performance to observe. It could be a performance by a professional musician you admire, or a peer (ideally you would observe both). Watch the segment you selected several times. Each time you watch, isolate one component of movement to observe. Respond to the following questions:

Body
What strikes you about the physical movements in this segment? Do the arms seem connected to the body? Does the head move independently of the torso? Do the feet seem connected to the ground?

Effort
In your own words, how would you describe the quality of the movement? Are the movements generally slow, fast, large, or small? Can you describe the movement qualities using Effort and Action-Drive terminology?

Space

How much space in their immediate bubble does the performer take up while they are performing? Do they tend to move forward or backward, sideways, or up and down?

Shape

To what extent does the breath guide the performer's upper body movements? Do you notice any expanding or pulling back of the ribs? How would you describe the body's spatial relationship to the instrument (where applicable)?

Teacher-Supported Movement Observation Exercise

The following questions provide guidance for a teacher-supported self-observation exercise that can be used in the lesson (Worksheet 6.2 ▶).

Instructions: Take time to observe your student's movements. It might be helpful to record a video and watch it together with your student. First take note of the neutral position. Does it look aligned? Are there any spots that seem (or feel) tight?

Isolate a portion of the performance that feels comfortable for the student and one that does not. Take note of each of the LMA categories (Body, Effort, Shape, and Space) and compare the quality of the movement in each of the sections. How does the movement flow in each section? Is it stuck, or does it seem connected to the core? Do the gestures communicate the musical intent effectively?

Detailed Self-Observation Exercise

If you are finding that your students would benefit from a more detailed self-observation, this next exercise provides guidance in that direction (Worksheet 6.3 ▶). Finding the beginning and end of a physical movement can be challenging, as movements tend to flow seamlessly from one to the next. Noticing what stands out is the most important aspect of the observation. The peaks of the movement are what the audience will notice too. This detailed exercise includes an arbitrary timing subdivision of five seconds. The duration will need to be adjusted depending on the piece and the phrasing. The idea is to analyze the movement in the smallest logical subdivisions for accuracy.

Instructions: Record yourself performing for approximately thirty seconds. Watch your recording multiple times and complete the following observation form using LMA terminology to the best of your ability. Analyze your movements in five-second segments (or another logical subdivision), addressing all four LMA categories (Body, Space, Shape, and Effort) (see Table 6.3).

1. Describe the prominent musical characteristics and emotional qualities of the music you are performing.
2. What are the current roadblocks that keep you from performing this piece to your full potential?
3. Divide the piece into short segments (five seconds each or another logical subdivision that makes sense with the musical phrasing) and analyze the recording using LMA terminology. Use the following guided questions to help with your analysis.

Guided questions for analysis:

Body
Do the body parts look connected to one another? How does your core relate to your limbs? Is there breath in your movement? Which body part initiates the movement?

Effort
Which Effort qualities or Action Drives do you notice in your movement? How do these relate to the musical expression? Do different body parts exhibit different Effort qualities?

Space
How does your approach to your physical and/or psychological kinesphere range change (short-, mid-, or far-reach)? Which planes do you tend to move in (vertical, horizontal, or sagittal)?

Shape
How does your body interact with your instrument and/or the space around you? Does your internal kinesphere grow, shrink, expand, narrow, bulge, or hollow? Do your movements follow straight lines, arcs, or curvilinear shapes?

Table 6.3 LMA Analysis

Timing	Body	Effort	Space	Shape
0–5"				
5–10"				
10–15"				
15–20"				
20–25"				
25–30"				

4. Reflect on your analysis. What did you notice? What was successful? What can you improve on?

5. Find spots in the music where you can improve your physical and/or musical communication. Make a note using a word that will trigger your imagination. Explore your options.

***

When we incorporate LMA into our lessons, our students' toolbox for healthy expression deepens and grows. Their musical understanding and technical skills become fortified with a wider range of movement vocabulary and a more efficient use of the body. This allows students to explore the interplay between their inner intent and their outward communication with the audience. Through an expanded and more refined physical movement vocabulary, students may be positioned to produce more visually communicative performances, gain more ownership over their performance, prevent injury through the use of more highly coordinated movements, and express their ideas in a healthy and effective manner.

7

The Power of the Mind

Mental Health Basics

Over the last several years, mental health centers at US universities have reported an ongoing increase in students who are seeking counseling for mental health needs.[1] According to the National College Health Assessment the most commonly diagnosed mental disorders among this population are depression and anxiety. Some of the common problems that students sought help for were use of medication, depression, academic skills, and grief.[2] A study by Benton et al. concluded that over the course of thirteen years, students were reporting more complex mental health problems. We can't know whether the reason behind this increase in reported cases primarily reflects an increase in the number of students who are dealing with problems, if universities have been more successful at destigmatizing the process of seeking help, or if both factors may be in play. In any scenario, the fact that students are not suffering in isolation, but rather are taking brave action toward seeking help, is certainly a positive step toward building healthier college campuses.

Music students face the same challenges as other students in terms of social and academic demands. Furthermore, each year of music school comes with its own set of difficulties. Freshmen may not be as concerned with employment and career development as seniors and graduate students. Yet they are dealing with a similar personal adjustment, transitioning from home life to campus life, and that comes with social and emotional stress, too. Depending on their course of study within music, students may at times deal with degree-specific demands. Those pursuing a performance or composition degree deal with isolation related to practicing or composing alone for several hours per day. Frequent required performances in front of their applied instructor and peers may be adding extra pressure, a heightened sense of performance anxiety, as well as perceived judgment of their innate talent. Music education preservice students experience the stress of dealing with intrapersonal conflict, having multiple people to report to, and the challenges of contributing in a meaningful manner to a program they are only interfacing with temporarily.[3] Lacking the appropriate tools to cope with such issues may result in early career teacher burnout.

Graduate students experience additional challenges that are not as common among undergraduate students (higher academic and performance expectations, transition to professional life, financial difficulties, etc.). Our own expectations may be that those who have completed bachelor's degrees have, through that process, figured out how to manage those challenges. The reality is that many individuals

Teaching the Whole Musician. Paola Savvidou, Oxford University Press (2021). © Oxford University Press.
DOI: 10.1093/oso/9780190868796.003.0007

continue on to pursue graduate study immediately after completing their under-graduate degree. Those few summer months between degrees are not necessarily enough to prepare for the greater challenges that lie ahead. In a study investigating mental health needs in graduate students, almost half of the students reported having experienced a stress-related problem in the past year, pointing to the need to extend a nurturing approach to all of our students, regardless of grade level.[4] School stressors are, generally speaking, likely more manageable for a healthy individual, yet they can be extremely challenging for a student who is also dealing with a mental health disorder. Seemingly low-pressure situations may cause high anxiety for the student living with generalized anxiety disorder, for example. The difficulty of man-aging such stress, compounded with certain types of disorders, may potentially put a student in a harmful situation.

In the most severe scenarios, they may even contemplate self-harm. With the right tools, as we will learn in this chapter, the instructor can support students dealing with all levels of distress and can become a powerful reference point to the appro-priate professional resources they may need to thrive.

As we embark on the mental health basics journey, we will first discuss contributing factors to mental distress, learn about practices for protecting mental health, understand common mental health disorders, and familiarize ourselves with tools for addressing some of the common challenges among music students.

Understanding Mental Health

Mental health refers to our emotional and psychological state. As described in Chapter 1, the dimensions of wellness are interconnected, which indicates a close relationship between our mental health and other areas of our well-being such as our social relationships, sleep patterns, and school or work performance. Having a healthy emotional and mental state means that we can weather the storms that come our way with resilience, maintain healthy relationships, and sustain an overall posi-tive sense of well-being.

Dealing with a short-term sadness or frustration does not necessarily mean that one is dealing with a mental disorder. Persistence of these moods that leads to im-pairment of thought, mood, or behavior is what may be a sign that a mental illness may be present.[5]

A mental disorder, as defined in the *Diagnostic and Statistical Manual of Mental Disorders* (DSM-5), is "a syndrome characterized by clinically significant distur-bance in an individual's cognition, emotional regulation, or behavior that reflects a dysfunction in the psychological, biological, or developmental processes underlying mental functioning. Mental disorders are usually associated with significant distress or disability in social, occupational, or other important activities."[6] This definition goes on to add that a response to a common stressful situation or loss is not a mental disorder, nor is behavior that is "socially deviant." In other words, there has to be a disturbance in the person's ability to function cognitively, emotionally, and behaviorally for the concern to rise up to the level of a mental health disorder. We will look at common disorders in more detail later in this chapter.

I can safely assume that we all very well understand that a diagnosis is not as simple as checking off a list of signs and symptoms. It involves assessment by a skilled professional who will develop a comprehensive understanding of that person's past, social environment, and biological factors. It is extremely important to remember that teachers who are not professionally trained as mental health clinicians—the vast majority of professional music pedagogues—should not be attempting to diagnose mental disorders. Untrained professionals could cause serious harm if they tried to provide guidance beyond their expertise. However, with baseline knowledge and the right tools, they can be instrumental in swiftly referring a student to the appropriate medical or mental health resource. My aim in this chapter is to strongly encourage teachers to become familiar with some of the common concerns music students deal with so that they can encourage protective behaviors and, where appropriate, provide information about resources.

Even mindful pedagogues are often reactive. We spend inordinate amounts of time going back to fix problems, rather than preemptively encouraging protective practices. In the emotional/mental health wellness dimension, we should apply the same approaches as we do in physical health by adopting a combination of preventive approaches and recovery support. Foundational knowledge of common mental health disorders that afflict college students is a first step. Preventive approaches involve encouraging self-care practices, being mindful of the workload assigned to students, and acknowledging how criticism and feedback land on the student. Get to know the resources on your campus and community for when a student needs professional help. Where available, reach out to mental health professionals to better understand the process of how to deal with an emergency, what their recommendations are for helping students in crisis, and how you can get in touch with a social worker or counselor who would be readily available to help. It is not uncommon to find an emergency crisis line available 24/7 at an on-campus center. In addition to learning about the campus mental health center, I suggest reaching out to your administrators to find out what the protocol is for when a student is dealing with a mental health emergency or expresses suicidal thoughts. Often, mental health concerns become known when the student is already in a crisis situation; therefore, acting quickly to connect the student to a place where they can get help is of the essence. This preparation will be important if and when a situation arises with a student.

Through your actions toward mental health support, you can help reduce the stigma your students may encounter around the process of seeking assistance, prevent minor concerns from becoming bigger ones, and direct students toward the resources they need.

Contributing Factors to Mental Distress

It might seem that the most obvious pedagogical approach is to keep an eye out for students who are expressing distress through behavior that demonstrates psychological turmoil. But acting as a supportive and effective pedagogue in these scenarios is not so simple. Many students who struggle with psychological challenges will not explicitly express the challenges they are facing. Therefore it is imperative to get to know our students and understand what underlying stressors may exist so that we may thoughtfully frame our feedback and adjust our expectations. In this section we will learn about several factors that may contribute to mental distress.

Stress

Although not a mental health disorder, stress can be an underlying contributing factor to other disorders such as anxiety and depression. When we are in a stressful situation, usually the first thing that is noticeably affected is our breath: it becomes faster and shallower. Accelerated breathing stimulates the sympathetic nervous system, which in turn stimulates the speed of the breath, thus continuing the stress response cycle.

The central nervous system, as mentioned in Chapter 3, consists of the sympathetic nervous system (SNS) and the parasympathetic nervous system (PNS). The SNS is responsible for activating the fight or flight or freeze reaction in response to perceived danger. The responses that occur within the sympathetic nervous system are designed to increase our speed and power to either stay and fight or run away. The pupils dilate, the blood flows to the large muscles, digestion slows down, and the heart and respiration rates increase.

Our SNS threshold can be lowered over time, if we find ourselves in chronically stressful situations. This could result in the triggering of our fight or flight responses, even in low-risk scenarios that do not present imminent danger. For example, taking an academic quiz or exam may trigger the SNS, even though we may be in a safe physical circumstance. While a valuable response when we are in situations of danger, this reaction is not helpful if it habitually persists over time. Chronic stress in these low-risk situations is dangerous to our health, as it wears and tears our body prematurely.

The term *distress* accurately represents the majority of such experiences. However, surprisingly, the umbrella term of *stress* also includes positive experiences known as *eustress*. An example of eustress would be planning a celebration such as a graduation party or a wedding, when we feel a combination of excitement and anticipation, as well as thoughts of whether everything will go as planned.

There are multiple stress factors that can cause negative stress in the higher education student. One example is the transition from the home environment to the university. This transition, for most students, involves a new living arrangement (often sharing a room with a stranger), which can affect sleep. Eating habits, including the frequency and quality of the meals, change as well. Poor eating choices triggered by stress can lead to feeling depleted of energy. For international students, this transition is even more stressful, especially when it involves functioning in a language other than their mother tongue.

Responding to stress varies among individuals and can involve any or all of the following components:

1. Emotional response, which may include experiencing fear, anxiety, and depression;
2. Cognitive response: how the individual assesses the situation at hand;
3. Behavioral response, such as snapping at others, sleeping to avoid the stressor, eating issues, drinking, smoking, and using other drugs;
4. Physiological response, such as increased heart rate, shaking, or headaches.[7]

The cumulative impact of stress on the body, called the *allostatic load*, causes suboptimal postures, such as chronically holding the shoulders up, tightness in the chest, and a rigid spine, as well as other negative physiological responses, such as chronic increased heart rate, higher levels of carbon dioxide, and muscle tension. The challenge with stress is that it has a way of becoming normalized within our psyche. We come to accept it as a way of being. There is real danger in developing more serious health conditions when stress becomes habitual and particularly when there is a reward, such as performing well on an exam that required disciplined study and preparation. The student may begin to believe that such distress is necessary for success, which can lead to serious health problems. To counteract this type of chronic stress load, we have to activate the PNS, which triggers the body's relaxation response through practices such as self-care (discussed in the next section) and breathing exercises (see Chapter 8).

Working While in School

Students with limited means face financial pressures to find employment to either entirely fund their education or support their living expenses. As a result, they spend the limited amount of time available outside of class, rehearsals, and lessons working in what is often an unfulfilling job that provides minimal compensation. Students who take out loans and don't work during their studies may not bear the same concerns in the moment, since they have time to pay back the loans. However, they may still account for this financial responsibility as an underlying stressor, knowing that their success now may determine their ability to pay back the loans over time. Because working is a necessity for many, it does call for sensitivity from the instructor in understanding scheduling issues, practicing limitations, and compounding tiredness. By fostering an environment of acceptance and consideration toward a variety of personal circumstances, we enhance the trust within our studios and set the stage for more effective advocacy when mental health stressors arise.

Lacking a Support Network

Prior to college life, a support network of friends and family appears to be one of the most important contributing factors to students' well-being. When students transition to school, they lose this sense of safety. Making new friends and fitting in take time, leaving many students without easy access to a close friend of family member to vent to and counsel with during a transition period into new and unknown challenges.

Cultural and Social Factors

International students deal with another set of similar challenges when they transition to university life in a different country. Every aspect of their new lives may feel different, from the food to their living environment, transportation methods, social relationships, language, and cultural expectations, along with the same lack of a family and social network that most college students encounter. For these reasons, international students are at an increased risk for depression, anxiety, and risky substance use.

Students who are functioning in a different language may also face the added barrier of communication difficulties. Misunderstandings can happen due to cultural differences. As an undergraduate international student myself, I vividly remember these experiences firsthand. I would become confused whenever anyone would walk past me in the hall and ask how I was, without pausing for even a second to hear my response. I couldn't understand why they would bother asking the question if they didn't have the time to listen. It took a while to realize that saying "Hi, how are you?" is just another form of greeting, no different than simply saying "Hi!"

Writing can also be particularly challenging for international students, and often, extra effort is needed to prepare writing assignments. Writing centers are readily available on college campuses, and often native-speaking peer mentors are available to provide assistance by providing feedback on idiomatic language and grammar.

Depending on the student's background, expectations of the student–teacher relationship may be different from the norms in the United States. For example, in the student's culture, it may be considered a flaw to admit experiencing stress associated with a performance. Students may be expected to remain strong and not reveal weakness to their teacher. Encouraging a supportive studio environment among the students is essential for international students to thrive. You might consider providing some type of basic training on how to support peers in distress to ensure that those students who are not comfortable sharing mental health challenges with any of their teachers still understand how to seek help from their peers.

Exams and Deadlines

How many times have we all heard the phrase "I just don't have enough time"? Many of our students may feel that they are constantly overextended in the face of a hefty academic workload, facing constant deadlines and struggling to complete assignments on time. Coupled with the all-too-common fear of failure, the intensity of just getting through each day can increase stress and anxiety. Particularly during examination periods, it may not be uncommon to see students show up bleary-eyed and exhausted to their lessons and class meetings. Many admit to not having slept or eaten properly in days. The stress of exams, exacerbated by poor coping skills, results in physical fatigue and a fragile mental state.

Perfectionism

There are several factors that contribute to amplifying perfectionistic tendencies in musicians. Two of these are the public nature of performance evaluation and the comparison with highly edited, "perfect" recordings. Striving for note-perfect performances only sets students up for failure—as a perfect performance simply does not exist. Perfectionism is thought to be adopted as a strategy toward self-acceptance. This was evident in one student's journal reflection: "For some reason, I put the pressure on myself to get all As every semester, even though my parents don't care (they want good grades, but all As aren't something they need to see). I think this is just a personal thing I have had since middle school, when letter grades became a thing." As she identified, the pressure to achieve perfect grades came from herself, not from an external force.

Striving for unattainable perfection can have a negative impact on students' mental health, compounding over time as everyday stressors intersect with a heightened, perhaps even unrealistic, sense of expectation. Pursuing excellence, on the other hand, is attainable for any student. According to research, excellence is achieved through the following: effective concentration during practice, setting specific goals, self-evaluation, designing effective practice strategies, and keeping in mind the bigger picture.[8] Excellence, in other words, is about developing self-reliance in the process of learning. The ability to accept mistakes is a productive way to adapt to what could be perceived as failure. Through a growth mindset, mistakes are viewed as opportunities to learn, rather than as character flaws. Researched most prominently by psychologist Carol Dweck, growth mindset applies to those individuals who develop an understanding of failure as a necessary part of the learning process, and an opportunity to move toward higher levels of potential. This attitude sits in opposition to a fixed mindset, which proposes that talent, or a specific predetermined ability level, controls your capabilities. Those with a fixed mindset perceive intelligence, creativity, and skills as static, and thus tend to avoid failures and measure their success against fixed standards. As a result, one may insulate themselves from failure. They may develop a fear that any failure, even a minor one, might expose their inferiority. Over time, this can stunt progress, eventually leading to feelings of inadequacy and low self-esteem.

The power of a growth mindset lies in its ability to embrace mistakes, and to develop a certain level of fearlessness in one's pursuits. One student I interviewed had come a long way in working through perfectionism and had this to say: "There is just this huge expectation of having to know all the answers to all the questions that are asked ever, and I think for me what's been helpful is to think, well, I don't know all the answers, and that's okay, because no one does." Cultivating a growth mindset not only requires openness to admitting what you don't know, it also requires suspending self-judgment, and increasing self-compassion.

Competition

Undoubtedly, the competition within our profession is fierce—both in terms of actual music competitions and also in terms of earning acceptance into top academic training programs, not to mention competing for opera roles, seats in orchestra, grants, ensembles, scholarships, assistantships, and even the unofficial perceptions of rank within a studio. The list goes on, and it does not even include the competitive dimension of building a professional career post-graduation. While some students thrive in a competitive environment, others struggle, especially when internal perfectionistic attitudes put more pressure on them.

Loneliness and Isolation

Several students I interviewed mentioned loneliness and isolation as two of the greatest challenges they faced while in school. They cited many of the factors we discussed earlier, including a heavy workload, a competitive environment, and the isolation resulting from countless number of hours spent practicing or composing alone. A graduate student mentioned experiencing a sense of "living in [her] own world and hyperfocusing on meeting the academic and performance demands." The lack of social interaction increased her sense of anxiety. Other students mentioned not being able to talk to their peers about issues they were dealing with because of fear of being judged as weak and undeserving of a spot in their program. Bearing the burden alone caused feelings of sadness and stress.

Time Management

One of the first life lessons students learn while in college is how to manage their time. Music students' schedules tend to be highly structured, requiring discipline and strong organizational skills. Staying on top of assignments and responding to the demands of applied lessons means that students have to set aside time daily to catch up on homework and, of course, to practice. Between homework and classes, their schedule is packed from morning to evening. If they get sick or don't follow their daily routine, they can fall behind, making it difficult to catch up. Assignments pile up, and so does stress. According to Nonis et al., it's not so much the actual time that students have available to them but the perception of control over that time that causes stress.[9] One of the undergraduate students in my class addressed this very point in a journal reflection:

> I have a tendency to drop out of certain things when life gets stressful. This is something I know about myself, and it is something I would like to change. Often, by skipping things, I can lose more time in the catch-up process than I gain by skipping in the first place. In these cases, sometimes I justify it to myself, saying I need the time now and can afford to sacrifice some later. Sometimes, I am right about this, but more often than I'd like, I am wrong to assume that I'll have more time in some vague sense of the future. That being said, I think it is important to know one's limits and respect them.

This student is not alone in his experience. Many students are faced with assignments piling up and, feeling like they are losing control, resort to skipping classes and dropping commitments.

Workload

The workload of a music student is both heavy and demanding. Coupled with fears of not being able to complete assignments on time and the fear of failure, students can feel paralyzed and unable to complete their homework in a timely manner.

A graduate student vividly described what a heavy workload feels like in terms of prioritizing:

> My biggest problem is prioritizing my tasks. I have difficulty concentrating on one task while there are others that are occupying my mind. I usually have multiple tabs open at the same time and complete a little bit of everything at the same time. I feel like I will forget what I am thinking if I don't put it down as soon as I think about it, and I keep thinking about multiple things at a time. I also sometimes use this as an escape from a task, with the excuse of completing the other one. It is complicated.

Indeed, confronting difficult tasks can feel overwhelming, causing a sense of disarray, not only in terms of time management, but also in terms of our thinking. Our brain is designed to tackle one thing at a time and does not handle multitasking very well.

In her study report on psychological distress among university students, Stallman brings up a good point: A sick day for students does not mean that assignments do not eventually need to be completed and that class time does not need to be somehow made up.[10] These tasks are just pushed off, adding to the already busy schedule of the weeks that follow.

Living Arrangement

Students who live alone or off-campus tend to have higher levels of stress when compared to students who live either on campus or with their partner or family.[11] We could surmise that this might be because living alone could mean having less social interaction after coming home from a stressful day. A conversation with a roommate or family member about the day is a way of processing how the day went and talking through difficult situations. Without someone at home to do that with, one could be accumulating more stress over time.

Physical Pain and Injuries

When the body is experiencing symptoms of injury, it makes sense that the mind and emotions will also experience distress. Research shows that physical pain and mental health disorders can, and often do, appear concurrently. In fact, a study by Kenny and Ackermann examined the relationship between self-reported performance-related musculoskeletal pain disorders, trigger-point pain, and depression, social phobia, and music performance anxiety in professional orchestral musicians. The results revealed a complex relationship between the physical experience of pain and the mental disorders of depression and performance anxiety. The musicians who reported the highest severity of depression were also experiencing the highest levels of playing-related musculoskeletal disorders. When depression and performance anxiety were present, high trigger-point scores were also reported.[12]

Although many musicians with a physical injury will experience severe psychological distress, others will experience milder forms of distress. They will worry about what their instructor and peers think of them and experience anxiety over the unknown timeline of recovery. A graduate student I spoke with had experienced injuries in her arms. Her description of what was going on through her mind during that time period was as follows:

It was such a major concern that I felt like it completely halted my first year of my master's degree. It became very frustrating because I knew that at each lesson, the instruction was going to be very rudimentary and very slow. I felt like I was not grasping concepts quickly enough and was still having arm pain. It was all so hard on me because I was worried about what my professor thought of me. I would tell myself, "What if he doesn't think that I'm a good student? Or that I'm not trying hard enough?"

By all accounts, her instructor was a supportive professor. Nevertheless, the negative self-talk and fear of judgment came to the forefront of her thought patterns during her injury. Thankfully, this story has a happy ending! The student relied on the expertise of healthcare professionals and followed the guidance of her teacher in retraining her technique. She was able to overcome the injury and thrive in her degree program.

Technology

Technology has dramatically changed the way that we live and interact with other people. We have an incredible amount of information at our fingertips, which, when amplified by the ubiquitous technological platforms that govern much of our day-to-day work, can lead to information overload. While technology has improved our lives in so many ways, it also comes with major drawbacks when it comes to mental health. Its addictive nature can get in the way of our deep engagement in other activities (whether they be practicing or enjoying lunch with a friend) for long periods of time without the need to check email or a social media platform at some point. Social media has affected the teenage and young adult population specifically in terms of increased feelings of isolation, depression, and envy.

Parents

Parents today are known to be highly involved in the observation and critique of their children's education, even into collegiate study. This type of overprotection can limit the young adult's development of independence, which translates into poor protective factors for dealing with distress. A student who comes from a household of overprotective parents may find the autonomy of college life disorienting and especially isolating. These students may be particularly eager to embrace a teacher–student mentor relationship to provide comfort and support during their transition toward independence.

***

We have explored several contributing factors toward mental distress in the applied lesson setting. While this list may seem overwhelming, it doesn't mean every student should expect to deal with every one of these stressors. Similarly, pedagogues may need to be flexible in terms of assignment parameters, workload, and other expectations when we discover students who are experiencing variable levels of mental distress. In any circumstance, the best approach while you are in conversation with your students is to encourage protective factors. Applying motivational interviewing techniques (as explored in Chapter 2) can help us better understand potential solutions to safeguard against overwhelming stress levels, which, if left unaddressed, could lead to more serious mental health conditions. But there are many other accessible techniques we can use to preempt more significant issues from arising. The following pages explore some of these mental health protection strategies in more depth, to help you develop a broader awareness of the ways you can support positive mental health awareness in your students.

Protecting Mental Health

Irrespective of the numerous factors and circumstances that may trigger distress, there are several practices that can serve to protect mental health. Remember that taking care of wellness means being deliberate about daily actions that lead to maintenance or improvement. In this section, I will discuss self-care strategies as tools for preventing long-term stress to the mind and body and how self-compassion serves as the gateway to actualizing them in our day-to-day lives.

Self-Care

There are certain misconceptions about the act of self-care that I would like to address before exploring applicable strategies. The first one is that self-care is a selfish act. Think about a caregiver to someone who is chronically ill. The kind of support given by a caregiver to someone sick is often both physically and emotionally demanding. It may seem that any time spent on self-care in this scenario is taking away from the person who is relying on their constant care. And yet it is imperative that the caregiver takes time to rejuvenate herself. It might actually be to the benefit of both parties. Without that commitment to self-care, looking after the other person may soon become even more challenging and could lead to burnout.

Another misconception is that self-care is an exclusive practice, requiring money to unlock services offered by fancy spas, resorts, or exotic getaways. While it certainly could, the great news is that many effective self-care practices are, in fact, free. Self-care is not about buying health; it comprises basic activities that we can all adopt as long as we find time to do so. It could involve something as simple as deep breathing, or pen and paper for journaling or drawing. And, finally, there's an attitude that self-care strategies that work for a friend should also work for me. But just like with all areas of our wellness, there isn't a one-size-fits-all self-care plan. Needs vary among individuals, and every person responds differently to different strategies. Therefore, it may take some experimentation before finding activities that are truly restorative.

I think about self-care as putting on a suit of armor. It's our protective mechanism against the wear and tear of life. Without it, we are vulnerable to the accumulation of stress, which in turn may lead to many serious health issues. By making time to take care of ourselves on a regular basis, we can restore balance in terms of our physical, emotional, and mental wellness.

Hopefully, if you've read this far along in the book, you are already convinced of the value of self-care. But if it is so important, then why don't we practice it? What are those barriers that are getting in our way? Well, the most common one that I hear about (and I can attest to) is time. Our days are crammed with teaching, work, writing, responding to emails, family responsibilities, and all sorts of last-minute and oh-so-very-important tasks. We ignore the limits of what we are able to handle, and may hold off until the weekend to allow ourselves some time to rest. Even then, we may not actively pursue an activity that is fulfilling and refreshing to our body and soul. Setting unrealistic expectations of what that self-care activity will look like (e.g., spending an hour at the gym every day, or forty-five minutes of meditation) can also cause feelings of disappointment. Feelings of guilt for engaging in an activity other than work (or practice or fill-in-the-blank) add to our resistance to taking care of ourselves. And since our students look up to us as role models, if we don't practice self-care, they are not likely to do it either (they tend to "do as we do," not "as we say"). Now let's explore a foundational attitude toward ourselves that enables us to overcome some of these barriers toward practicing self-care.

Pause for Self-Compassion

If we look at the psychology behind these barriers, we might notice that they stem from feeling like we don't matter enough to be paid attention to. Other activities end up taking up our time, leaving little to no time for ourselves. As musicians, we are accustomed to living with a highly critical internal voice that often extends beyond the practice room and into other areas of our lives. We judge ourselves for our imperfections and compensate for them by working harder and filling up our schedules with even more things to do. But what would it be like if, instead of being so harsh with ourselves, we extended kindness and self-compassion? Instead of telling ourselves, "What's wrong with you? Why can't you get that passage right?," we would say something like "This is a difficult section, and I can see why you are struggling with it." Talking to ourselves from a place of kindness allows us to see a situation and our reaction to it more objectively. Accepting all of it (the good, the bad, and the ugly) gives us permission to engage ourselves in a more positive dialogue.

Reframing our inner critic takes practice (which is why it's called the *practice* of self-compassion). One of my favorite approaches for finding that comforting inner voice is to imagine that I am talking to a younger version of myself. I would never dream of saying those same mean things to a child! In my own teaching of younger students, I constantly reaffirm their strengths and extend compassion freely. Directing these attitudes toward myself means pausing and inserting moments of mindfulness when those negative self-talk moments arise. Through observing them and reframing them with kindness, I can be gentler and more understanding with myself. I can reframe the guilt and talk myself into self-care rather than out of it. Through the lens of self-compassion, we can begin to allow ourselves to find the time to refill our vessel. Let's look at some strategies for making it possible.

Self-Care Strategies

When you are making time for and selecting self-care activities for yourself, or exploring options with your students, consider the following guidelines:

- Let go of guilt and practice self-compassion instead.
- Carve out time for self-care every day (block time in your calendar), even if it's only fifteen minutes.
- Set realistic goals (what will you feel like doing, and for how long, during the time you have blocked off? You know yourself better than anyone else.).
- Start with a tiny step (even just putting on your walking shoes and then taking them off is a start toward building a habit).
- Decompress throughout the day (don't wait until the weekend or until the end of the day).
- Select activities that are enjoyable (you are less likely to follow through if the activity is not enjoyable).

At this point, you might take an inventory (either for yourself or with your student) to think about what self-care practices you already have in place. For me, taking a siesta has long been a part of my life, thanks to my upbringing in a warm Mediterranean climate. I cannot imagine weekends without naps, and that is one way I take care of myself. Naps are not possible during the week, so I have to get creative with mini stretching and breathing breaks throughout the day. Here are a few ideas to explore:

- Practice a guided three- to four-minute meditation. There are several available on YouTube or through several podcasts.
- Enjoy a comforting cup of tea or coffee while reading a poem or reflecting on a favorite quote.
- Try adult coloring books (repetitive movements are calming).
- Bring an attitude of mindfulness to your meal or snack, savoring the experience (see Chapter 9 for a mindful eating meditation).
- Connect with a friend or family member.
- Pick up your favorite hobby (knitting, sewing, brewing kombucha).

I am certain you have your own ideas of what you need to care for your well-being. I encourage you to develop a list of your favorite activities so that in your times of stress, you can refer to it and quickly have ideas of what you know works well for you.

So far we have explored contributing factors to mental distress, as well as protective practices to prevent spiraling into more serious conditions. However, because mental health disorders are reliant on genetic predisposition, familial environment, and current situations, the focus may be more on managing conditions through the support of a healthcare professional. A mental health disorder can significantly impact day-to-day life. Even for a person who is taking all the right steps toward managing her condition, there may be relapses or other challenges. Being familiar with symptoms of some of the most common disorders among college students may inform our approach toward those students.

Overview of Mental Health Disorders

For this section, I consulted the *Diagnostic and Statistical Manual of Mental Disorders* (DSM) and the *International Classification of Diseases* (ICD) by the World Health Organization, which are widely regarded as the most comprehensive and reliable resources for clinical and research purposes. If you would like more in-depth information, I suggest looking at these resources.

Anxiety

Anxiety is a normal reaction to perceived danger, and it is the most frequently diagnosed psychological disorder in both adults and children.[13] There are several types of anxiety: generalized anxiety disorder, social anxiety, obsessive-compulsive disorder, post-traumatic stress disorder, and panic disorder. Music performance anxiety also falls under the anxiety category. Anxiety could be triggered by actual danger, or by something that is perceived as dangerous. The inability to complete a heavy workload in a timely manner, concerns over future employment, the fear of failing on stage, current financial troubles, and social issues, such as fitting in, are all potential causes of anxiety. A chain of physiological, psychological, and behavioral responses are set forth by the activation of the fight-flight-freeze response (discussed under the section on stress) in order to quickly respond to the stressor. The difference between stress and anxiety is that stress is usually temporary, and it goes away when the stressor ends (for example, after taking an exam). Stress can be motivational, whereas anxiety is not. In fact, avoidance behaviors are common in people who experience anxiety, causing perpetuation of those feelings. Anxiety can cause significant distress and disruption to daily life. Now let's look at some of the most common forms of anxiety.

Generalized Anxiety Disorder

Signs of generalized anxiety disorder (GAD) include worrying excessively about several areas of one's life; avoiding situations that are viewed as threatening; having sleep difficulties; experiencing physical pain, such as tension, headaches, and digestive problems; fatigue; and having trouble focusing. You may have encountered a student who constantly avoided performing or tackling a new and challenging piece. Procrastination is a way of coping with situations that are perceived as difficult.

GAD can affect multiple dimensions, such as one's occupation, social life, family, and education. Complaints about physical pain, such as muscular tension, may be attributed to the disorder. Cognitive behavioral therapy, which addresses the thoughts, feelings, behaviors, and physical sensations associated with the anxiety, is considered the most effective way to treat anxiety. Calming exercises such as diaphragmatic breathing can bring about a sense of calm to the physical body, thus positively affecting thoughts, feelings, and behaviors.

Social Anxiety

In campus-wide surveys on mental health, social anxiety was the most reported concern experienced by students, alongside academic distress. Social anxiety is characterized by fear of public or performance situations in which students will be around unfamiliar people or will be subject to scrutiny that lasts for six or more months. The anxiety is caused by fear of embarrassing oneself in front of others. As a result, the person avoids the situation or endures it with a great amount of distress. Social anxiety can greatly interfere with a student's academic success and social relationships. Cognitive behavioral therapy is the most effective form of treatment for social anxiety.

Post-Traumatic Stress Disorder

Post-traumatic stress disorder (PTSD) is caused by ongoing, high-stress circumstances such as parental divorce, living in a financially insecure household, and neglect, among other factors. Experiencing or witnessing one-time traumatic events, such as physical or sexual assault, robbery, torture, or kidnapping, are also causes of PTSD. Memories of the event can trigger flashbacks as if it were happening again, overriding one's awareness of safety in the present moment. In these cases, one may actively avoid situations or people that trigger memories and feelings related to the traumatic event or situation. Negative emotions, such as guilt, fear, or anger, can be persistent, making it difficult to experience positive emotions. Extreme sensitivity to stimuli, such as jumpiness to loud sounds, is common, as are angry outbursts and self-destructive behavior such as excessive alcohol or drug use.

Panic Disorder

Panic disorder is often confused with panic attacks. For one to be diagnosed with panic disorder, one must experience panic attacks frequently, with each panic attack followed by about a month of fear of experiencing another one, resulting in avoiding situations that may trigger one. Panic attacks are categorized into expected (i.e., a specific, known fear causes them) and unexpected (i.e., appearing seemingly without a trigger). Symptoms include a sudden increase in heart rate (sometimes similar to the feeling of a heart attack), sweating, shaking, nausea, and chest pain.

If you are around someone who is having a panic attack, it is important to seek medical care immediately, as the symptoms may be caused by panic or another medical condition. A doctor will be able to run tests to determine if there are other conditions present. Treatment for panic disorder includes a combination of therapy and medication.

Obsessive-Compulsive Disorder

Millions of Americans are affected by obsessive-compulsive disorder (OCD). The most recent estimates show that approximately 1 in 40 adults between ages 15 and 44 years of age and 1 in 100 children are affected by OCD. The disorder is characterized by obsessions and compulsions that take up at least one hour every day. Obsessions are unwanted, persistent thoughts or images. Compulsions are repetitive behaviors or mental actions, such as counting or praying, meant to get rid of the obsessive thoughts or images and the distress caused by them. It is common for OCD to be accompanied by other disorders, such as anxiety, depression, and bipolar disorders.

As the public has become more aware of OCD, so has the labeling of conditions that are not OCD become common. It is important to understand that OCD causes a high level of distress. Individuals with OCD are trying to stop the obsessive thoughts through the compulsive behavior. This is markedly different from Obsessive Compulsive Disorder Personality, in which individuals take pleasure in creating an extremely organized and neat environment in their home. OCD is also not associated with other obsessive behaviors such as lying, which is more associated with impulse control difficulties.

A person with OCD is likely very aware of his behaviors and probably understands that they are problematic and interfere with his normal functioning. OCD can be treated through Cognitive Behavioral Therapy; therefore if the need arises to have a conversation with a student about this issue, your recommendation should be to schedule an appointment with a qualified mental health professional who can provide this type of therapy.

Music Performance Anxiety

In order to perform optimally, one's musical competence, physical well-being, and psychological well-being must be at a high level. The increased heart rate and nervous energy that are associated with a live musical performance may be interpreted either as excitement and a necessary component for elevating performance to higher levels of achievement, or as a threat to one's success. Negative music performance anxiety (MPA) is considered to be the number one threat to the psychological well-being of musicians. Whether viewed in a negative or positive light, MPA affects every musician and can never be eradicated, as it is part of what makes us human.

MPA causes physiological, behavioral, and cognitive symptoms. Negative thoughts include fear of being evaluated negatively, fear of an imperfect performance, and a poor self-image. Negative self-talk feeds these patterns, continuing the cycle of unhelpful thoughts. Physiological symptoms are similar to the symptoms experienced when the fight-flight-freeze response is activated. These include increased heart rate and blood flow, quick breathing, sweating, lightheadedness, dry mouth, and a feeling of having butterflies in the stomach. One of the students I talked with described a "very strange" physical symptom of his hands feeling "completely cold and empty," which can make the thought of performing a piano recital absolutely terrifying! Behavioral responses include avoiding performance situations and social environments that may involve discussions about performance anxiety.

There are several factors that place students at a higher risk for experiencing MPA. According to Kenny, a researcher in music psychology, six causes of MPA are most commonly cited among music students: inadequate preparation, self-imposed pressure, lack of self-confidence, playing repertoire that is too difficult for the student's skill level, and excessive physical arousal before or during a performance.[14] Research by Sadler and Miller have demonstrated that musicians with a negative emotional temperament (e.g., distressed, upset, nervous) are predisposed to experiencing MPA.[15] Perfectionism and setting unrealistic expectations for a performance are also factors that contribute to MPA. Inability to control MPA can be detrimental for the musician. Many talented musicians have given up music altogether, citing the difficulty of overcoming the stress of public performance. With support from a mental health professional and/or the instructor, it is certainly possible to not only manage MPA, but to use it as a tool to fuel thrilling performances.

Although often framed in a negative light, MPA, to the degree that it does not disrupt the performance, has many advantages, such as heightening our senses, releasing stored energy, and maintaining stamina during long and demanding performances. The goal of treatment is not to eliminate MPA completely, but to harness it by straddling the balance between activation of the sympathetic and parasympathetic nervous systems. There are various methods for treating MPA, including behavioral, cognitive, cognitive-behavioral, pharmacological, and alternative therapies. The most effective method of managing MPA is through a combination of cognitive and behavioral techniques. A therapist can help students develop the skills to be in control of their psychophysical reactions to performance anxiety.

When students experience stress related to performance, the first person they usually go to for help is their applied instructor; therefore, the instructor must be prepared to have those conversations and should have a toolkit to help students with coping (see the toolkit section at the end of the chapter and the breathing exercises in Chapter 8 for ideas).[16] Having open conversations with students early on creates a safe environment for them to discuss their experience and develop coping strategies.

The language you use in such conversations can make the difference between empowering students to rely on their strengths to deal with the performance and leaving them feeling disempowered and weak in the face of what is perceived as a terrifying situation. I suggest using prompts that open the door for students to feel more comfortable to talk openly about their feelings around the performance. They may be too nervous to bring them up. You might ask, "How does your breath move when you think about performing in studio class?" or "How are you feeling about Sunday's performance?" or "What do you anticipate your concentration being like right before playing next week?" You can decide how pointed you want your questions to be, but the more you can help them connect to their experience, the more they will become aware of their response to the stress of the performance and learn to accept it as part of the process. Resisting anxiety only makes it worse. It's only when we accept, notice it, and breathe through the anxiety that we can learn to use it as a powerful tool for generating energy in a performance.

In your conversations with students around MPA, they may ask you if you think beta-blockers could be the right course of action for them to help reduce their symptoms. While some musicians benefit from their use, they certainly don't work for everyone. A common complaint is that they help calm down the physical response, but not the cognitive one. Thoughts could still be racing, but the body's inability to respond to the mental state may create a strange, disjunct experience of busy mental chatter with a calm heartbeat and physical sensations. When considering beta-blockers, suggest that a student talk to her physician to get a prescription, since they are prescription medications that should not be freely shared between people, as often happens. If a student has a prescription and wants to use beta blockers for an upcoming performance, you might suggest that she try them out ahead of time to ensure there aren't any adverse effects.

Students who are given tools to aid them in managing performance anxiety have the potential to have positive outcomes. Osborne, Greene, and Immel facilitated two lectures and a masterclass, supplemented with a workbook, to help students with audition and performance anxiety.[17] Thirty-one students participated in their study, which compared pre- and post-intervention responses on self-reported performance anxiety. The results showed that working through strategies for developing skills such as improving self-talk, recovering from mistakes, and channeling per-formance energy improved their "performance preparation, confidence, courage, focus, concentration and performance resilience." The mental health toolkit section at the end of the chapter includes exercises for coping with MPA ⊙.

The students in my wellness class attend an educational talk by our on-site coun-selor on performance anxiety and complete several of the exercises available on the companion website. They come up with a plan for managing performance anxiety that involves both long-term and short-term goals, which they reflect on in their journals. One student reflected on previous experiences with performance anxiety and identified a plan for her next performance:

> Performance anxiety can have a major effect on my performances, no matter how well pre-pared I am. One thing [the counselor] said in the clinic was to acknowledge the signs of performance anxiety without letting them lead to panic. I think this strategy will help my mind stay calm and focused. I have learned to overcome the physical effects of anxiety, like shallow breathing, shaking, and cold hands. I don't normally feel those effects anymore, but most of my anxiety is mental and emotional. I tend to think about what other people are thinking while I am playing, and it gets very distracting. I have had dress rehearsals crash and burn because of nerves, leading to a successful performance because I become so de-termined to defeat the nerves. For my next high-pressure performance, I want to prepare by recording myself, playing for other people, and recreating performance environments as much as possible to incrementally practice overcoming anxiety.

Her response indicates that an intervention such as access to educational talks, exercises, and, of course, instructor support can help students better understand their response to performance anxiety and develop ways to work with it. It is im-portant to recognize that performance anxiety is likely borne by many, if not a ma-jority, of our students. By regularly integrating resources that could assist in dealing with performance stressors as a fundamental pedagogical value, rather than acute interventions with individuals already experiencing high levels of stress, we can nor-malize that aspect of our discipline and empower our students to feel safe in pursuing help when needed. Destigmatizing conditions in this way is a critical strategy to-ward building a confident, trustworthy relationship with your students, and may pay dividends when more severe disorders appear.

Depression

Depression is a serious mental illness that can deeply impact a person's ability to func-tion and connect with other people. The CDC estimates that between 2013 and 2016, 8.1 percent of Americans over twenty years old suffered from depression.[18] The dif-ferent types of depression are persistent depression, bipolar disorder, psychotic de-pression, peripartum (postpartum) depression, premenstrual dysphoric disorder, seasonal depression, situational depression, and atypical depression.[19] Research studies focusing on the music student population indicate that music students experience a higher rate of anxiety and depression compared to their peers pursuing other degrees and that first-year students experience higher rates of depression, stage fright, and fatigue compared to older students.[20] This is not surprising, considering the competition, intense schedule, and high demands that music students have to live up to.

According to statistics from the World Health Organization, major depression is the leading cause of disability in the United States for those aged fifteen to forty-four. For a major depressive disorder diagnosis to occur, five or more of the following symptoms must be present consistently for a period of at least two weeks: reduced interest in activities that were previously pleasant, weight loss without dieting efforts, low energy or fatigue, feelings of worthlessness or guilt, difficulty concentrating, and sleep difficulties. Thoughts of death and suicide attempts are common, especially in those who live alone and have previously attempted suicide. When a student says things like "My life doesn't matter anymore," or "I might as well be dead than go through this," it could be a sign that they may be having suicidal thoughts. The upcoming subsection "Helping Students in Severe Distress or Crisis" offers tools for responding to such language.

Major depression causes significant impairment in many areas of functioning, although impairment may not always be noticeable by others. It's possible that you may notice some of the symptoms mentioned previously, but they may also go completely unnoticed, especially if the student is able to complete her work as required. Again, symptoms must be persistent for at least two weeks, so if a student occasionally comes in feeling tired and having difficulty concentrating, it could be a result of occasional poor sleep, not necessarily a more severe disorder. If, however, you are noticing several of these symptoms for a long period of time, a more serious issue, such as major depression, may be at hand.

Impostor Phenomenon

The impostor phenomenon (also known as impostor syndrome) was first identified in the 1970s by Suzanna Imes and Pauline Rose Clance, who recognized the syndrome in high-achieving women. The impostor phenomenon (IP) refers to feeling like a fraud in one's profession and that one's accomplishments are attributed to sheer luck, or incredible amounts of effort. Thoughts related to IP include "I don't belong here," "Someone will eventually figure out I am here because of a big mistake," and "I'm never going to be as good as ____." These thoughts reflect an inability to internalize accomplishments, convincing the individual he is a phony, even though his achievements demonstrate otherwise. Although not a recognized disorder in the DSM-5, IP has been studied in several contexts and has been linked to perfectionism and social anxiety. The need to appear perfect to others increases the feelings of fraudulence and contributes to an avoidance of communicating in a social setting out of fear of making mistakes and appearing as a fraud.[21] Musicians who are accepted at elite institutions, for example, may feel that they don't belong in such a place and that soon they will be revealed as incompetent. These feelings may result in self-doubt and a low sense of self-worth.

It is common to experience IP in the academic environment because of the pressure to achieve and the constant comparison to others. Transitioning into the academic environment also brings about these feelings as students try to find their place. Fear of failure and perfectionistic tendencies cause students who experience IP to either work much harder than they need to or spend little time completing tasks because they perceive failure as inevitable. As such, IP can become a barrier to academic success and can lead to higher stress and burnout.

I have yet to encounter a student in my wellness class who has never dealt with feelings of IP. It is quite possible that you also have students who feel they are not talented enough and don't deserve a spot in their academic program. If such conversations come up in lessons, you could suggest using some of these activities for processing and reframing negative thoughts as well as affirming strengths and values:

- Jot down your thoughts before a stressful event.
- Create an inventory of your accomplishments: spend five minutes writing down evidence of your success.
- Reaffirm your core values by writing them down to promote your self-worth.
- Consider your complexity as an individual: think about all the things that make you who you are, which will ease pressure off one aspect of your life that may be stressful.
- Affirm your strengths: complete a strengths test such as the Gallup Strength Finder; ask a friend or a family member to affirm the results for you and provide concrete examples of how these strengths show up.
- Reframe your thoughts: think about ways you can reframe negative automatic responses into positive ones.

As your student works through building her self-confidence and overcoming IP, you or a peer can provide affirmation of her strengths and values (e.g. "You are such an excellent communicator and I can see that in how you lead your quartet rehearsals. You address your group with maturity and clarity."). By practicing consistency in these responses, the pedagogue strengthens her capacity to empower students over their broader set of skills, and, over time, may help all students see their total potential.

Attention-Deficit/Hyperactivity Disorder (ADHD)

A persistent pattern of inattention can manifest itself in different ways: making mistakes in schoolwork or during other activities, having trouble staying focused for long activities (lectures, reading, etc.), seeming inattentive when spoken to, having trouble following through with completing assignments, having difficulty getting organized and appearing to be messy, and being easily distracted by others (or by thoughts). Hyperactive behaviors that can be visible are fidgeting, not being able to remain seated when needed, excessive talking, impatience in waiting one's turn during conversation, and interrupting others during conversation, which may cause conflict with others. The student's schoolwork and social life are affected. Following through with tasks and accomplishing larger projects are daunting, and as a result, a student with ADHD will tend to avoid them.

Autism Spectrum Disorder

This disorder's common signs can be noticed in the responses given in a conversation. The body language and verbal communication of someone with autism spectrum disorder (ASD) do not correspond very well, and understanding social relationships can be difficult. Repetitive speech and movement patterns are also present. A person with ASD also exhibits intense fixations on objects, has restricted interests and activities, and experiences stress when even small changes in routine occur. The manifestation of this disorder varies greatly depending on the severity. The most essential component is the deficit of socio-emotional reciprocity in conversations.[22]

Maintaining a routine is crucial to avoid frustration and outbreaks. Academic success may be affected negatively if the individual has trouble with organization and coping with change. Due to the social and emotional deficits, social isolation may occur. Since autism is not a curable disorder, as pedagogues we can counteract social isolation and create space for students on the spectrum to be vibrant contributors to our musical community.

Bipolar Disorder

Bipolar disorder is characterized by periods of depression, followed by periods of intense emotions and activity. These episodes can last for about a week, during which they can be present for almost the entirety of the days. Characteristics include high levels of energy, needing much less sleep than usual, an increased sense of self-esteem, irritability, and engaging in activities that could potentially cause harm.

Hypomanic or major depressive episodes may precede or follow manic episodes. The characteristics of hypomanic episodes are similar to those of manic episodes; however, the symptoms do not impair one's functioning. Depressive episodes are characterized by depressed mood, weight loss, insomnia, low energy, thoughts of death, or even suicide attempts.

The intensity of the manic episode may result in social and occupational difficulties. Drug abuse is also common and may result in self-harm or harming others. The suicide risk of someone with bipolar disorder is fifteen times higher than for the general population. The mean age for developing bipolar disorder is eighteen, which means that college students who have bipolar disorder may be experiencing some of these symptoms for the first time.

***

Now that we have learned some of the challenges our students face and the basics of common mental health disorders, let's turn to some tactics and exercises that will help us support our students, regardless of which issues they may encounter.

Seeking Help

Why Students Don't Seek Help

Needless to say, in spite of nationwide efforts, there is still a stigma attached to seeking help for mental health concerns. Even though college campuses, in general, do have adequate resources, students may not take advantage of them. Some students may not want to be seen by others as they walk into the clinic for treatment, others don't know how to access the right assistance, and in some cases there is a limit to the support available.[23] There may be pressure from family not to disclose mental health problems, or even family members who don't believe they exist. Such attitudes can also come with lack of access to health insurance for treatment. Additionally, some students are resigned to accepting stress as a normal part of being a student. Functioning under stress becomes a habit and may even be viewed as necessary to get through one's academic career.

Recently, there have been campus-wide efforts to start the conversation around mental health, specifically with the aim of destigmatizing the act of seeking help. Organizations such as Project375, Bring Change to Mind, and We Are All a Little Crazy have partnered with universities to bring artists and celebrities who are championing mental health conversations to their campuses. These unprecedented efforts aim to normalize the acceptance of mental health issues, highlight the importance of seeking appropriate resources, and share stories of those who have found success in coping with their conditions. By being part of these conversations, we can play a role in advocating for mental health awareness in our communities and bring about positive change.

The Teacher's Role

Mental health professionals agree that the instructor's support of a student in distress can be immensely beneficial. At this point, I want to reiterate that supporting students in distress does not mean providing therapy, diagnosis, or medical advice—none of which most music teachers are trained to provide. The type of assistance you as the teacher can provide is to create a supportive environment, model appropriate responses to emotionally stressful situations, improve your ability to listen with compassion, and provide information about resources for help. Proactive preparation to support students' well-being will ensure that when the situation arises, you already know what resources are available and what steps are needed to guide students to the appropriate professional assistance.

Throughout the course of the semester, you can promote wellness and self-care by having occasional check-ins with students, particularly when stressful situations are approaching (e.g., exams, high-stakes performances, auditions). Encourage adequate sleep, nutrition, and exercise even during those stressful times. An email to the entire studio with reminders that it is okay to take time to sleep and eat properly may give students the permission they need to take care of themselves.

Students with a perfectionist attitude will inevitably place importance on everything they do and thus do not deal with failure very well. You can support these students by encouraging a growth mindset. You might share challenges you faced while honing your skill or specific instances in which you had to deal with failure and continue to work toward your goals. Degree recitals can often feel like the be-all and end-all of a student's performance career, when in reality they are just one step in the larger process of growing as a musician. To take the pressure off this one recital, you could provide several lower-stakes performance opportunities throughout the semester that are graded.

Helping Students in Mild or Moderate Distress

You may encounter students who are experiencing different levels of distress, ranging from mild to severe. Behavior can be a useful indicator that helps us better understand what students are dealing with. Knowing how to talk to students at each level of distress and how to help gives you the chance to have a positive impact on students' lives and may even prevent students from putting themselves in a harmful situation.

Common behaviors exhibited by students who are dealing with mild distress (as identified by the University of Michigan's Counseling and Psychological Services) include a sudden change in performance, grade problems, falling asleep during class, low energy (or excessive talking), and visible anxiety when called upon to answer questions. In my experience, many students fall into this category at one point or another during the academic year. Dealing with stress can be challenging and can cause them to drop assignments, not show up on time, and demonstrate visible signs of anxiety during their class or lesson. If you are noticing behavioral changes, such as the student repeatedly asking for special considerations or extensions, behavior that is disruptive to the flow of the class or the lesson, or strong emotional responses to feedback, then the student may be in moderate distress.

To help students in mild or moderate distress, a face-to-face conversation is the first step. Give the student space to speak and explain what he is dealing with, while you practice active listening. In your conversation with the student, respect what he has to say, even if it doesn't make sense to you. Allow the student to do about 80 percent of the talking, and spend your 20 percent identifying problems that you are hearing by asking questions and reflecting back what the student has told you (see the discussion on motivational interviewing in Chapter 2). Students can often feel overwhelmed by homework and other responsibilities. They may be having trouble breaking their work down into manageable steps. Normalize this and help them identify small steps they can take to make progress. Although the phrase "Everything will be okay" may sound reassuring, it may cause even more stress to a student who doesn't feel that everything is okay at the moment. Instead, try something like "Let me help you figure out solutions." A few questions you can ask are "How can I help you the most?," "Have you dealt with a similar situation in the past?," and "What are some options you can use to deal with what you've been feeling?" Such conversations offer opportunities for practicing the motivational interviewing tool of elicit-provide-elicit (see Chapter 2). Once the student has shared what she has experienced before and how she has dealt with such situations in the past, you can then offer a menu of ideas by saying, "Would you be interested in hearing what has helped other students who were in similar situations?" If the response is positive, then you can share three to five ideas.

A way to encourage the student to elaborate or go into more depth about her experience are the three simple words, "Tell me more." While the student is speaking, notice the emotion behind the thoughts and ideas she is sharing with you. Maintain a calm demeanor, even if what she is sharing might be a trigger for you. Avoid judgment and giving advice. Instead, let the student rely on her strengths and previous experiences to find solutions. If she is struggling to come up with something, you might ask if she is comfortable with you sharing suggestions that have worked for other students. Some suggestions might be journaling, deep breathing, getting more sleep, exercising, reaching out to family and friends for support, and checking in with a counselor.

If this student's performance is affecting other classes, especially if he may be facing the possibility of significantly underperforming or failing other courses, contact the appropriate colleagues or the department's administrator. This would be a good time to refer the student to campus resources, such as a counseling center, for help. Reaffirm to the student that seeking help is actually an act of strength, not weakness. Explain that a social worker is better suited to help with what they are dealing with than you are, although you are there to support them and help them with any course-related changes they might need to make.

Helping Students in Severe Distress or Crisis

Students in severe distress can exhibit behaviors that are threatening to themselves or people around them. Crisis mode, according to the National Alliance on Mental Illness (NAMI), means getting in trouble with the law, injuring oneself accidentally or on purpose, or coming up with a suicide plan or a plan to hurt others.[24] According to the JED Foundation research, over one thousand suicides occur on US college campuses every year, and approximately 20 percent of the student population have considered suicide at some point while in college.

A student in severe distress or crisis mode has lost touch with reality and may have trouble communicating clearly. Panic attacks, extreme anxiety and depression, PTSD episodes, and medication complications are all triggers that can potentially place a student with a mental health condition in crisis mode. Not knowing about a student's condition makes it harder for faculty or staff to better understand what he is going through.

If the student is injured and needs immediate medical attention, call 911 right away. If the student is saying things like "I wish I were dead" or "I hate my life," follow the Question-Persuade-Refer (QPR) protocol. The QPR response was developed by Dr. Paul Quinnett, executive director of the QPR Institute, to help save lives through the process of questioning, persuading, and referring. Questioning refers to asking the student if he is thinking of harming himself. It may sound like you would be overstepping boundaries by asking this question, but this is the one proven way to prevent suicide. As you are getting ready to ask this question, be prepared to respond in an understanding and empathetic way. Disbelief of the student's experience is only going to make matters worse and increase the distress. Once you have communicated that you understand the student is in a situation in which he needs urgent help, then ask the question of what feelings he is experiencing and if he is thinking of harming himself.

It is likely that the student might not want help, either because he is ashamed or doesn't recognize that he needs it. These conversations are usually very difficult to have, especially for people who are not trained professionals. The goal is to persuade the student to see a mental health professional. Taking a small step toward getting help is a big achievement in this situation. Listen carefully to what the student has to say about what he is experiencing and then respond by telling him, "Let me help," or "Let's go together to find help." Perhaps offering to find the phone number for the student, or reassuring him that your knowing about his distress will not affect his grade or how you view him, might be of assistance.

If he is already seeing a therapist, he may need to schedule an urgent appointment. If not, he may need to visit the nearest hospital. If the student doesn't know where to go, the most accessible place is usually the twenty-four-hour crisis hotline (on campus or at the local hospital). On campus, the mental health center may take walk-in appointments. If you are concerned about suicide, you can recommend either the hospital psychiatric emergency service or the National Suicide Prevention Hotline (1-800-273-8255). At the end of the conversation, be sure that the student has committed to following through by either visiting in person or talking with a professional as soon as possible.

The student may find herself in a crisis situation again in the future when she's on her own. Encouraging her to come up with a plan of action that she can keep on her phone or in her wallet might help save her life. That plan might include phone numbers of health professionals, hotlines, or loved ones to call, as well as tools for staying calm (breathing exercises, mantras, taking a walk, or exercising). The National Alliance on Mental Illness Helpline (1-800-950-NAMI) also offers support and local resources.

If a student discloses to you suspicion of a mental health condition but has not been diagnosed, encourage her to take advantage of on-campus resources as soon as possible. Sometimes, it can be uncomfortable to tell someone to seek such help. You could use language such as "I have heard other students have benefited from an appointment with the mental health center," or "I wonder if there's someone who is familiar with resources at the mental health center. Do you have their number to call?" I would also suggest following up with the student in a week or so. This will reinforce to the student that you care and support her mental well-being.

Responding to Accommodations

According to a study by NAMI, nearly 50 percent of students with mental health conditions did not disclose their condition, nor did they request the necessary accommodations.[25] Some of the reasons for not disclosing were concerns that their mental health status would not remain confidential and that it would affect perceptions from the faculty on their capabilities and character. Given the context laid out in this chapter, perhaps it is not surprising that many students might choose not to disclose this information in a music school environment. No one wants to be perceived as weak or flawed, especially in highly competitive educational circumstances. Students who did choose to disclose did so primarily in order to receive accommodations, to gain access to campus mental health resources, and to help with destigmatizing mental health.

It takes a great deal of courage for students to go through the process of disclosing their mental health condition and requesting an accommodation. In my experience, the disabilities office may not always be fully aware of what performance examinations or applied courses look like for music students and may not be able to advise students on what accommodations would be appropriate to request. Open communication between the student, the instructor, and the disabilities office is key in working out accommodations.

Mental health conditions are just as real as physical injuries and can interfere with performance in similar ways. We don't expect a student with carpal tunnel syndrome to prepare a Chopin étude as quickly as someone without an injury. We should be bringing the same flexibility and patience to our students dealing with mental health conditions that we do to our students dealing with physical injuries: giving them more time, excusing lessons when treatment is needed, and understanding what they need to be successful in their studies.

The research we covered in this chapter shows that students do better when they are in a supportive environment where they have social support and a positive relationship with their advisors. As faculty mentors, we can't assume that our students know where to go for help on campus. When they disclose a mental health concern, we must be aware of the available resources and be able to guide them in the proper direction for help. Preemptively, this information can also be listed as part of a syllabus and given out to students at the beginning of the semester (see sample syllabus statement in Chapter 2).

✱✱✱

As we have learned in this chapter, students may deal with a range of mental distress, from mild to severe. Awareness of the broad set of challenges students face while in school, as outlined earlier, may inform your approach toward your students. Compounded with a mental health disorder, getting through a music degree can become very difficult. However, with the right professional support, it *is* possible to not only manage one's conditions but to design and fulfill a thriving musical life. Although music teachers are, for the most part, not mental health professionals, they can provide critical assistance by encouraging students to seek professional counsel and treatment when needed. We should also commit to encouraging protective practices, such as self-care, to all students. In the final section of this chapter you will find additional exercises that may be useful in a lesson setting to support your students' mental and emotional well-being.

Mental Health Toolkit

The exercises in this section address the following topics: cultivating mindfulness, developing time-management tools, and coping with impostor phenomenon, anxiety, and performance anxiety. These are also available on the companion website ▶. The breathing exercises available in Chapter 8 complement this toolkit.

Mindfulness of Breath

The goal of the exercise is to focus on the present moment by counting breaths. Guide the student with the following instructions (Audio 7.1 ▶):

> *Instructions:* Come to a seated position and close your eyes, if you are comfortable doing so. If you prefer, you can keep your eyes open and keep your gaze soft and lowered. Turn your attention to your breath. Notice the inhalation and the exhalation. Notice the pause between the two. Pay attention to the quality of your breath. Is it slow, fast, or average speed? Is it smooth or bumpy? Simply notice your experience without judgment. Once you are aware of your breath, I invite you to start keeping track of each breath by counting. Inhale . . . exhale . . . one. Follow your breath, counting up to five. If your mind wanders and you've forgotten which number you are on, simply begin again with one. If you've reached five, go back to one, and take a long pause here. Notice which number you are on and let go of counting your breath. Notice how you are feeling now and the quality of your breath. Gently open your eyes if they are closed.

Coping with Anxiety

Instructions: Think about a situation that triggers stress. Once you have identified that situation, observe how your mind responds. What images or thoughts appear in your mind? Are those thoughts or images that feed a negative thought pattern? Are they helpful in dealing with the situation, or are they causing further stress? The following exercise (Table 7.1) will help you replace your negative thought patterns with positive affirmations. In the far left column, write the stressful situation you thought of. In the middle column, write or draw your automatic response to that situation. In the far right column, write a more rational thought that is more helpful to you, or an affirmation that will help you get through the situation. You will find this exercise on Worksheet 7.1 on the companion website ▶.[26]

Table 7.1 Coping with Anxiety Exercise

Stressful Situation	Automatic Thought (Draw or Write)	Rational Thought (or Affirmation)

Time Management

Setting SMART goals is a useful tool in prioritizing tasks and managing time. SMART is an acronym that stands for specific, measurable, achievable, realistic, and timed goals. The questionnaire can be filled out on a Sunday as the student plans for the week. Considering that practicing is central to the student experience, the first step is to fill out the following questionnaire to set SMART practicing goals. The second step provides students with a template for setting up a manageable and realistic schedule. This exercise is available on the companion website on Worksheet 7.2 ▶.

Instructions
Step 1: Set your goals for your practicing sessions.

Specific
What do you want to accomplish during the course of the week? What are your priorities in terms of technical exercises? What are your priorities in terms of your repertoire? By when do you wish to be able to perform in studio class? What do you want to play in your next lesson?

Measurable

At what point will you feel satisfied with the results? For example, what is your performance standard for the week? To be able to play a portion fluently, under tempo, from memory?

Achievable

How many hours of practicing do you think you'll need to be able to accomplish your specific goals noted in the previous section? Do your expectations meet the time you are setting aside for practicing?

Realistic

Is it possible for you to learn the amount of repertoire you are setting out to learn, or is it too much for the amount of time allotted? Are you accounting for time to process, mentally rehearse, and consolidate what you are learning?

Time

How will you build up to your week-long goal each day? What are your mini-goals for each practice session?

Step 2: Develop your schedule around your practicing goals.
Consider the following questions:

- What are your best practice times (e.g., morning, afternoon, late night)? Are you able to practice during those times?
- How much time do you need to warm up and cool down?
- How long will each practice session last, and when will you take a break (ideally practicing no more than twenty-five minutes without a short break for hydration and stretching)?
- When do you do your best work? Schedule the most important tasks during those times.

Fill out your weekly schedule. Start by filling in your obligations first (e.g., classes, lessons, other important meetings). Then set aside your practice time. Estimate how much time you'll need for homework and work out when you'll be able to do it. Plan your meals, exercise, naps (or rest time), and social time.

Take a look at your schedule and notice how you feel. Does it feel manageable? Is it overwhelming? If so, is there anything that you can cut back on?

Body Awareness in Performance

The purpose of this exercise is to help students observe some of the physiological aspects associated with the experience of performing. These physical responses might be associated with excitement or other heightened states of attention. This exercise is available on Worksheet 7.3 on the companion website ⊙.

Instructions: Complete the first part of the exercise approximately fifteen to twenty minutes before performing and the second part immediately after performing. Try to sit in a quiet place and not talk to anyone while you are completing the exercise.

Part 1
Find your best seated alignment and, if you are comfortable doing so, close your eyes. Notice how each part listed in the following list feels. Spend a few seconds simply noticing, without judgment. Label the sensations in your mind, such as sweating, burning, warm, tingling, etc. Then write these sensations down next to the body part.

a. Note the physical feelings or sensations in your
    - Feet
    - Lower legs
    - Knees
    - Thighs
    - Pelvis
    - Lower back
    - Upper back
    - Shoulders
    - Neck
    - Upper arms and forearms
    - Hands and fingers
    - Neck
    - Jaw
    - Eyes
    - Mouth
    - Throat
    - Chest
    - Stomach
    - Lower belly
b. How would you describe your breath (smooth, bumpy, deep, shallow, etc.)?

c. What state is your mind in right now (focused, calm, erratic, etc.)?

d. Describe your mood as related to the upcoming performance.

Part 2

Take a few minutes to reflect on your performance and to notice the physical sensations that are coming up.

a. What did you notice about your mental, emotional, and physical state while you were walking on stage?

b. What did you notice about your mental, emotional, and physical state while you were performing?

c. How do you feel now after some time has passed? How would you compare your physical state now with before you walked on stage?

d. What have you learned from this observation experience?

Positive Self-Talk

What do you usually tell yourself when you are practicing, right before or during a performance? Are you using negative language, such as "Don't mess up!" or "Don't lose it on stage!"? Or are you telling yourself positive affirmations, such as "I am ready for this" or "I can do this!"? Keep a journal of what you tell yourself both during practice and performance situations in the left column (see Table 7.2). Reword any negative self-talk into positive self-talk in the right column and start using those expressions instead. You can find this exercise on the companion website on Worksheet 7.4 ⊙.[27]

Table 7.2 Positive Self-Talk Exercise

Current Self-Talk	Positive Self-Talk

Mental Rehearsal

Successful preparation for a performance is as much reliant on the time spent physically practicing as on the time spent mentally preparing. Mental rehearsal can help students prepare for the emotions they will experience during their performance and help them stay positive. If this is a new skill, it is best for students to mentally rehearse short segments of their performance at a time. For example, they can start with working through their pre-performance routine up to walking on stage. Another time, they can rehearse the first ten minutes of their performance, and so on. Breaking mental rehearsal up into smaller sections helps with maintaining concentration.

Instructions: To start your mental rehearsal, find your best seated alignment and close your eyes, if you are comfortable doing so. Quickly scan your body from head to toe, noting any points of tension or other sensations that are coming up. Notice your breath. In your mind's eye, go through your pre-performance routine. Where will you be? How will you warm up? What will you play, and for how long? Be as specific as possible. Conjure up as many sensations as you can (What will the temperature feel like? What will the room smell like? How will your body feel? What will you be wearing?). Imagine yourself standing in the green room and then the stage entrance. How do you feel now? Go through the process of walking on stage, taking a bow, and playing the first few notes. How does that feel? What are you telling yourself? Are you smiling? What do your first few notes sound like? Were you breathing before you started playing? What are you thinking about right before playing? Let go of your rehearsal and rest. Repeat this process, focusing on more segments of your performance.

Impostor Phenomenon Quiz

Your students may find it helpful to learn about the impostor phenomenon and explore whether they may be impacted by it to a degree. The following questionnaire is a shortened version of the Clance Impostor Phenomenon Scale. You may choose to have your students respond to the questionnaire in their own time and not share the results with you, simply using it as a tool for them to be aware of how impostor syndrome may be affecting them. See link to the full questionnaire on the companion website ▶.

Instructions: Respond with a Yes or No to the following questions. If you have answered more Yes than No, you may be dealing with Impostor Syndrome.

1. I have often succeeded on a test or task even though I was afraid that I would not do well before I undertook the task.
2. I avoid evaluations if possible and have a dread of others evaluating me.
3. When people praise me for something I've accomplished, I'm afraid I won't be able to live up to their expectations of me in the future.
4. At times, I feel my success has been due to some kind of luck.
5. I often compare my ability to those around me and think they may be more intelligent than I am.

From Pauline Rose Clance, *The Impostor Phenomenon: When Success Makes You Feel Like A Fake* (Toronto: Bantam Books, 1985), 20–22. Copyright 1985 by Pauline Rose Clance, Ph.D., ABPP. Used by permission of Dr. Pauline Rose Clance. Do not reproduce/copy/distribute without permission from Pauline Rose Clance, drpaulinerose@comcast.net, www.paulineroseclance.com.

Performance Plan Based on Subjective Units of Distress (SUDs)

The Subjective Units of Distress Rating Scale is a common cognitive therapy tool for measuring distress in people with social anxiety. This tool may be applied to performance anxiety management. Often, students will only practice performing in low-stress situations without any intermediary steps to prepare them for a high-stress performance. The following exercise can help students develop a performance plan aimed at building resilience to performance anxiety by gradually increasing the stress level of the performance.[28] This exercise is also available on the companion website on Worksheet 7.5 ▶.

Instructions: Use the following scale to create a list of performances that gradually increase your level of distress until you can work up to the highest-stress performance. Here are examples:

Low-stress performance: Playing for a friend in a practice room – 10 SUDs
Mild-stress performance: Playing for studio class – 30 SUDs
Moderate-stress performance: Performing in a departmental recital in a large venue – 60 SUDs
High-stress performance: Performing degree recital – 70 SUDs

Distress Rating

    0 – No stress at all; relaxed

  10 – Alert; good concentration

  20 – Minimal distress

  30 – Mild distress, but it does not interfere with performance

  40 – Mild to moderate distress

  50 – Moderate distress; feelings of discomfort but can continue to perform

  60 – Moderately to quite anxious

  70 – Quite anxious; distress interferes with the performance

  80 – Very anxious; unable to concentrate

  90 – Extremely anxious

100 – Highest amount of distress ever experienced

Final Performance (venue, date, format, etc.): _____

1. _____ SUDs (0–100) _____

2. _____ SUDs (0–100) _____

3. _____ SUDs (0–100) _____

4. _____ SUDs (0–100) _____

5. _____ SUDs (0–100) _____

6. _____ SUDs (0–100) _____

7. _____ SUDs (0–100) _____

8. _____ SUDs (0–100) _____

9. _____ SUDs (0–100) _____

10. _____ SUDs (0–100) _____

8

Turning Inward

Contemplative Practices

As we have seen in the previous chapter, stress and other conditions can worsen if left unchecked. In our culture, we are expected to push through and get the job done, often at the expense of our own well-being. Productivity takes precedence over anything else. Every single day, we encounter conversations that imply "I'm busier than you." And it's true, we tend to base our self-worth on our productivity, or proving to our acquaintances that we are busier than they are. We buy into the busy lifestyle, perhaps to keep up with expectations in our field, or to stay one step ahead of our peers. Yet through this constant juggling act we may lose the crucial time we need to ask some basic questions: Is this what I need right now? Is this project fulfilling? Why am I pursuing it? The problem with this productivity-focused mindset is that it robs us of the experience of the present moment, exacerbates stress, and over time may lead to burnout.

Within the college setting, many students deal with busy schedules and a heavy workload, all while still trying to learn time-management skills. As a result, they superficially engage with their learning by cramming information the night before an exam or preparing new repertoire as quickly as they can. This surface-level approach does not include the learning processes that are impactful in the long term. To make matters worse, we live in a world where we are constantly bombarded with new information. The constant flow of thoughts and emotional reactions to this information add to the distractions we must contend with. By incorporating contemplative practices into the educational experience, we give our students the gift of increasing their focus and attention. Students can connect with the material in a more meaningful way—learning practices that will ground them in the present moment, while strengthening their connection to core values and advancing the pursuits that truly feed their intellectual wellness. Through such practices, students may also improve their emotional regulation.[1] Observing the way in which emotions arise and disappear in a nonjudgmental way is a powerful tool for learning how to let thoughts and emotions float by while choosing which ones to engage with.

Many cultures around the world embrace some form of contemplative practice, such as meditation, dancing, prayer, yoga, or a combination thereof. Figure 8.1 shows some of the more commonly known traditions. A commonality among these traditions is the cultivation of a centered, self-aware inner world through seated meditation or movement-based meditation. This chapter offers a practical guide to how contemplative practices may be incorporated into the applied music lesson.

Teaching the Whole Musician. Paola Savvidou, Oxford University Press (2021). © Oxford University Press.
DOI: 10.1093/oso/9780190868796.003.0008

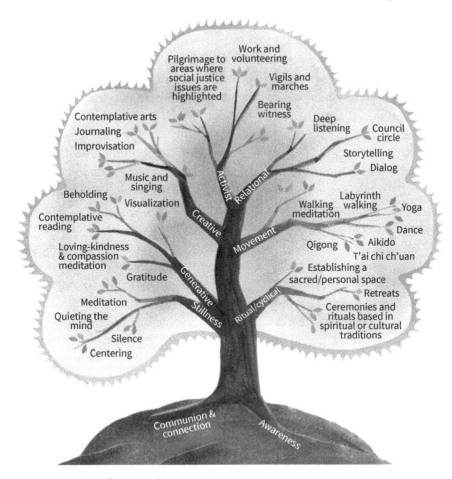

Figure 8.1. The tree of contemplative practices.
Reproduced by permission from the Center for Contemplative Mind in Society, www.contemplativemind.org.

Contemplative Practices in Higher Education

Educational systems that tend to be highly focused on external goals, such as grades and awards, miss out on the opportunity to engage students' internal connection with the material. According to Ambrose et al. in *How Learning Works: Seven Research-Based Principles for Smart Teaching*, students who are able to monitor their own progress and explain what they are learning are more successful at problem-solving and "have greater learning gains."[2] Incorporating contemplative practices into the educational process is a way to help students validate and connect with their inner experience.

When students approach their education more mindfully, they engage with their own learning and digest new material more effectively. Contemplation allows students to take ownership over the material, and through this process, they also learn more about themselves. They gain the requisite space to think about their own values and how what they are learning fits into their priorities and perhaps even the world at large. Moreover, students who are introverted by nature appreciate the opportunity to learn through an assignment that is within their comfort zone, such as a reflection paper or a journaling exercise. Having such varied opportunities to engage with the material thus presents the additional benefit of promoting inclusivity in the classroom.

An indispensable component of music students' training is teaching them how to nurture their creativity. One aspect of creative thinking within music involves considering multiple solutions to problems and engaging with various answers before deciding on the best one. This is a process that students go through on a daily basis in the practice room; for example, when choosing fingering for a passage or making expressive choices in a particular phrase. Although students are far better served if they take time to consider many possibilities, this doesn't always happen because the process of engaging with creativity is time-consuming. And it may also be difficult to justify spending time considering all the possibilities when it's so much easier to make a quick decision and move on to the next task at hand. However, maintaining an attitude of openness to the possibilities, albeit sometimes a challenging process, is more advantageous in the long run. Practicing this approach will help students achieve deeper learning while fostering more ownership over their artistic process and creative choices.

Meditation and Mindfulness

Meditation and mindfulness are two terms that have come to be used interchangeably, even though they are not quite the same concept. Meditation has its origins in ancient, prehistoric religions. The earliest records are found in the Vedas, which are Hindu texts, dating back to 1700–1100 BCE. Different forms of meditation developed in religious practices such as Buddhism, Taoism, Christianity, Judaism, and Islam, aiming to reach a calmer sense of being, spirituality, and transcendence. With the adoption of Eastern meditative practices in the West during the twentieth century, the primary purpose of these practices has become stress reduction and overall improvement of well-being.

Lutz et al. categorize meditative training into two common types: focused meditation and open monitoring.[3] In focused meditation, practitioners direct their attention to a specific object, such as the breath or a candle flame. In open meditation, one maintains an open awareness in the environment, continuously re-engaging with the awareness when the mind wanders or engages with other stimuli. Hearing meditation is an example of open meditation (see the end of this chapter for a guided practice).

Some form of meditative practice exists in most cultures around the world, making it the most common and widely researched form of contemplative practice. Research studies on the effects of meditation on students and teachers in classroom settings indicate that its benefits include stress management, better concentration and attention, improved mental health and psychological well-being, increased connection and generosity, deeper understanding of the course material, and increased creativity.[4]

Both focused and open meditation practices have been shown to improve emotional regulation, which has enormous benefits for our students' mental health.[5] Labeling thoughts as they occur (a practice common in mindfulness instruction) appears to help emotional regulation processes by reducing both the intensity and the duration of the emotion. When we practice meditation, we train our mind to quickly transition from negative emotions to positive ones, thus growing our ability to regulate our emotions. Consider your student's emotional state after a performance in which he didn't play his best. Negative thoughts of self-doubt and worthlessness could linger for days. A meditation practitioner could more quickly shift his thinking to a positive state by distancing himself from the experience and transitioning to a more positive emotional state. Wadlinger and Isaacowitz cite meditative practices as being "among the most effective training methodologies in enhancing emotional well-being."[6]

Meditation is a way of practicing mindfulness. Jon Kabat-Zinn (the founder of the Center for Mindfulness in Medicine, Health Care and Society) defines mindfulness as "the awareness that arises by paying attention on purpose in the present moment nonjudgmentally."[7] His signature course, Mindfulness-Based Stress Reduction (MBSR), has demonstrated improvements to participants' mental health. A study by Anderson et al. demonstrated that participants in an MBSR course were much more successful in regulating emotions related to depression, anxiety, and anger compared to participants in the control group.[8] Even though MBSR training is usually only eight weeks long, it has been shown to have positive results that outlast the duration of the course.[9] What this means is that even a short meditation experience can have a longer-lasting positive impact on our students.

Mindful breathing practices are among the most accessible and common practices. The benefits of ancient breathing practices have been accepted by Eastern cultures for thousands of years and were introduced to the West in the late nineteenth century, with their popularity increasing in the twentieth. It's truly a wonder that the simple act of deep breathing, when done mindfully, can have a significant impact on one's psychophysiological state. Western medicine now has the tools to scientifically prove the benefits through rigorous testing. Research studies have investigated the effects of yogic breathing, with supportive positive outcomes on reducing stress by improving the autonomic nervous system response, positively affecting immune function and psychological disorders.[10] When applied to performance, a situation we perceive as threatening, breathing exercises can serve as a tool for lowering the body's stress response.

Jon Kabat-Zinn, in his book *Full Catastrophe Living*, identifies seven fundamental attitudes of the mind toward mindfulness practice: non-judgment, patience, beginner's mind, trust, non-striving, acceptance, and letting go.[11] Later, he added two more to the list: gratitude and generosity. These attitudes are the foundation from which to grow mindfulness and, for many, the base ingredients for building a fulfilling life. Although they are listed as separate, they coexist and rely on one another. They invite us to set aside any expectations that meditation will be the instant miracle cure to all our troubles. For meditative practices to have such an impact, they must be cultivated over time, with these nine attitudes at the forefront of our attention, as described in the following.

Non-Judgment

Our brains are wired in such a way that we are quick to judge—not just other people, but also our inner experiences. We often harshly criticize our performance and don't give ourselves a chance to step back and view it more objectively. An attitude of non-judgment means we can observe those thoughts without labeling them as positive or negative, but simply recognizing them as thoughts and letting them go.

Patience

It's not uncommon to learn a large amount of music in a short amount of time! This can be a hasty choice, causing us to be harsh on ourselves; eager to see immediate results, we can become impatient even though the task at hand is not realistic. The reality is that processing new information takes time. Absorbing new repertoire takes multiple performances, space to reflect, and enormous patience for the inevitable mistakes that are part of the learning process. Patience involves allowing things to unfold in their own time and acceptance that the timeline will likely be different than we anticipated.

Beginner's Mind

This refers to having an open mind in our approach to the world. Imagine that you are receiving instruction for a new skill like cooking or salsa dancing. If you don't have any experience in the area, you are probably wide open to what the instructor has to say. You are taking it all in, paying full attention from moment to moment. With no preconceived ideas or expectations, you can more fully embrace the possibilities. My undergraduate professor used to tell me, "Every time I practice, I try to notice something new." Even in a piece of music we already know well, there are still new things to notice and different connections to make when we view it as if for the first time.

Trust

Cultivating trust starts with something as simple as following the breath, knowing that the breath will be there, no matter what, to serve as an anchor in the present moment.[12] From this foundation, we can then begin to trust our intuition. We can have the confidence that our gut reactions are valid, even when others around us might be saying the opposite. Through developing this attitude, we learn to trust our body when it's telling us it's time to stop practicing and take a break. This self-guidance needs cultivation, especially when we are used to external validation.

Non-Striving

Striving for success and validation is a common attitude among musicians. But what would it be like if we allowed ourselves to be present in each moment without trying to be somewhere else, or somebody else? What if we were content with how things are? Non-striving teaches us to focus less on trying and to come to terms with our present experience. Essentially, meditation is a practice of non-doing and simply being with ourselves.

Acceptance

Think about how many times you've told yourself, "I'll feel better after this recital," or "Once this semester is over, I'll finally be able to relax." We always think the next moment will be better than the one we are living in right now, getting stuck in a perpetual rut. Accepting the present moment as it is helps us release the tension of resistance and find peace.

Letting Go

Our mind tends to ruminate on past events, rehashing what we could have said or done differently. When it's not thinking about the past, it worries about the future. Being sad about the past and anxious about the future steals our attention from our present experience. Learning to let go is crucial in performance settings, when all the preparation has already been done and all that is left to do is to fully enjoy each moment.

Gratitude

Even in the midst of chaos, recognizing small things we can be grateful for brings about a sense of optimism about the future. Our mind is wired to think negatively as a protective mechanism against threatening situations. But negative thinking does not actually yield productive outcomes; instead, it results in higher stress. Gratitude is a powerful, positive force that helps settle down the negative thoughts and raise the positive ones. One of my students who incorporated this practice in her journal had this to say about her experience:

> I have adopted the gratitude journal at the start of my morning. I have to say five things I'm grateful for before I leave my bed. Then I have to write them down before I leave my room. It has definitely had a positive impact on my mornings, especially since I'm not a morning person and it is very hard for me to get out of bed. I need to start trying to incorporate these types of things throughout the day to keep my mood up so I don't lose the momentum that I created in the morning.

Gratitude practice can be adapted to each person's schedule. For this student, writing in the morning works well. For others, the evening is preferable, as it offers a small block of time to reflect on the day.

Generosity

Being of generous spirit means giving others the gift of our full attention and presence. You have probably felt it, too, when you were in the presence of someone who wasn't checking his phone constantly or diverting the conversation toward himself at every opportunity, but rather was paying attention to you and what you had to say. Generosity lies in the way we make ourselves present and see others for their intrinsic goodness.

Each semester, the students in my wellness course experience various types of mindfulness practices, both in class and as part of their assignments. I often bring a bag filled with strips of paper, each of which has one of the nine attitudes written on it. Students draw a random "attitude" to apply toward their meditation practice for the rest of the week. They are asked to reflect on their experience in their journals. In the years I have been teaching this class, the attitude of "non-striving" is one that keeps being mentioned by students as a powerful one. Here is a quote from one student's journal:

> I have a very hard time doing things without expecting a specific result, and I will continue to go after that result until I achieve it. So, I set aside thirty minutes for this meditation to try not to feel pressured to achieve this kind of mindset in a short amount of time. Going into it, I was very scared because I really didn't know how to go about not trying to achieve anything. I just tried to focus on my breath and the way my hands felt. Not focusing on a mantra or a goal feeling, just sitting with myself and allowing myself to just be. I don't know if I was able to fully achieve that, but it was kind of nice to just be and have no expectations.

I find it intriguing that the student chose the word "scared" to express the resistance against the feeling of release, allowing himself to stay present in the moment without expectations. Being open to the experience of the unknown can certainly cause feelings of discomfort and even fear. With continued practice, we may grow more comfortable with the experience and perhaps notice that fear may loosen its grip. The power of contemplative practices lies in this ability to "just be" with ourselves, as this student pointed out. Now let's talk about a few essential guidelines for integrating contemplative practices in the applied lesson setting.

Guidelines

Incorporating meditation, or any other contemplative practice, could be a simple one- to two-minute activity at the beginning or the end of studio class, or a full-blown semester-long integrated approach. If a longer-term approach is the right thing for your students, then you may need to consider whether it will be part of the grade. Obviously, grading a subjective experience can be challenging. However, there are effective ways of doing so. For example, if you ask students to practice hearing and breathing meditation on a weekly basis as part of their music practice, you may also ask them to keep a journal in which they reflect on their experience. The journal can then be graded on a pass/fail basis based on completion and carry a percentage of the semester grade. Another approach is to assign a reflection paper for the end of the semester in which students write about their overall experience with contemplative practices throughout the semester.

One student in my class suggested pausing while doing homework to set a timer for ten minutes to practice meditation with a self-affirmation component. A positive self-affirmation could be as simple as one word (such as "peace"), or a sentence ("I am safe and calm") that is repeated internally. Here is how she describes in her journal the way this worked for her:

> One discovery I made is the addition of self-affirmation during my meditation breaks. When I have been doing homework for a long time, I set a timer for ten minutes and turn on meditation ambiance sound and go into a meditative state where I repeat a self-affirmation to calm down the thoughts and reset my mind so that I can be more attentive with the rest of my day or work. It's a good way for me to make sure my thoughts and internal monologue are in a positive state and helping me, rather than hindering me by being mean and negative.

This demonstrates that students, given a variety of tools, will discover for themselves what works for them in their own process and daily workflow.

The intention of any contemplative practice assignment must always be clear to the students. Communicate the reasoning behind the assignment either before or after, depending on your goals. Explaining the intent afterward may make more sense in exercises where you want the students to maintain an open mind. One more thing to consider is giving students the opportunity to opt out if they are uncomfortable for any reason.[13]

Verbal Instruction

If you are guiding your students through a meditation practice, there is no reason to use fancy language that both you and they will be uncomfortable with. Simple and familiar language is better. Closing the eyes during seated practices allows one to focus inwardly without the distraction of the visual sense. However, some students may feel unsafe when closing their eyes. Offer the option of keeping the gaze soft toward the ground, about six feet away.

Follow-up Discussion

Following the meditation practice, you may ask what that experience was like (or you can completely skip this part of the process if you are nervous about navigating uncharted territory). Verbalizing their experience helps students gain a deeper understanding of their own process. Remember that one grows in one's own awareness throughout the lifetime. Deeper insight will come with time and practice.

It is important when listening to students' comments to allow them to have their own responses without any expectations from your end. If the meditation was done during studio class and you sense that they are uncomfortable sharing in a group setting, you might give them the option of sharing their experience with a partner. Embrace the gaps in conversation and resist the temptation to fill them in with chit-chat.

If you are worried that sharing out loud may cause discomfort for your students (or if you are uncomfortable with it), you could instead offer the opportunity for students to write down a reflection as a way of processing their experience. It could be as simple as responding to prompts such as:

- Write down what you noticed during your meditation practice.
- What drew your attention? What distracted you? How did you feel (e.g., curious, impatient, etc.)?
- How do you feel now?

Or, if your students prefer, they can freely respond to the experience without prompts.

Potential Challenges

If you have never meditated before, I would suggest developing your own practice before incorporating meditation in your lessons or classes. This will better equip you to guide your students through the process. Perhaps for you it might be movement-based (such as t'ai chi) or a seated meditation. The best type of meditation for you is likely the one with which you are more comfortable. That is because you are more likely to consistently implement it, which is even more important than the specific modality you choose to adopt. If you prefer, you could enlist the help of a local expert to come in and lead your class through a meditation or yoga class.

When shifting attention inward to thoughts, emotions, or the body, it's possible that triggers might come up, especially for those who have experienced trauma. Always give students the option to opt out if they become uncomfortable during the meditative practice. They may choose to leave the room or distract themselves with doodling or other thoughts.

It's important to be mindful of both your own biases and pre-existing beliefs related to contemplative practices, as well as your students' backgrounds and the attitude they bring to such practices. Some may not see the value in such activities, while others may enthusiastically embrace them. For those students who are coming to these practices with resistance, simply notice the resistance without trying to affect it. Music students may be interested in the subjective experience; those with a science background may also need to see data in order to be convinced of the effectiveness of a practice. Remain sensitive to your students' responses and remain open to trying new things, as the same exercise will likely not work equally well for even two different groups of students.

The religious association of many of these practices can make it difficult to know which can be incorporated without unwittingly making students feel uneasy because of their own backgrounds and beliefs. On the flip side of this coin, students of different backgrounds may feel that the learning environment is more inclusive when a variety of practices are made available. In either case, you might clarify for your students that no specific faith is required to practice meditation.

Now that we have learned foundational guidelines, let's explore hands-on tools, along with scripts, that you can use with your students.

Contemplative Practices Toolkit

Breathing Techniques

Breathing techniques and meditation inhibit the release of the hormone cortisol, which is known as the stress hormone. This stimulates the parasympathetic nervous system by releasing the relaxation hormones norepinephrine and oxytocin, thus creating a better balance. Considering that approximately 80 percent of students consider themselves "moderately stressed" or "burned out," breathing exercises can be helpful to them.[14]

One of the most fundamental yoga practices, with many benefits to the body and mind, is *pranayama* (as discussed in Chapter 5). Through controlled breathing, we can improve the balance of our nervous system and affect a positive change in our psychological state. Yogic breathing practices vary in type and benefits, depending on the depth and length of the breath cycle.[15] Types of breaths you may be familiar with are the breath of fire, alternate nostril breath, and ocean breath. In this section, you will find several breathing practices borrowed from yoga. These are also available on the companion website ⏵.

Breath Awareness

Instructions: You can practice breath awareness sitting on the floor, on a chair, or lying on your back. If you are sitting on a chair, begin by grounding through your feet and sit bones and finding length in your spine. Close your eyes if you are comfortable doing so, or keep your gaze soft. Bring your attention to your breath. Notice the sensation of the breath entering the body at the tip of your nose. Feel the air as it travels down your throat. Take a moment to pay attention to your head and neck muscles. Check that you are releasing any unnecessary tension. Place one hand on your chest and one hand on your belly. Notice the movement of your chest as you breathe in and out. Now notice how your belly moves as you breathe. Follow the path of the breath from the inhalation at the tip of the nose, down the throat, into the chest and belly, and then out again. Now hug your thumb and fingers around the bottom sides of your ribcage. Notice the movement of your ribs as you breathe in and out. Notice the movement of your belly. Shift your attention to your upper back. Note the movement of the ribcage as it widens and narrows. With your mind's eye, travel up and down the spine, noticing any micro-movements of the spine as you breathe. Release your arms and continue to breathe (Exercise 8.1 ⏵).

Diaphragmatic Breathing

Instructions: Lie on your back with your arms by your sides. Place your feet flat with your knees pointing up. Allow your spine to lengthen and to "sink" into the floor. Notice the curvature of your spine and each point of contact with the floor. Place one hand on your belly and one hand on your chest. Notice your breath without trying to change it. Pay attention to the length of the breath and which parts of your body move as you breathe in and out. Now lengthen the exhalation with each exhale. Explore shifting your attention from the chest to the belly and sinking deeper as you exhale. Shift your attention to noticing your inhalation. Notice how the front of your body moves as you inhale. Slowly start to increase the amount of air you inhale, making sure that you are always comfortable. After a few long breaths, slowly roll over to lie on your belly with your arms at your side and your head facing in either direction. Continue to breathe deeply, and notice how as your belly is pushed out, your back curves upward. Take a few breaths here, noticing the movement of your lumbar spine. Roll onto your back and end with a few more breaths, noticing how your chest, belly, and back move with every breath cycle (Exercise 8.2 ⏵).

Coherent Breathing

This deep, slow variation of a breathing yogic technique (also known as "resonant breathing") was developed by engineer, inventor, and life scientist Stephen Elliott. The instructions for this type of breathing are simple: breathe in and out for an equal duration of time, amounting to approximately five breaths per minute. Where the typical rate is between ten and twenty breaths per minute, slow breathing is defined as "any rate from 4 to 10 breaths per minute."[16] For maximum benefits, the recommendation is to practice this type of breathing for fifteen to twenty minutes per day.

> *Instructions*: Find a comfortable position lying on a mat, or the floor. Your knees could be bent falling toward each other, or raised, resting on a chair or a bench. Start evening out and lengthening the breath. Count slowly to five on the inhale, and to five on the exhale. Repeat a few times. Gradually slow down your pace of counting to where you are taking slow and easy breaths. If it would be helpful to keep track of your breathing, you could use an interval timer app that chimes every minute, or you can set a timer to chime after a certain duration of time to signal the end of your practice. You will probably experience deep relaxation at the end of your breathing practice. Move slowly to transition out of your practice, especially if you might be feeling a little lightheaded after this practice. Slowly wiggle your fingers and toes and move into a seated position (Exercise 8.3 ▶).

Ocean Breath

The ocean breath, or *ujjayi pranayama*, is used during yoga pose practice to focus the attention and increase the benefits of the pose. This breath has a calming effect and can be used to activate the parasympathetic nervous system.

> *Instructions*: To learn how to practice the ocean breath, start by finding a comfortable seated position, either on a chair or on the floor. Shift your attention to your breath. Now, continue breathing through your mouth. Place the palm of your hand a few inches in front of your mouth and imagine that with your breath you are fogging up an imaginary mirror in your hand. This will cause your throat to constrict and result in your breath sounding like the gentle waves of the ocean. Now close your mouth and continue applying that throat contraction in both the inhalation and the exhalation. You can take a few ocean breaths while seated, or you can move to your favorite yoga poses and practice breathing with the ocean breath (Exercise 8.4 ▶).

Three-Part Breath

The three parts refer to the belly, the ribcage, and the chest. This breath has a calming effect and also helps bring awareness to the different moving parts of the breathing mechanism.

Instructions: Begin in a seated position or lying on your back. Close your eyes if you are comfortable doing so. Bring your attention to your breath. Notice the inhalation and the exhalation without trying to change anything. Allow the breath to simply be. If thoughts creep in and distract you from your breath, gently escort your attention back to your breath. Continue to breathe for a few moments. Place one hand on your belly and one hand on your chest. On the next inhale, direct your breath to the bottom of your lungs, allowing your belly to expand. Draw the belly toward the spine as you exhale, letting go of as much air as you can. Repeat. On the next inhale, fill up the bottom of the lungs and then sip some extra air to allow your lower ribs to move apart. On the exhale, start by pulling the ribs closer together and drawing the belly toward the spine. Repeat. Breathe in again, filling the bottom of the lungs, expanding the lungs, and then sip in some more air to allow your chest to expand. On the exhale, lower your chest, draw the ribs together, and pull the belly toward the spine. Repeat this long, three-part breath a few times. Inhale belly, ribs, chest, and exhale chest, ribs, belly. Try for a smooth breath, without any pauses in between the different sections of the breath (Exercise 8.5 ▶).

Breath of Fire

The breath of fire is a more advanced type of yogic breath usually practiced in Kundalini yoga. Due to the quickness of the breath and the use of the abdominal muscles, it can have an energizing effect on our mood and a toning effect on the muscles. The speed and intensity of this breath may cause lightheadedness after practicing it. It is contraindicated for people who are pregnant, have a heart condition, experience vertigo, or have a respiratory infection.

Instructions: Begin in a tall seated position. Place both hands on your belly and check that your belly is expanding when you inhale. Pause at the top of the inhalation. Activate your abdominal muscles and push air out of your lungs with ten quick exhales panting like a dog. Inhale, allowing the air to rush into the lungs without forcing it. Now close your lips and repeat this process two times (Exercise 8.6 ▶).

Alternate Nostril Breath

The alternate nostril breath has a calming effect through the activation of the parasympathetic nervous system.

Instructions: Find a comfortable seated position, either on the floor, on a chair, or on a bench. Start by noticing your breath. With your right thumb, press on your right nostril. Place the pointer and middle fingers on your forehead and float the ring finger by your left nostril. Inhale through the left nostril, then close the left nostril with your ring finger. Hold the breath for a moment, release the thumb from the right nostril, and exhale slowly. Inhale through the right nostril, close with the thumb, release the ring finger, and exhale through the left nostril. That completes one cycle. Repeat the process for two more cycles, alternating breathing in and out from each nostril, pausing between inhalation and exhalation. Release the arm down and breathe normally (Exercise 8.7 ▶).

Body Awareness
Body Scan

Our body is in constant motion, activated further by a pervasive pressure to stay busy. We pride ourselves on doing a million things a day and never stop to check if our body is feeling up to it. As a result, we carry hidden tension in our bodies. We may be feeling aches and pains but not even realize it until we start to pay attention to them. The body scan meditation is a way to drop into the present moment by noticing sensations that arise in one body part at a time. Often, this meditation will elicit a relaxation response, but it may also bring into conscious awareness parts of the body that may be experiencing pain, or that may be blocked. Emotional stress that we hold in our muscle tissue may come up as well. Mindfulness practice teaches us to maintain objectivity in the observation of sensations, thoughts, and emotions as they come up.

Instructions: Start by lying down supine (face up) in a warm and comfortable place. Close your eyes if you are comfortable doing so. Tune in to your breath, noticing the inhalation, the exhalation, and the pauses in between. Start by noticing your left toes. Notice any sensations that arise. Then move on to paying attention to your left sole, heel, and top of the foot. You might trace the contour of your foot in your mind's eye. Then proceed to noticing your ankle. Then your lower leg, your knee, and your thigh. Pause at each body part and pay attention to how the muscles feel. Then repeat the same process with the right foot and leg, scanning the left foot, to the lower leg, knee, and upper leg. Move on to the pelvis. Notice the weight of the pelvis and where it makes contact with the ground. Slowly move up the spine, bringing one vertebra at a time to your attention. Follow the contour of the spine. Pause at the thoracic spine and notice the shoulder blades. Move up to the neck and down the left shoulder. Observe the sensations in the left shoulder, then the upper arm, elbow, forearm, wrist, hand, and fingers. Repeat the same process starting with the right shoulder. Shift your attention back up to your face. Notice any tension you might be holding in your forehead, eyes, cheeks, chin, mouth, tongue, and throat.

Travel with your attention down to your chest, experiencing the up and down movement of the ribcage as you breathe. Move down to your belly, noticing any movement there. Finally, return to your breath. Notice its quality, length, and tone. Gently wiggle your fingers and toes, waking up the body. Open your eyes, keeping your gaze soft. (Audio 8.1 ▶).

For beginning meditators, the body scan may be practiced by squeezing the muscles of each body part and then releasing, as it's easier to draw attention to various body parts in this way.

Kindness to Self and Others
Lovingkindness Meditation

Lovingkindness meditation, also known as *metta*, develops compassion toward other beings by wishing them well. The meditation involves sending well-wishes to yourself, then to a person close to you, to a neutral person, and finally to someone you have a difficult relationship with. A research study by Pace et al. showed that compassionate meditation lowered stress responses after standard laboratory tests.[17] At the University of Southern California, Immordino-Yang explored the central role of emotions and social connection in decision-making and learning through a series of research studies. In her work, she has found that positive feelings and compassion can increase learning.[18]

Instructions: Start by finding a comfortable place to sit and taking a few deep breaths. Close your eyes if you are comfortable doing so. Focus your attention on the first phrase (listed in the following), silently repeating it to yourself over and over again. Take time to notice how saying this phrase makes you feel. After a while, move through each of the phrases, silently repeating them to yourself. Notice your breath, how your body feels, and any emotions that arise. Simply observe them, refocusing your attention to the phrases.

> *May I be free from danger.*
> *May I have mental happiness.*
> *May I have physical happiness.*
> *May I have ease of well-being.*

Once you have repeated all these phrases in sequence to yourself, take a few moments to notice your breath and how you feel. If you would like to continue the meditation, you can progress to bringing to your awareness to a person close to you or a pet. Repeat the phrases, sending lovingkindness to the person or pet. The next step is to bring to your attention a neutral person. This could be someone you saw walking down the street, or at the grocery store. Repeat the phrases, sending this person kind thoughts. Finally, and only if you are comfortable doing so, you can bring to mind a person you have a difficult relationship with. Repeat the phrases toward this person. Pause and notice your breath. Gently come out of your meditation by opening your eyes and taking a couple of deeper breaths (Audio 8.2 ▶).

Affectionate Touch

See Chapter 7 for a discussion on self-compassion as a protective mechanism for mental health.

> *Instructions*: Find a comfortable seated position. You may choose to close your eyes if you'd like. Start noticing your breath, following the inhalation and the exhalation. Take a few breaths. Then, slowly place one or both hands over your heart. Feel the warmth of your hands. Notice the natural rhythm of your breath. You may choose to follow the up-and-down movement of the chest. Enjoy this feeling of self-soothing for a minute or two. Then release your hand(s) back down and gently open your eyes (Audio 8.3 ▶).

Movement-Based Practices

In this section, you will find introductory activities for movement-based contemplative practices. These are also available on the companion website ▶.

Yoga

See Chapter 5 for more information about yoga and sample poses.

Qigong

Qigong is the umbrella term for several Eastern mind–body practices aimed at cultivating *qi*. *Qi* refers to the life energy that permeates all living things (i.e., life force). *Gong* translates to cultivating or achieving skill through self-discipline and dedication. Therefore, qigong means balancing life energy. Some styles of qigong are quiet and introspective, focused on health and spirituality, while others are more martial arts oriented. Aligning the breath with physical movements, aided by visualization, is a central component of the quieter forms of qigong. Through the practice of unification of the breath with movements, energy flows through the body to regain balance, inherently connecting with nature.

The purpose of this qigong exercise, called "pulling down the heavens," is to stabilize the body. On a more philosophical level, it helps to purify and cleanse the energy in the body.

> *Instructions*: Stand with your feet hip-width apart and your arms by your sides with your palms facing your body. Inhale, lifting your arms laterally with your palms facing down. Once you reach shoulder height, rotate at the shoulders so your palms face toward the sky. Continue to raise your arms overhead. As you exhale, bend your elbows, turning your palms to face you and pressing your arms down. Inhale, lifting your arms up while keeping your palms down. At shoulder

height, rotate your palms up, continuing to lift your arms. Bend your elbows, turn your palms to face you, and press your arms down as you exhale. Once more, inhale bringing the arms to the shoulder (palms down), rotate up, exhale (palms facing you), press arms down (Movement-Based Practice 8.1 ▶).

T'ai Chi

T'ai chi is a mind–body practice influenced by Chinese medicine, philosophy, and martial arts. Its complex history is obscured by both historical facts and mythical stories. It is a martial art whose movements were influenced by the movements of animals. Traditionally, t'ai chi provided a means for monks to exercise and practice self-defense. T'ai chi continues to evolve, especially since its introduction to the West in the 1960s, blending with other forms of other mind–body practices such as yoga.

T'ai chi is considered one of the soft arts of qigong, exemplifying softness and internal power against physical force. Its practitioners often seek healing benefits in balancing the opposing, yet complementary, forces of yin and yang in the body. There are several short- and long-form movements, which are all designed to integrate the body with the mind and the breath. A set of movements takes ten to fifteen minutes to perform. Through slow and controlled motions, the rhythm of the breath synchronizes with the body to achieve harmony. The path toward restoring balance and harmony comes from self-cultivation through practicing forms aimed at improving one's weaknesses and limitations while also appreciating one's strengths.

"Wave hands like clouds" is a classic t'ai chi movement common to different t'ai chi styles. In this variation for beginners, your feet will stay in a standing position, without any additional steps.

Instructions: Stand with your feet shoulder-width apart and your knees slightly bent. Allow your arms to drop by your sides. Breathe and feel a sense of ease and relaxation in this starting position. Rotate your right palm to face the earth, while lifting your left hand to face your heart with the elbow slightly bent. Use your hips to rotate your upper body toward the left. Rotate and lift your right arm toward your heart while rotating your left palm down toward the earth, essentially switching the position of the arms. Repeat the cycle two more times, keeping your movements calm and fluid (Movement-Based Practice 8.2 ▶).

Walking Meditation

The purpose of walking meditation is to slow down the automatic act of walking to focus on the present moment. The first time I practiced walking meditation, I felt awkward and clumsy. My gait felt wobbly, and I had trouble finding a "natural" way of walking at a slow speed. As I continued with the practice, I found an increased sense of calm and embodiment. Walking meditation can be practiced in a formal slow practice, or by turning the attention toward movement.

Instructions: Find a quiet spot to practice, either indoors or outdoors where you feel comfortable and can walk back and forth. Decide on where the beginning of the walking path will be and take a comfortable stance with both feet securely placed on the ground. Allow your hands to rest by your sides. You may close your eyes if you are comfortable doing so. Tune in to the sounds around you and other sensations that you may be noticing, such as the temperature or the breeze. Shift your attention to your breath and follow it for a couple of cycles. Now notice your body and how your feet are connected with the earth. Notice how the rest of your body is balanced on your feet. Slowly start to shift your weight onto one leg, preparing to walk. Gently lift the other foot and begin to walk slowly. As you walk, notice the sensations of lifting the leg and placing it back on the earth. Feel each step as you continue to walk. Once you've reached the end of your path, pause for a moment. Breathe. Realign yourself and slowly turn around. Pause again. Start to shift your weight to one side and begin to walk slowly and mindfully. Stay present with each step. When the mind begins to wander, gently escort your attention back to your body. Continue to walk until you reach the end of your path. Pause there and repeat your walk for five or ten minutes. Pause at the end and notice how your breath, heart, and body feel after practicing walking meditation (Movement-Based Practice 8.3 ⓟ).

Contemplative Practices Applied to Music Learning

Contemplative Score Study

The purpose of this activity is to examine a score from a fresh perspective. Choose a section of the piece to focus on before you start. Find a comfortable place to sit with your score near you, limiting distractions as much as possible. Sit in silence for a few breaths. Turn your attention to your score and the section you selected. Think about questions like, *How does this music speak to me? What kind of sounds do I want to create? What do I want to communicate?* Pause to reflect on your reactions to the score and the music. Look for something new each time you look at the score. Imagine a different possibility to your expression or technique. Allow yourself to pause and breathe if you notice your thoughts becoming judgmental or difficult. Once you have reflected on the music and your interpretation, develop a practice plan for the next few days.

Hearing Meditation

As musicians, we are constantly exposed to music. Coupled with the ongoing daily "noise" coming from the TV, cars, dishwasher, etc., our ears get overloaded. Hearing meditation is a way to tune in to the silence and notice the sounds that we tend to block out. This increases our sensitivity to the sounds around us and allows our ears to rest. I find that listening to music after this experience gives us greater awareness of nuance.

Instructions: Begin by sitting in a comfortable position. Close your eyes, if you are comfortable doing so, and tune in to your breath. Become aware of sounds in the room, such as the clock ticking or the air vent. Then become aware of sounds outside of the room: people walking in the hallway, the traffic, a dog barking. As the sounds arise, listen to them nonjudgmentally. You might notice that you have a reaction to those sounds, such as an instinctive tightening of the muscles in response to a loud noise. Observe without judgment. Shift your awareness between sounds, noticing qualities such as pitch and volume. Notice if the sound has a beginning, a middle, and an end. Identify any sounds that are barely audible. Are there moments of complete silence in the space between sounds? What is it like to rest your awareness there? Take a couple of deep breaths and wiggle your fingers and toes. When you are ready to come out of your meditation, gently open your eyes, keeping your gaze soft (Audio 8.4 ▶).

Contemplative Listening

In tandem with the hearing meditation, one could practice a contemplative listening meditation. What would the experience be like to listen to a recording of the piece you are playing with a heightened sensitivity to sound?

Instructions: Sit quietly and take a few deep breaths. Play the recording you have selected and shift your attention to it. Inasmuch as possible, listen without an agenda to judge or compare yourself to the recording. Notice the sound as it is created in a similar manner to what you were practicing in the hearing meditation. When your attention shifts, simply notice it and escort it back to listening to the recording. When the music ends, continue to sit in silence. Note the impact of the music on how you feel and your reactions to the recording. Write a few notes and then listen to a different recording. Repeat the same process.

Contemplative Journaling

Keep a daily practice journal and treat it as a time for contemplative writing. Before you practice, take a few minutes for mindful breathing. In that time, think about the music you are about to practice and make a plan for the next fifteen minutes of practice. After you practice for fifteen minutes, pause and respond in your journal about how that practice felt to you. Describe what you noticed about your focus during your practice, thoughts (or other events) that distracted you, effective strategies you used, challenges you faced, emotions you felt. You can continue with this process, varying the intervals at which you pause to reflect on your practice.

Gratitude Practice

Maintaining a gratitude journal is a simple practice of writing down a list of things (big or small) that you are grateful for every day. Gratitude practice is a way to focus more on the positive and less on the negative aspects of life. Studies have shown that the practice of keeping a gratitude journal has positive and long-lasting mental health benefits, such as lowering stress and improving sleep. A gratitude journal could consist of just writing down three things you are grateful for, or a letter of gratitude to someone else. Whether it is shared or not, the benefits are just the same. Students may choose to take some time after they practice to write down a short list of what they are grateful for in terms of their practice. Perhaps they were grateful for the two-hour block of time they had to practice, the fact that a practice room was available for them, or that they were able to get through their practice plan for the day.

Mantra

Harvard University professor Herbert Benson says that there are physical benefits to reciting mantras. These benefits include a lower pulse rate, lower blood pressure, a sense of relaxation, a slower breath rate, more control over the mind and senses, and inner peacefulness.[19] Using a phrase or a word as a meditation mantra provides an opportunity for reflection and can affect a change in the state of mind. Traditional yogic mantra meditation uses a Sanskrit word; however, the word could be anything that you want to immerse yourself in. You could start by writing down several words such as "peace," "love," and "joy," and then form those into a short sentence. Repeat your word or sentence several times, noticing the feelings that arise.

Affirmations

Affirmations are short sentences repeated internally to oneself about a positive outcome. For example, an affirmation could be "I am peaceful." It is important that affirmations be stated positively instead of negatively, as negative language can be confusing to the mind. It is therefore better to say "I am peaceful" than "I am not upset."

Affirmations can be used as a tool for musical performance preparation. Examples of such affirmations are "I am feeling excited and in control" and "My performance is connected and successful." As with any contemplative practice, the greatest benefit is achieved when affirmations are practiced frequently and well ahead of the performance.

***

In this chapter, we have learned about several ways to practice mindfulness through both breath- and movement-based practices and music-oriented activities. Based on recent scientific research, incorporating mindfulness in higher education has a long list of benefits for our students in terms of both their personal and their intellectual well-being. You don't have to be an expert meditator to share mindfulness. Simply encouraging your students to focus on their breath for one minute before they start practicing can be a powerful tool in deepening their overall awareness.

9

Fueling the Body and Mind

Nutrition and Sleep

Nutrition and sleep are rarely discussed in applied lessons. Admittedly, the connections between these two topics and performance are probably not as obvious as those of the other wellness dimensions we have discussed in this book. However, they do deserve attention, since disturbed sleep and poor eating habits are linked to stress, thus affecting mental health and overall well-being. Understanding what constitutes a healthy diet, coupled with the development of sound sleep hygiene habits, is key to fueling students through their long, busy days. In this chapter, we will discuss nutrition and eating habits, as well as sleep challenges and related solutions. Nutrition and sleep are addressed together because of the significant amount of research demonstrating the effects one has on the other, further strengthening the need to simultaneously address seemingly separate dimensions of our wellness.

Nutrition

Perhaps more than any other topic related to our well-being, nutrition has dominated the media, with promises of diets that will help us achieve peak performance, acquire our dream bodies, and manage our compulsive cravings and addictions. Some diets encourage limiting food groups, while others invite adding food groups and supplements such as superfoods, omega-3s, and probiotics. There is an overwhelming amount of dietary information readily available to us. Influential platforms like social media promote many diets, but are not reviewed by an external body for credibility, making it difficult to know what is scientifically accurate and what is appropriate for each individual. We all have different body types, sensitivities, and nutritional needs.

Challenges

One major adjustment that students must deal with when they transition to college is having to make their own decisions about what to eat. More often than not, the meals they had available at home were decided upon and prepared by their parents. Access to fruits and vegetables was likely much easier before college. Since most freshmen live on campus, they are required to eat in the on-campus cafeteria, which

Teaching the Whole Musician. Paola Savvidou, Oxford University Press (2021). © Oxford University Press.
DOI: 10.1093/oso/9780190868796.003.0009

can be a big change. Cafeterias are generally open for limited hours, which means that students have to plan their day around when they can have their meals (often resulting in skipping meals, or grabbing fast food when schedules get busy). The food available in cafeterias is not always nutritious, and students may not have the necessary information to make the right choices as to what constitutes a well-rounded and nutritious meal. When you are a sleep-deprived college student, a burger may sound much more appetizing than a salad! Also, the all-you-can-eat style of cafeterias may lead to overeating due to the unlimited quantities of food available. Some cafeterias have found creative solutions to help students with this issue, such as not supplying trays, so students can only carry a plate of food and a drink.

The weight gain during the transition year to college is traditionally known as the "freshman fifteen." A study by Deforche et al. indicated that in their first year in college, on average, female students gained 1.9 kg, and male students gained 4.2 kg.[1] Although these numbers are lower than the "freshman fifteen," studies throughout the course of the undergraduate degree show that weight gain continues to increase steadily throughout the four years.[2]

If and when students transition to off-campus living, healthy eating becomes even more of a challenge. Lack of personal transportation limits the grocery shopping options. The perceived higher costs of meal preparation using fresh ingredients at home leads many students to instead opt for purchasing pre-packaged one-time meals. Such easy-to-prepare food products are typically highly processed and low in nutrients. Difficulties with access and cost perception are likely major reasons why students typically eat fewer than three servings of fruits and vegetables per day (far less than the recommended five servings per day).[3] Another challenge students face is busy schedules that only seem to get busier as their academic careers progress. Their perceived lack of time is another barrier to purchasing and preparing nutritious meals.

A study by Small et al. tracked students' eating and physical activity over seven semesters, making comparisons between on- and off-campus living. The results support what we could already assume about students' eating behavior when they move off campus: the consumption of fruits and vegetables reduced significantly over the course of the seven semesters, as did the total amount of time spent exercising.[4] Meanwhile, the total consumption of sweetened drinks, such as soda, increased over time. While there are challenges with eating at the on-campus cafeteria, clearly moving off-campus has its own set of challenges when it comes to healthy eating.

As we are well aware, obesity has risen to the level of an epidemic in the United States. The most recent statistics available from the Centers for Disease Control and Prevention show that obesity affected 39.8 percent of US adults in 2015–2016, which translates to approximately 93.3 million adults.[5] Swanson indicates that the body mass index (BMI) of young adults at ages twenty-one (women) and twenty-four (men) can reliably predict their BMI later on in life, which means that the food choices college students make while in college will impact their health down the road.

Overeating is not the only culprit in gaining weight, though. A sedentary lifestyle becomes the norm among college freshmen due to the increased requirements of studying and practicing. Building exercise into their routine often falls by the wayside in favor of spending more time in the practice room. Other sedentary activities common among college students are playing video games and watching movies or TV. One in three college students are considered sedentary, with their level of activity slowly declining over the course of their time in college.[6]

Increased consumption of alcohol is another contributing factor to weight gain, particularly in males.[7] In a study by Das and Evans, college students indicated that weight gain could potentially have a negative effect on their mental health because of the impact it could have on their social relationships and potential employment opportunities.[8] Low self-esteem resulting from weight gain, as well as the impact of a culture that celebrates thin and fit body types, may be the underlying reasons for these beliefs. Beyond the dangers of unhealthy weight gain, a lack of awareness relative to nutrition research poses threats to the student population.

It is alarming that a high percentage of students so readily accept information they find online and assume that it is well researched and accurate. In fact, a research study by Emily Abbott indicated that, despite being some of the most active social media users, college students are quite ineffective at distinguishing credible information from opinion.[9] The study, which surveyed eighty-three students at two universities, collected information on how students used social media to find information about nutrition. Students tended to search for topics related to nutrition tips, weight loss, and healthy recipes. Fifty-one percent of the students surveyed used social media for nutrition information, with Instagram being the most common source, followed by Facebook and Pinterest. The most common search site for students was Google, as opposed to sources that include peer-reviewed content, such as the university's library or medical portals.[10] It is not surprising that students were trusting of both credible and non-credible information, considering that they tended to base their judgments on the quality of the images and the length of the post, rather than the content.

Vitzthum et al. investigated thirty-seven musical theater students' nutrition knowledge.[11] The results showed that 81 percent of students answered only 30–59 percent of the General Nutrition Knowledge Questionnaire correctly. Knowing that low nutritional knowledge results in poor nutritional choices, universities must ensure that students are receiving appropriate information about nutrition.

During this critical time of transitioning to college, students should be provided with the tools they need to be able to make smart eating choices. Although the applied instructor is not responsible for students' nutrition, there are some ways in which these conversations may come up in the lesson, with questions such as "What and when should I eat before I play?" or "How much water should I drink before my voice lesson?" Or perhaps a student might make a comment such as "I get so hungry when I practice, but there's never anything good in the vending machine." Such questions and comments could be entry points for discussion. The section that follows presents foundational information about nutrition, eating disorders, and guidelines for addressing nutrition concerns specific to music students.

Components of a Healthy Diet

Macronutrients: Carbohydrates, Protein, Fat

These consist of the three types of food that make up our main diet: protein, carbohydrates, and fat. "Macro" refers to the fact that we need larger quantities of these nutrients for our body to function properly.

Carbohydrates

Carbohydrates get a bad reputation among dieters these days! As the body's primary source of energy (except for those on specialized diets such as the ketogenic diet), they are a crucial component of our everyday intake. Carbohydrates consist of starch, sugar, and fiber. The body breaks down carbohydrates into glucose for energy. Daily consumption of carbohydrates varies per person. The recommendation of the National Institutes of Health is to consume approximately 136 grams per day. Sources of carbohydrates include fruit, bread, pasta, rice, dairy products, beans, legumes, starchy vegetables, and processed food such as cookies and candy.

Complex carbohydrates, such as whole-grain rice, are preferred over simple carbohydrates because they are more nutritionally dense and take longer to digest. A longer breakdown process means the body can maintain its energy for longer periods of time.

Protein

Proteins are popularly known as the building blocks of life. This is because they are critical for maintaining the health of our muscles, bones, and skin. In fact, they are found in every single cell of the body. Sources of protein include both animal and plant products. Animal proteins are complete, meaning they contain all the amino acids the body needs, whereas plant proteins, such as beans, peas, and nuts, are incomplete. Eating a variety of proteins daily ensures that the body will be supplied with all the amino acids it needs. The daily amount of protein needed varies depending on the person's age, sex, and physical activity. The recommendation for protein consumption by the US Department of Agriculture for women ages nineteen to thirty is 5.5 ounces per day, and for men ages nineteen to thirty, 6.5 ounces per day. Protein density per ounce for various food sources should be considered when deciding portions. For example, one ounce of cooked meat or poultry is equivalent to one-quarter cup of cooked beans. The ChooseMyPlate website includes a table with amount equivalents for the protein food group.[12]

Fats

Contrary to popular belief, fat is not the enemy of nutritious eating! In fact, fat is critical to our health, as it supplies our body with energy and helps us absorb micronutrients. Much like protein, it is an essential component of every single cell in our body, regulating substances that go in and out of cells. The important thing to take note of is the type (and of course quantity) of fat we are consuming: saturated, unsaturated, or trans. An easy way to distinguish saturated from unsaturated fats is to observe their consistency at room temperature. Saturated fats are solid at room temperature (e.g., butter, cheese, meats, and plant-based foods such as coconut and coconut oil). Unsaturated fats are liquid at room temperature (e.g. olive, canola, safflower, and corn oils). They are also prevalent in many solid foods, including fish (such as salmon and trout), avocados, walnuts, and olives.

Trans fats (also known as partially hydrogenated oils) are primarily created through industrial processes and are found in fried food, pastries, pizza crust, cookies, and crackers. The American Heart Association suggests eliminating trans fats when trying to lower bad cholesterol (LDL).

The ratio of carbohydrate-to-fat consumption in musicians is determined based on the intensity of their activity. Campbell, in *Sports Nutrition: Enhancing Athletic Performance*, demonstrates that at low intensity, we use fat as the main source of energy, whereas at high intensity, we use more carbohydrates.[13] Music-making can include both low- and high-intensity muscular energy depending on the instrument, which means that musicians need to consume both fats and carbohydrates to have appropriate levels of energy for the activity.[14]

Micronutrients

Micronutrients refer to vitamins and minerals. Even though we only need small amounts of these substances, their presence is critical to prevent disease and maintain health. Minerals are further divided into macrominerals and trace minerals. We need larger quantities of macrominerals, such as calcium, and less of trace minerals, such as iron. Deficiencies in micronutrients can have a significant negative impact on growth. The National Institutes of Health have a helpful site that includes health information for each vitamin and mineral (a summary is provided in Tables 9.1–9.3).

Probiotics

Probiotics have come to be widely used by US adults as the third-most-common dietary supplement, following vitamins and minerals.[15] The health benefits of probiotics are acknowledged as a way to promote healthy functioning of the digestive system. Probiotics are "good" bacteria that help the gut digest food properly. There are two

Table 9.1 Vitamins

Vitamins	Benefits	Sources
Vitamin A	Supports vision, immune system, and reproduction; ensures proper functioning of the heart, lungs, and kidneys	Beef liver, salmon, green leafy vegetables, cantaloupe, mango, apricot, dairy products
Biotin (Vitamin B)	Helps convert macronutrients into energy	Meat, eggs, fish, seeds, nuts, sweet potatoes, spinach, and broccoli
Thiamin (Vitamin B_1)	Helps convert macronutrients into energy; important for proper cell functioning	Whole grains, pork, fish, enriched breads and cereals, legumes, seeds, and nuts
Riboflavin (Vitamin B_2)	Needed for metabolism, vision, and skin health	Milk, leafy green vegetables, whole grains, enriched breads and cereals.
Niacin (Vitamin B_3)	Needed for metabolism, contributes to nervous system, digestive system and skin health	Meat, poultry, fish, whole grains, enriched breads and cereals, mushrooms, asparagus, leafy greens, and peanut butter
Pantothenic acid	Needed for metabolism	Meat, eggs, legumes, milk, mushrooms, avocado, kale, and broccoli
Folic acid	Needed for making DNA and red blood cells	Leafy green vegetables, legumes, seeds, orange juice, and liver
Cobalamin (Vitamin B_{12})	Maintains healthy nerve and blood cells; produces DNA in all cells	Beef liver, clams, fish, meat, poultry, eggs, and milk
Pyridoxine (Vitamin B_6)	Needed for metabolism and proper brain development	Poultry, fish, organ meats, potatoes, carrots, spinach, bananas, and avocado
Vitamin C	Serves as an antioxidant, makes collagen to heal wounds, supports iron absorption	Citrus fruits, broccoli, strawberries, cantaloupe, red and green peppers, kiwifruit, papayas, and tomatoes
Vitamin D	Maintains strong bones by absorbing calcium, fights off infections, necessary to transfer neural messages between the brain and body parts	Fatty fish (tuna, salmon), egg yolks, beef liver, cheese, mushrooms, and fortified milk
Vitamin E	Acts as an antioxidant, fights off infections, prevents blood clots	Wheat germ, sunflower and safflower oils, peanuts, hazelnuts, almonds, sunflower seeds, whole grains, and leafy green vegetables
Vitamin K	Prevents blood clotting, maintains healthy bones	Green leafy vegetables, vegetable oils, blueberries, figs, meat, cheese, eggs, and soybeans

Sources: "Vitamins: Their Function and Sources," *Michigan Medicine Health Library* (https://www.uofmhealth.org/health-library/ta3868#ta3868-sec); "Vitamin and Mineral Supplement Fact Sheet," *National Institutes of Health Office of Dietary Supplements* (https://ods.od.nih.gov/factsheets/list-VitaminsMinerals).

Table 9.2 Macrominerals

Macrominerals	Benefits	Sources
Calcium	Maintains strong bones, supports structure of bones and teeth and nervous system, blood pressure regulation, supports immune system	Milk, yogurt, cheese, kale, broccoli, chinese cabbage, fish with soft bones, and grains
Phosphorus	Found in every cell; used to make energy	Yogurt, milk, cheese, grains, meats, poultry, fish, eggs, nuts, cashews, sesame seeds, lentils, kidney beans, potatoes, and asparagus
Magnesium	Regulates muscle and nerve function, blood sugar levels, and blood pressure; makes protein, bone, and DNA	Legumes, nuts, seeds, whole grains, green leafy vegetables, milk, and yogurt
Sodium	Needed for proper fluid balance, nerve transmission, and muscle contraction	Table salt, soy sauce, processed foods, breads, vegetables, and unprocessed meats
Potassium	Necessary for proper kidney and heart function, muscle contraction, and nerve transmission	Dried apricots, prunes, raisins, orange juice, bananas, acorn squash, potatoes, spinach, tomatoes, broccoli, lentils, kidney beans, soybeans, nuts, milk, yoghurt, meats, poultry, and fish
Chloride	Needed for proper fluid balance, stomach acid	Table salt, soy sauce, processed foods, milk, meats, breads, and vegetables
Sulfur	Found in protein molecules	Meats, poultry, fish, eggs, milk, legumes, and nuts

Sources: "Vitamins: Their Function and Sources," *Michigan Medicine Health Library* (https://www.uofmhealth.org/health-library/ta3868#ta3868-sec); "Vitamin and Mineral Supplement Fact Sheet," *National Institutes of Health Office of Dietary Supplements* (https://ods.od.nih.gov/factsheets/list-VitaminsMinerals).

Table 9.3 Microminerals

Microminerals	Benefits	Sources
Iron	Carries oxygen in the body; necessary for metabolism	Organ meats, red meats, fish, poultry, shellfish, egg yolks, legumes, dried fruits, dark leafy greens, fortified cereals, and iron-enriched breads
Manganese	Used to make energy, protects cells	Whole grains, clams, oysters, mussels, nuts, legumes, leafy vegetables, pineapple, blueberries, tea, and black pepper
Copper	Used to make energy, maintains nervous and immune systems, needed for brain development	Beef liver, oysters, cashews, wheat-bran cereal, whole grains, potatoes, mushrooms, avocados, chickpeas, tofu, and water
Iodine	Needed to make thyroid hormones which control metabolism, growth, and development	Seafood, dairy products, bread, cereal, and iodized salt
Zinc	Fights off infections and viruses, makes protein and DNA, helps heal wounds, and contributes to taste perception	Oysters, red meat, poultry, crab, lobsters, fortified cereal, beans, nuts, and whole grains

Sources: "Vitamins: Their Function and Sources," *Michigan Medicine Health Library* (https://www.uofmhealth.org/health-library/ta3868#ta3868-sec); "Vitamin and Mineral Supplement Fact Sheet," *National Institutes of Health Office of Dietary Supplements* (https://ods.od.nih.gov/factsheets/list-VitaminsMinerals).

main types of probiotic bacteria, which have different functions: *Lactobacillus* and *Bifidobacterium*. In healthy people, probiotics have not been shown to have any negative side effects. Common sources of probiotics include fermented foods such as yogurt, kombucha, non-pasteurized sauerkraut, kefir, tempeh, and traditionally fermented pickles.

Fundamentals of Proper Nutrition

Eat Colorful Food Leisurely

Keeping track of all the nutrition information available is overwhelming and confusing. It doesn't come as a surprise that, as a society, we've lost sight of what a healthy diet looks like. In fact, eight in ten Americans believe that the advice available about what to eat is conflicting.[16] In spite of all the confusing and ever-changing information that's out there, the fundamentals of proper nutrition have not changed. The Dietary Guidelines for Americans present the following simple guidelines for eating[17]:

- Eat food within an appropriate caloric intake.
- Consume vegetables from all subgroups and colors (dark green, red and orange, legumes, starches, etc.), fruits, grains (preferably whole), low-fat or fat-free dairy (milk, yogurt, cheese), a variety of protein (seafood, poultry, lean red meat, eggs, beans, nuts, seeds, soy products), and oils.
- Keep saturated fats, trans fats, and sugar intake to less than 10 percent of daily calorie intake.
- Alcohol, when consumed, should be in moderation: one drink per day for women and two drinks per day for men. One drink is defined by the US Dietary Guidelines as 12 oz. of beer, 5 oz. of wine, or 1.5 oz. of hard alcohol.

The ChooseMyPlate campaign by the US Department of Agriculture provides a simple visual guide for what a healthy plate should look like: fruits and vegetables should be half of the meal, grains and starches one-quarter, and meat/protein the remaining quarter.[18] A quick way of knowing how much food to put on your plate is to account for fruit and vegetables taking up about as much space as the size of your palm, while protein and grains or starches should each be approximately the size of your fists, and fats should take up no more than the size of your thumb. This quick guide is easy to remember and can provide an approximate ratio of the different food groups in a meal.

Encouraging slow eating promotes a mindful approach to food intake. We can potentially eat less than we think we need and feel more satisfied after the meal because we've taken the time to taste the food. One of my favorite activities in my wellness class is a mindful eating exercise. The only prop you need is one raisin for each student (unless you are feeling generous, in which case you can swap the raisin for a piece of chocolate). The purpose of the exercise is to slow down the habit of scarfing down food and fully experience eating this humble dried fruit. It begins by observing its shape and ridges, feeling its weight and texture, hearing the sound it makes when pinched between the fingers, smelling it, and finally slowly eating it (Audio 9.1 ⏵). This has been a consistently successful experiment, in my experience. The responses are usually along the lines of "Wow! I never thought that a raisin could taste so good!," "I could taste the dirt of the earth in that one," or "I just realized I haven't really tasted my food, I mean really tasted, in a long time." Take a few minutes to try out this meditative eating practice. You might be surprised at what you will discover!

There is a wealth of information available out there about nutrition, and it can be difficult to remember all the details about food portions and to keep track of meals, especially for busy college students. If I were to boil down the advice I give my students, I would say this: Eat leisurely so you can actually taste the food you eat, and go for as much variety of color on your plate as you can.

Assessing Hunger Cues

How many times have you been in a situation where you grabbed a snack not because you were hungry, but because you were procrastinating on doing your work? I'm certainly guilty of it. Eating is often used as a distraction from working, or as a way to deal with difficult emotions. A good first step toward noticing hunger cues is to close the eyes and notice how the body feels. Are you actually hungry? Or thirsty? Or looking for a way out? If you are unsure as to whether you are hungry or not, it is usually helpful to wait for a few minutes to see if your hunger persists.

If you or your students are curious about keeping track of eating habits, consider using a nutrition diary such as the one in Worksheet 9.1⏵, or an app (there are several available on the market). Noticing what you eat, when, your mood, and your hunger levels can be useful in becoming aware of habits that may or may not be helpful.

Snacking

Snacks for college students should be easy to find and convenient to transport in a backpack or lunchbox. Ideally, snacks would be a combination of a carbohydrate and either protein or fat. A few examples of such snacks are apple slices and cheese cubes, apricots and cashews, baby carrots and hummus, a banana and almond butter, and berries and Greek yogurt. These healthy snacks provide longer-lasting energy than snacks consisting of refined foods and sugar.

Pre-Performance Meal

We can draw valuable information from sports nutrition to determine what and when musicians should eat before a performance. This information should always be calibrated to account for each individual's pre-performance rituals and needs, which vary widely. Eating a heavy meal just before performing is obviously not ideal because digestion causes drowsiness, and you need focus and energy to perform. A meal two to three hours before performing is preferable, as it gives the body enough time to digest the food that is being consumed. It is important that the meal consumed during this time be well-rounded, consisting of complex carbohydrates, protein, and vegetables. The combination of these nutrients will fuel the body with the energy it needs to perform. Hydration, to the degree that feels comfortable, is also necessary to help with digestion and to guard against lightheadedness. Caffeine and alcohol are best avoided right before performing.

As far as what to eat is concerned, we can turn to the recommendations for athletes. While I'm not suggesting a musical performance is equivalent to an athletic performance, there are certainly parallels in terms of the endurance, strength, and flexibility required. Athletes are encouraged to start planning their competition-day meals several days or even weeks in advance to set themselves up for success. Considering that carbohydrates are the main source of energy (again, for those who are not on specialized diets), they should be consumed the day before as well as prior to the event (one to four hours ahead of time). Many athletes tend to "load up" with carbs by eating pasta the night before a competition. Although white pasta is a good source of carbohydrates, complex carbohydrates (such as whole-grain pasta or rice) will provide longer-lasting energy, as they take more time to digest. As a side note, wheat tolerance must be considered, as wheat products may have an undesirable calming effect.[19] On that note, one should also avoid any potential allergens or other foods that could lead to potential GI distress.[20]

Hydration

The amount of daily hydration needed to maintain *euhydration* varies as much as each of our bodies' water composition, which ranges between 45 and 75 percent. Euhydration is a fancy word for normal levels of hydration (when neither dehydration nor hyperhydration is present). Signs of dehydration are yellow urine, headaches, dizziness, fatigue, dry eyes, and dry mouth. Factors that affect fluid intake include sweat rate, food intake, and environmental factors that affect sweat.[21] The recommended water intake, as suggested by the Institute of Medicine's Dietary Reference Intakes, is 125 oz. for men and 91 oz. for women (these numbers include water in food, which accounts for approximately 19 percent of our fluid intake).[22] Again, the amount will vary depending on the person, individual activity levels, and the climate. Dehydration is obvious in hot climates but less so in cold climates. The urge to drink water is not as strong when you are feeling cold; however, dry forced air can have a dehydrating effect.

Water is not the only fluid that counts toward euhydration. Other fluids include juice, milk, and coffee. There is controversy over whether caffeine is considered hydrating, since it has a diuretic effect. However, it has not shown to exhibit long-term negative effects on hydration.[23] Too much water should be avoided, as it can cause constipation, mineral depletion, and other imbalances.[24]

My strategy for staying hydrated in any climate is to always carry a water bottle with me and refill it approximately four times during the entire day, which will help me accomplish my water drinking goal of between 90 and 100 ounces per day. There are also several apps and smart watches that can help keep track of water intake, sending reminders when it's time for a sip of water. I also enjoy fresh, juicy fruits and vegetables that are both satisfying and hydrating.

Nutritionist or Dietitian?

There seems to be confusion among the general public in understanding the differences between nutritionists and dietitians. Even though these terms are often used interchangeably, the two professions are in fact different in terms of both their training and governmental oversight. Registered dietitians (RD) are also often designated as registered dietitians and nutritionists (RDN), but not all nutritionists are necessarily dietitians. Formal training, certification, or licensing is not required in all states in order for someone to call himself a nutritionist. However, it is illegal in any state for persons to call themselves a dietitian without the proper credentials. In order to become an RD or RDN, one has to complete necessary training (e.g., a bachelor's degree), hundreds of hours of supervised practicum, a registration exam, and continuing education credits. RDs or RDNs can also specialize in different areas (e.g., sports nutrition) through the Center for Dietetics Registration. A nutritionist may or may not have sufficient training or practical experience to be able to advise as such. When seeking a provider for nutrition, be sure to caution students to read through their credentials and specialization before making an appointment.

Eating Disorders

Eating disorders (EDs) affect less than 5 percent of the worldwide population. The most common age for onset of EDs is between eighteen and twenty, which means that traditional-age college students are at high risk. In the United States, approximately 9–13 percent of female and 3–4 percent of male college students are affected by EDs. Of those students, less than 20 percent receive treatment.[25] In a study by Eisenberg et al., students who did not seek help for symptoms of EDs cited that they did not need to or did not have time, or that it is normal to have stress in college.[26] This means that students who are untreated remain at risk for suffering the physical, psychological, and academic impacts of these illnesses.

The two most common EDs are anorexia nervosa and bulimia. The third recognized category is called "eating disorders not otherwise specified" (EDNOS). Anorexia nervosa is characterized by distorted body image, excessive dieting resulting in significant weight loss, and fear of gaining weight. In order to control body weight, the person may diet, use laxatives, and/or vomit. Anorexia nervosa mostly affects females who are in their teenage years.

Bulimia nervosa, a more common disorder than anorexia, is characterized by binge eating, followed by self-induced vomiting to avoid gaining weight. A person with anorexia nervosa may be visibly underweight, but someone with bulimia may be either underweight or overweight. For a diagnosis of bulimia nervosa, the binge eating followed by vomiting threshold is at least twice a week for three months or more. As with anorexia, bulimia affects mostly females, often starting in their adolescent years.

The third category, EDNOS, consists of disorders that don't fully fit under either the categories of anorexia or bulimia, such as binge eating disorder. The main difference between this disorder and bulimia nervosa is that there is no attempt to vomit to compensate for the overeating. A formal diagnosis is based on binge eating about twice per week for over six months.

Eating disorders are serious mental disorders and can pose risks to one's life caused by kidney failure, heart failure, or brain dysfunction. Often, people with an ED also suffer from another mental disorder, such as depression, anxiety, or substance use.[27]

People with perfectionistic tendencies are considered to be at risk for developing EDs.[28] Patients diagnosed with either bulimia nervosa or anorexia nervosa tend to demonstrate perfectionistic tendencies as related to their self-image or maintaining a perfect body shape and weight. Even in individuals who recover from the disorder, perfectionism still remains at elevated levels.[29] The types of perfectionism that these individuals were found to retain even after recovery, according to a study by Bardone-Cone et al., are setting expectations of perfection for themselves, trying to appear perfect to others, and having frequent "perfectionism-related" thoughts.[30] Knowing that many musicians suffer from an unhealthy dose of perfectionism, this is valuable information, as we may be able to advise students or even prevent any damage if we are aware of the requisite warning signs.

Warning Signs

With EDs, warning signs can manifest in outward appearance, behavior, or psychology. In terms of behavioral signs, these could involve dieting, fasting, binge eating, frequent visits to the bathroom after meals to vomit, cutting out entire food groups from the diet that the person previously enjoyed (such as fats or dairy), skipping meals, being overly focused on food preparation, obsessive interest in body shape and weight, and avoiding social settings. Some physical warning signs could be fainting, weight loss (or fluctuating between losing and gaining weight), always feeling cold (even when it's warm), and swelling in the cheeks or jaw. Psychological warnings include being overly concerned about physical appearance; worrying about being overweight, despite being underweight or normal weight; being sensitive to comments about body weight, food, or exercise; and a feeling of extreme dissatisfaction with one's appearance.[31]

How to Respond

As with any physical or mental illness, the sooner an ED is treated, the easier the process of recovery will be. When approaching someone with an ED, try to first educate yourself about the disorder as much as possible. Find a time when you are not frustrated or angry when approaching the person. A conversation like that is best done in a calm environment. When talking to the person, the recommendation is to use "I" statements instead of "you" statements.[32] "You" statements come across as accusatory and could be perceived as blaming the person for their disorder. For example, it's better to say, "I am concerned about you," rather than, "You worry me." If the person is responding in a way that makes you concerned about their safety (e.g., suicidal thoughts), or you are noticing disorientation or vomiting, it is best to call 911 immediately. If the situation you are in is not a crisis situation, then proceed to listen to the person nonjudgmentally, as difficult as it may be (refer to guidelines in Chapter 2). If the person is open to support and acknowledges struggling with an ED, offer options for professional help, such as a primary care physician, psychiatrist, or nutritional counselor. If, on the other hand, you are met with resistance, anger, or denial, continue to offer your emotional support and point out the person's strengths.

***

As with all things wellness, there are no hard and fast rules, only guidelines that we can follow. Dr. Evan Engelstad, a pianist and nutritional therapy practitioner, gave an excellent piece of advice during a recent conversation: "We all have different reactions to different foods. There is a lot of self-experimentation that we need to undertake to find out what works best for our individual system and our genetic predisposition." For example, eating bananas right before a performance may work well for someone, but may give someone else a sugar rush followed by a dip in energy. Experimenting with variety, quantity, and eating schedule is key to finding what works best for each individual in terms of maintaining consistent energy throughout the day and ensuring a holistic supply of necessary nutrients and hydration.

***

Sleep

Sleep is the most predictive factor of well-being. Difficulty with memory, concentration, social relationships, and food cravings are but a few of the effects that sleep deprivation has on our overall wellness. In my attempt to better understand the culture around sleep, I asked this same question to all the students I interviewed for this book: "In what ways does sleep deprivation affect the well-being of university students?" I didn't even ask if they thought sleep deprivation was an issue, because it is. Thousands of students cite sleep deprivation as one of the top three impediments to academic success.[33] And the few music students I interviewed agreed, or so I assume based on the way they rolled their eyes and snickered at the question ("Isn't it obvious that it affects us in every way?"). One of the students had this to say about her experience with sleep:

> I've been struggling with sleep all semester, trying to change my routine and just go to bed earlier. But because I would wake up late and then go to bed super late, I have to force myself to be productive. I end up getting sick all the time. Yesterday, I got sick again because I slept only two hours the night before. I know I need to work on this, but it's getting worse and worse. I have this conflict, too, because I want to be productive, but if I don't sleep, I can't get work done.

It is deeply concerning that students consider sleep as a commodity, not as a basic need for functioning at their best.

Sleep appears to receive less attention from university health centers than alcohol and drug use, even though it has a much higher impact on academic success. Monica Hartmann, professor of economics at the University of St. Thomas, and Roxanne Prichard, professor of psychology and neuroscience at the same university, demonstrated that sleep is an accurate predictor of academic problems. More specifically, for each additional day per week that a student reported sleep difficulties, their probability of dropping a course increased by 10 percent, and their cumulative GPA lowered by 0.02.[34] This study cites sleep as a "modifiable risk factor," which thus has the potential to positively impact academic success when addressed effectively.

Sleep Cycles

Circadian rhythm refers to our sleep/wake cycle, which is controlled by the hypothalamus in the brain and central nervous system structures.[35] Neurotransmitters send messages from the brain to neurons about when to sleep and when to wake up. This system is responsible for the feelings of alertness and sleepiness that occur at regular intervals throughout the day. The highest level of sleepiness usually occurs between

2 and 4 a.m. while we are asleep. Another alertness dip occurs just after lunch time, between 1 and 3 p.m., which explains the timing of siesta in Mediterranean countries. Our circadian rhythm is sensitive to disruptions, though. Jetlag, daylight saving time, and staying up late to watch TV can all interrupt our cycle, making it difficult to stay awake and focus during our usual waking hours. If we are well rested, these feelings of sleepiness are not as intense during the day.

Zeitgebers are environmental cues that tell us when it is time to be awake or asleep. The strongest *zeitgeber* is daylight; others include exercise, social life, and food/drink intake. Before the time of electricity, humans' sleep cycle would follow the natural cycles of sunrise and sunset. But now, because we spend most of our days indoors, we are exposed to less natural light during the day and more artificial light at night. This change has shifted our sleep cycle as a society. We are now sleeping approximately 20 percent less than we did about one hundred years ago.

Sleep cycles consist of five stages. The first stage consists of falling asleep and light sleep. During the second stage of sleep, eye movement and brain waves begin to slow down. When entering the third stage, the brain waves are much slower (also referred to as delta waves). The fourth stage consists of deep sleep. There is no muscle or eye movement during this stage, and it can be quite difficult to be woken up from. The last stage of the cycle is called the rapid eye movement (REM) stage. The eyes usually move fast, breathing is irregular, and blood moves to the brain. The brain explores the events of the day, deciding which memories to keep and which to discard. Vivid dreams usually occur at this stage. Each cycle lasts between 90 and 110 minutes and repeats between four and six times per night, with deep sleep decreasing in length and REM increasing.

Factors That Affect Sleep

Actually, everything can affect sleep. If I were to modify the eight dimensions of wellness image from the first chapter to include a category for sleep, I would draw a circle encompassing the spot in the middle where all the petals intersect and label it "Sleep." Family situation, work or class schedule, geographic location, physical and psychological health, and environmental factors all contribute to habitual sleep patterns.

There are several reasons that students lose sleep: incongruent roommate schedules that cause tension and difficulties falling asleep, new and different noises at night (e.g., doors closing, people talking in the hallways), alcohol, hanging out late with friends, late-night eating, and certain types of prescription medication. Surfing social media and checking email just before going to bed can stimulate the brain, rather than producing the calming effect needed to fall asleep. Not only can receiving a work- or school-related email just before sleeping increase levels of stress, but the blue screen light emitted from the screen is thought to suppress melatonin (the sleep hormone) and to promote wakefulness.

Students tend to sacrifice sleep when assignments and practice time pile up. A recent study by Brown, Qin, and Esmail indicated that while a large percentage of students did not sleep enough, 80.6 percent did not seek help to address their issues.[36] The same study, which surveyed approximately 1,300 students, showed that 30.5 percent of students reported sleeping less than six and a half hours per night (mostly undergraduates), 61.5 percent slept between six and a half and eight hours per night, and only 8 percent slept for eight or more hours. About a third of the respondents indicated getting enough sleep. When students couldn't sleep, their three most common self-help tools were reading a book, listening to music, and adjusting the heat. Alcohol and cigarettes were used by about 30 percent and 29 percent, respectively, to aid with sleep. These percentages demonstrate just how troubling the issue of sleep is for university students. It is particularly concerning that, at least based on this study, only one-fifth of the students considered sleep important enough to seek help.

One of the doctoral students I interviewed reflected on how the combination of coursework and teaching made it difficult to get enough sleep:

> I think sleep deprivation is tricky because there's just so much work to do. I've noticed recently that my sleep has been better now that I'm done with my coursework because I'm not staring at a screen late at night anymore, whereas before I would be writing papers and I would have to be up at that late hour because I didn't finish teaching until a certain time. It's a huge struggle.

Poor planning can get in the way of sufficient good-quality sleep, but sometimes there's just too much to do! Addressing overcommitment and providing guidance on how to prioritize the projects at hand are conversations to have with our students.

But even when organizational skills and thoughtful project commitments are addressed, there still remains the issue of combating the culture of pride around sleep deprivation that plagues our campuses. I have been present during many student conversations that went something like this:

STUDENT A: "Did you get your paper in?"

STUDENT B: "Yeah, I stayed up all night to write it. You?"

STUDENT A: "Yeah, me too. I got like one hour of sleep, and now I have to go to rehearsal. I have another paper due tomorrow, so probably won't sleep again tonight."

STUDENT B: "Yeah, I have to stay up late to practice tonight too. Probably till 3 a.m., my usual."

In this imaginary (but close to reality) conversation, you can see how students one-up each other on how little sleep they got. It is not okay to sacrifice sleep, and it is definitely not okay to egg each other on to sleep less and to perpetuate a culture of sleep-deprived zombies! It is my hope that through education around sleep hygiene and modeling the importance of sleep, we can start to shift this attitude.

Sleep Difficulties and Disorders
Sleep Deprivation

Sleep deprivation has a negative effect on cognitive and physical functioning. The body responds with decreased reaction time, often accompanied by tremors and aches, and a compromised immune system, which explains why we might get sick after a period of less sleep. We have difficulty focusing and memorizing and tend to be irritable. Because of the similarity in symptoms between inadequate sleep and anxiety, a sleep-deprived person is nine times more likely to screen positive for depression and seventeen times more likely to screen positive for anxiety.

Chronically sleep-deprived people tend to gravitate toward eating food that is high in sugar and fat. The brain responds to sleep deprivation as a state of emergency, and it wants us to load up on calories. These cravings usually occur in the afternoon when we are sleepy. Replacing these foods with nutrition-dense foods and healthy fats (e.g., nuts, avocados, hummus), as opposed to processed, sugary foods, gives the body energy for longer periods of time.

Although not a disorder, microsleep often occurs in sleep-deprived people. Microsleep lasts between a fraction of a second and ten seconds, and it occurs when part of the brain falls asleep. One may notice it as a temporary lapse in concentration or loss of muscle control. While not a dangerous condition when experienced at home, if experienced while driving, it may cause an accident. The best way to avoid microsleeps is to ensure that you get restful and adequate nighttime sleep.

Insomnia

Insomnia affects approximately 30 percent of the US population. It is no surprise, then, that it is the most common sleep disorder. Insomnia can affect an individual in three different forms: difficulty falling asleep (the most common one), trouble staying asleep, and not getting restorative sleep. For someone to be diagnosed with insomnia, they have to report both difficulty with nighttime sleep and sleep-related issues during the day. Daytime symptoms include sleepiness, mood disturbance, tension headaches, low energy, fatigue, and difficulty with concentration and memory.

According to Bonnet and Arand, causes of insomnia can be divided into four categories: (1) situational insomnia (caused by environmental changes or stress); (2) behavioral or learned insomnia (related to poor sleep hygiene, which could have developed in response to a stressful experience); (3) insomnia associated with other medical problems (for example, mental disorders such as depression, anxiety, and substance abuse); and (4) primary insomnia (not associated with any of the previously listed insomnias, psychological, or medical factors).[37] Insomnia poses serious threats to one's health, increasing the risk for hypertension and cardiac disease.[38] Prescription and over-the-counter medication, herbal supplements (such as valerian, kava-kava, and chamomile), and sedating antidepressants are all used to treat insomnia, to varying degrees of effectiveness. Melatonin supplements are commonly used to aid in regulating sleep cycles. Melatonin is a hormone produced naturally at nighttime that signals our body to get ready for sleep. A doctor should be consulted when considering herbal supplements, as they may have adverse side effects when combined with certain types of medication.

Obstructive Sleep Apnea

Obstructive sleep apnea, a condition that could potentially lead to life-threatening complications, causes frequent sleep interruptions due to the airway being blocked and the breath stopping multiple times during the night. Common symptoms are loud snoring, daytime sleepiness, and a sore throat upon awakening. A treatment that is frequently used is wearing a device while sleeping that keeps the airways open.

Circadian Sleep Disorders

Circadian sleep disorders (CRSD) occur when one's sleep/wake schedule does not align with one's actual habits. There are four types of CRSDs: (1) Advanced sleep phase syndrome is characterized by going to bed early at night (between 6 and 9 p.m.) and waking up very early in the morning (between 2 and 5 a.m.). (2) Delayed sleep phase syndrome can be viewed as the opposite of advanced sleep phase syndrome. It occurs when the individual has a delayed bedtime (between 1 and 6 a.m.) and delayed wake-up time (10 a.m.–2 p.m.). (3) Free running disorder is a rare condition that involves desensitization to *zeitgebers* that results in sleep–wake cycles that are longer than the 24–hour cycle. (4) Irregular sleep–wake rhythm is another rare disorder characterized by a lack of a consistent sleep–wake rhythm from day to day.

Delayed sleep phase syndrome (DSPS) is common among teenagers and is characterized by a delay in the circadian rhythm. The melatonin needed to trigger sleepiness is not released until two or more hours later than in the general population. Approximately 15 percent of eighteen- to nineteen-year-old males have this syndrome.[39] People with DSPS often describe themselves as "night owls." They have difficulty falling asleep at night and waking up early in the morning. A few public school districts in the United States have started to shift start times for high-school students, resulting in positive outcomes such as reduction in absences and improved grades.[40] If you have students dealing with DSPS, it would be helpful to offer them the option of having an afternoon lesson, as opposed to early in the morning when they might be having difficulty waking up.

Food Intake and Sleep

Difficulties with sleep have a negative effect on eating behavior. There is high comorbidity between eating and sleep disorders, and there are also syndromes that consist of both eating and sleeping difficulties, such as sleep-related eating disorder and night eating syndrome. Patients diagnosed with anorexia nervosa wake up early in the morning or have disturbed sleep.[41] Bulimia nervosa causes one to fall asleep right after binge eating at night and also may lead to longer periods of sleep.

The hypothalamus is responsible for regulating both eating and sleep cycles. It makes sense, then, that lack of sleep would also affect our eating patterns. Our body goes into alarm mode when we don't get sufficient sleep, causing our brain to think that we need to load up on food. Staying awake for longer than our body is used to means that we are using more energy (as opposed to the little energy we use when we are asleep). The body wants to consume more energy-rich food in order to conserve energy. This urge causes us to want to eat sweet and fatty foods. Even though our food intake increases, our lifestyle continues to be largely sedentary, meaning that the extra food intake causes weight gain. Dr. Plamen Penev, assistant professor of medicine at the University of Chicago, recommends that people who want to reduce the amount of food they eat should be getting adequate sleep.[42]

Another component that adds to the complex relationship between food intake and sleep is stress. Difficulties coping with stress can cause a heightened state of psychophysiological arousal, which in turn affects sleep.[43] Stress could be situational and also heightened because of personality traits such as perfectionism (for more information on stress, see Chapter 7). Fear of failure, excessive self-criticism, and sensitivity to criticism cause greater stress, leading to disturbed sleep and eating difficulties in people with perfectionistic tendencies.[44]

Milder habits can also have an impact on sleep. For example, caffeine intake (whether it's in the form of coffee, caffeinated tea, or food, such as chocolate) can have a negative impact on one's ability to fall asleep; however, individual responses vary. Factors that determine the effects of caffeine on each individual include how much and when caffeine is consumed, tolerance, and metabolism. A sudden increase in caffeine intake may also affect one's response to the drug and cause sleep disruption. Other negative effects of caffeine involve heightening preexisting feelings of stress and anxiety. A study by Lichstein et al. found that taking supplemental vitamins also affected the continuity of nighttime sleep with increased awakenings.[45] While caffeine and vitamins can negatively affect sleep, so can common downers, such as alcohol, which are used as a form of self-medication to help with falling asleep.

Alcohol does generally achieve its purpose; however, it also negatively affects the quality and continuity of sleep. Once alcohol is metabolized at some point during the night, it leads to "rebound increases in sleep fragmentation or nighttime wakefulness, increases in dreams and nightmares."[46] The amount of alcohol consumed has an impact on the effect, with lower doses increasing sleep time and higher doses leading to more disrupted sleep.[47] But there are also ways one can cultivate healthier sleep habits through physical activity. Any discussion on behaviors that affect sleep wouldn't be complete without addressing the positive role and impact of exercise.

Exercise and Sleep

Exercising elevates body temperature, which then creates a bigger temperature drop in preparation for sleeping. An added benefit of exercising is that it helps lower anxiety and guards against depression, which also contributes to better sleep.[48] If physical activity occurs too close to bedtime, though, it may have the opposite effect—stimulating, rather than calming, the body. Although the research is not entirely conclusive on the impact of exercise on sleep habits, the general consensus is that morning or afternoon are preferable times to exercises (as opposed to just before bedtime).

Exercising outdoors (e.g., biking, running, walking) contributes to regulating the sleep–wake cycle as it exposes the body to natural light—the strongest *zeitgeber*. The National Sleep Foundation recommends moderate to vigorous exercise for 150 minutes per week to help with improving sleep quality. Depending on your personal circumstances, it may seem challenging to incorporate thirty minutes of daily exercise. The good news is that even ten minutes of daily exercise, such as walking or biking, can still positively affect sleep.

A meta-analysis of several studies that investigated the relationship between the intensity of physical activity and sleep quality revealed that moderate intensity exercise might even be more effective in improving sleep, as opposed to vigorous exercise.[49] In one of the studies analyzed, a low-intensity t'ai chi exercise program improved participants' self-reported quality of sleep. Another study showed that secondary students who increased their weekly step count reported a high increase in sleep quality. College students reported sleep improvements as well following moderate-intensity exercise such as bicycling, walking, and running, as opposed to non-exercisers. These results suggest that even small amounts of low-impact exercise can make a difference. While we are on the topic of exercise, let's take this conversation one step further to learn more about the relationship between sleep, exercise, and injury.

Sleep and Physical Injury

During sleep, the body repairs and regenerates damaged tissues, a critical process for both injury prevention and recovery. Getting less sleep means that muscles, bones, and ligaments are not given the necessary conditions to heal from microtrauma. At the absence of sufficient recovery, a full blown injury may develop over time.

Even though musicians' energy expenditure is different from that of athletes, there are similarities in terms of the training regimen that allow us to use research on sleep and athletes when educating our students on this topic. A study by Johnston et al. demonstrated that athletes with lower quality and quantity of sleep (in addition to psychological factors) were at a higher risk of experiencing a new injury.[50] Some of the negative effects that were identified as contributing to this higher risk were increased muscle tension, slower recovery of muscle tissues, lowered immune response, and negative impact on motor and cognitive functions. When I think about times when I had to practice after not sleeping enough (more frequently than I care to admit!), I recall my thoughts were foggy, my shoulders felt tight, and I probably slipped into a few moments of microsleeping here and there. It certainly did not yield the most productive music learning results! It's possible that pushing my tired body to continue to practice may have been the cause for additional shoulder pain the following day. This is the beginning of a dangerous cycle that many performing artists encounter; it is important to note how making time to sleep and recover, especially during periods of stress, can be a powerful injury-prevention tool.

Another study correlated duration of sleep with injury risk in adolescent athletes.[51] The results showed that athletes who totaled less than eight hours of sleep per night were 1.4 times more likely to have had an injury, as compared to those who slept for eight or more hours per night. The association between injury risk and sleep was strong even after other factors such as year in school and time spent in sports participation were accounted for. The evidence points to the need for sufficient sleep (i.e., at least eight hours) to allow for effective healing of the tissues and to lower the risk of injury. Combating sleep issues can be more effective in contexts where we also understand the importance of sleep hygiene.

Good Sleep Hygiene

Providing students with accurate information and suggestions about good sleep hygiene can, by extension, ripple into benefits to their mental health. Sleep tends to be a low-stigma topic, meaning that conversations around sleep may be easier to initiate than those focused on other mental health topics.

In the study mentioned previously by Brown et al., 78.1 percent of students indicated they would like to receive more information about sleep from their institution.[52] When students come to us with concerns about their sleep, a good starting point for helping them would be to identify what they are already doing that promotes healthy sleeping behaviors (in line with the motivational interviewing approach discussed in Chapter 2). It could be that the students already have some effective tools, such as reading a book, listening to music, or a breathing meditation practice before bedtime. Having an established ritual helps the brain know that it's time to start transitioning to sleep. There may also be practices they use that are not optimal (e.g., listening to their own recording or someone else playing a piece they are working on may have the opposite effect of triggering anxiety rather than relaxation). Through such a strengths-based approach, students can become empowered to continue the helpful practices they are already doing and to make positive changes.

Having consistency in rising and bedtimes is key for optimal neurotransmitter and hormonal functioning. Ideally, sleep would not be interrupted, allowing for a feeling of being rested upon waking up. Generally, we need approximately one hour of sleep for every two hours that we are awake. Thus, the recommended duration of sleep is between seven and nine hours.

Knowing when to sleep involves not only looking at the clock and deciding to go to bed by a certain time, but also being sensitive to the signals the body is sending about falling asleep. Some of these signals include a drop in the body's temperature, droopy eyes, and difficulty concentrating or reading.

Sedentary activities such as watching TV, internet surfing, playing video games, and working on the computer for extended periods of time have a negative effect on physical activity energy expenditure.[53] In other words, food intake outweighs the energy spent during those activities. Particularly when watching TV, one may get in the habit of snacking even when hunger cues are not present. The negative effects of this behavior may include weight gain and high cholesterol. Exercise is recommended as an activity that can counter this behavior and has been proven to promote better sleep quality (see Chapter 5 for more information on exercising).

There seems to be a strong cultural belief in the United States that time not spent working is a waste of time. Naps tend to fall into this category. Why sleep when you can be productive? The 9 a.m. to 5 p.m. workday is certainly not conducive to napping in the middle of the day. The National Sleep Foundation recommends short naps as a way to get a boost of energy and increase alertness. A twenty-minute nap is ideal for refreshing the mind. Sleeping longer than that may have the opposite effect of feeling more tired and sleepy, especially if one is awakened from deep sleep. A long nap, or one that occurs after 3 p.m., may also interfere with nighttime sleep.

Here is a summary of guidelines for good sleep hygiene that you can share with your students:

- Maintain a sleep/wake routine as best you can.
- Respond to sleepiness cues and sleep when your body is telling you to do so.
- Keep screens and technology out of the bedroom.
- Avoid looking at screens about an hour before bedtime, or use blue-light blocking glasses to mitigate the waking effect of screen light.
- Dim the lights one hour before sleeping.
- Keep your room very dark (almost like a cave environment).
- Avoid eating a heavy meal close to bedtime.
- Limit alcohol and avoid caffeine intake.
- Exercise regularly, but not too close to bedtime.
- Go outside for at least one hour per day.
- Investigate if prescription drugs may be affecting your sleep.
- If you have trouble falling sleep, get up and do a relaxing activity until you feel sleepy.
- Try a calming activity before sleeping, such as
  - Journaling
  - Listening to music

- Reading a book (not related to coursework preferably!)
- Enjoying a cup of herbal tea
- Having a warm shower or bath
- Lying on your bed or floor with legs up the wall
- Practicing breathing meditation.

Nutrition and sleep are topics that deserve more attention among musicians. Fueling our body with a well-rounded diet and respecting our basic need for sleep help us take steps toward a more balanced life.

Sleep and Nutrition Toolkit

Sleep Diary

I recommend using the National Sleep Foundation's detailed sleep diary, which is available on their website (visit the companion website for the link ▶). The diary is to be completed in the morning and at night. Information tracked includes sleep/wake-up times, naps, exercise, medication, mood, and sleep quality. This is a useful resource for students trying to improve their sleep patterns and to understand what gets in the way of them getting restful and sufficient sleep.

Insomnia Resources

Epworth's Sleepiness Scale is a useful tool for measuring sleepiness and whether there is a need to seek medical attention. Another resource is the Insomnia Severity Index, which is a validated and reliable questionnaire for detecting insomnia. Links to both resources are available on the companion website ▶.

Nutrition Diary

Keeping a nutrition diary, such as the one shown on Table 9.4, can be a helpful way to monitor meals, hunger cues, and mood. The diary can be kept for one or two weeks, followed by a reflection on eating habits as they relate to mood and sleep (Worksheet 9.1 ▶).

Mindful Eating Meditation

Mindful eating calls for slowing down the eating process and tuning into the sensations of the body right before, during, and after eating. Through paying

Table 9.4 Nutrition Diary

Date:	
Meal 1/Snack 1	What I ate and drank:
	Why I ate:
	Hunger rating: 1 2 3 4 5
	Mood:
	Feeling right after:
	Feeling 2–3 hours after:
Meal 2/Snack 2	What I ate and drank:
	Why I ate:
	Hunger rating: 1 2 3 4 5
	Mood:
	Feeling right after:
	Feeling 2–3 hours after:
Meal 3/Snack 3	What I ate and drank:
	Why I ate:
	Hunger rating: 1 2 3 4 5
	Mood:
	Feeling right after:
	Feeling 2–3 hours after:
Meal 4/Snack 4	What I ate and drank:
	Why I ate:
	Hunger rating: 1 2 3 4 5
	Mood:
	Feeling right after:
	Feeling 2–3 hours after:
Meal 5/Snack 5	What I ate and drank:
	Why I ate:
	Hunger rating: 1 2 3 4 5
	Mood:
	Feeling right after:
	Feeling 2–3 hours after:

Reflection

Total hours of sleep:

Describe the quality of your sleep:

Did you have any cravings today?

Were there any triggers in your thoughts or environment that urged you to eat?

What were your reasons for eating?

Did you try something new today?

attention to the sensations that come up, we can stay focused on the present moment and fully enjoy the food we are eating. I always include a mindful eating experience as part of my class with either a raisin or a small chocolate. Some students absolutely hate the fact that they are instructed to be patient and not immediately chow down on a delicious piece of chocolate. Others find it relaxing and thoroughly enjoyable to savor every bite of their treat. One student reflected in her journal about the experience of mindful eating:

> This class really opened my eyes of how I would go about eating food. I would never really enjoy a meal when things are busy, because I didn't think it was really possible when there was little time to enjoy it. I am very glad to be wrong on that thought. When we practiced mindful eating in class with a piece of chocolate, it reminded me that I've felt this feeling before, of enjoying something in the moment, but it has been a long time since I have. It really reminded me that I can go back to that kind of practice because I've done it before; even if I have a busy day or I'm restricted with time to eat, now I take steps to really enjoy every time I have a meal or eat something small. I make sure that I'm not distracted by anything else and I can have a nice place to sit and just be mindful of how food tastes, what it smells like, all of the enjoyment from it makes simple things like eating such a better experience.

One key point the student talked about in this reflection is that we don't necessarily need to set aside more time for eating; rather, the mindfulness comes from the way we pay attention to the sensations that come up while eating. Please visit the companion website for a guided mindful eating meditation (Audio 9.1 ▶).

✳✳✳

Nutrition and sleep, although traditionally not discussed within the context of health for the musician, deserve to be addressed concurrently with other dimensions. If we are to remain true to the Eight Dimensions of Wellness model introduced in Chapter 1, we must acknowledge the impact of food and drink intake on sleep (and vice versa), as well as the cumulative effects of these two areas on the other dimensions. What we eat affects our physical strength and mood. Financial stability drives the quality of the food we can afford. In some cultures, meals are a social affair, a time to reconnect with others, which in turn has stress-relieving effects. Similarly, sleep affects all areas of our well-being. Restful sleep positively affects our concentration, memory, ability to handle strong emotions, and food cravings. Considering the enormous impact these two areas have on students' overall well-being, when questions come up about pre-performance meals, hydration, snacking, or sleep routine, they deserve to be addressed to the degree that you are comfortable with. The suggestions in this chapter regarding eating wholesome, colorful meals in a leisurely manner, and developing good sleep hygiene habits, may be pieces of advice you can readily share with students. As always, when you suspect a high-level concern (such as an eating disorder or disturbed sleep that significantly impacts learning), encourage your student to speak to a healthcare professional.

***

If you are reading this, pat yourself on the back. You must be a committed teacher who deeply cares about your students' well-being and professional success. You took the time to sift through research, background information on all-things-wellness, and explored hands-on activities you can use in your lessons (and maybe you even tried some out yourself). You are now equipped with tools and strategies to tackle difficult conversations, teach your students injury-prevention techniques, encourage protective mental health practices, and help them connect to their inner world through movement and contemplative practices. In other words, you are ready to teach the whole musician. Your students will remember the impact you had on them long after their lessons are done. Through the power of a mentorship practice that supports wellness in a personalized, holistic manner, your students will attain the capabilities to realize their full potential and sustain thriving careers in the arts. Go forth and be well!

Notes

Chapter 1

1. World Health Organization, "Constitution of the World Health Organization," 2000, https://www.who.int/governance/eb/who_constitution_en.pdf.
2. World Health Organization, "Health Promotion Glossary Update," September 2005, https://www.who.int/healthpromotion/about/HPR%20Glossary_New%20Terms.pdf.
3. Matthew Gallagher, "Well-being," in *The Encyclopedia of Positive Psychology*, ed. Shane J. Lopez (Malden, MA: Blackwell, 2009): 1030–1034.
4. Mihaly Csikszentmihalyi, *Flow: The Psychology of Optimal Experience* (New York: Harper Perennial Modern Classics, 2008).
5. Richard M. Ryan and Edward L. Deci, "On Happiness and Human Potentials: A Review of Research on Hedonic and Eudaimonic Well-being," *Annual Review of Psychology* 52 (2001): 141–166.
6. John Coffey et al., "Multi Study Examination of Well-being Theory in College and Community Samples," *Journal of Happiness Studies* 17, no. 1 (February 2016): 187–211.
7. Gallagher, "Well-being."
8. Corey L. M. Keyes, "Promoting and Protecting Mental Health as Flourishing: A Complementary Strategy for Improving National Mental Health," *American Psychologist* 62, no. 2 (February–March 2007): 95–108.
9. Richard M. Ryan and Edward L. Deci, "Self-Determination Theory and the Facilitation of Intrinsic Motivation, Social Development and Well-being," *American Psychologist* 55, no. 1 (January 2000): 68–78.
10. Ryan and Deci, "On Happiness and Human Potentials," 146–147.
11. Ibid., 145.
12. National Wellness Institute, "Six Dimensions of Wellness," accessed 11 November 2020, https://nationalwellness.org/resources/six-dimensions-of-wellness.
13. David J. Anspaugh et al., *Wellness: Concepts and Applications* (New York: McGraw Hill, 2011), 7.
14. Ibid.
15. American College Health Association, "American College Health Association–National College Health Assessment II: Reference Group Executive Summary Spring 2019," *American College of Sports Medicine and the American Heart Association* (Silver Spring, MD, 2019): 12.
16. Ibid., 5.
17. Liliana S. Araújo et al., "Fit to Perform: An Investigation of Higher Education Music Students' Perceptions, Attitudes, and Behaviors toward Health," *Frontiers in Psychology* 8 (October 2018): 1–19; Ron Roberts et al., "Mental and Physical Health in Students: The Role of Economic Circumstances," *British Journal of Health Psychology* 5 (December 2010): 289–297; Sarah Stewart-Brown et al., "The Health of Students in Institutes of Higher Education: An Important and Neglected Public Health Problem?" *Journal of Public Health* 22, no. 4 (December 2000): 492–499.
18. To view the most recent survey data and highlights, visit www.acha-ncha.org.
19. Jane Ginsborg et al., "Healthy Behaviours in Music and Non-music Performance Students," *Health Education* 109, no. 3 (2009): 242–258.

20. Claudia Spahn et al., "Health Conditions, Attitudes Toward Study, and Attitudes Toward Health at the Beginning of University Study: Music Students in Comparison with Other Student Populations," *Medical Problems of Performing Artists* 19, no. 1 (March 2004): 26–33.

21. Araújo et al., "Fit to Perform," 1.

22. Ibid.

23. Horst Hildebrandt et al., "Increment of Fatigue, Depression, and Stage Fright during First Year of High-Level Education in Music Students," *Medical Problems of Performing Artists* 27, no. 1 (March 2012): 43–48; Ioulia Papageorgi et al., "Perceived Performance Anxiety in Advanced Musicians Specializing in Different Musical Genres," *Psychology of Music* 41, no. 1 (2013): 18–41.

24. Rosie Perkins et al., "Perceived Enablers and Barriers to Optimal Health among Music Students: A Qualitative Study in the Music Conservatoire Setting," *Frontiers in Psychology* 8, article 968 (June 2017): 1–15.

25. Ibid., 7.

26. Spahn et al., "Health Conditions"; Kreutz Gunter et al., "Health-Promoting Behaviours in Conservatoire Students," *Psychology of Music* 37 (2009): 47–60.

27. Kris Chesky et al., "Health Promotion in Schools of Music: Initial Recommendations for Schools of Music," *Medical Problems of Performing Artists* 21, no. 3 (September 2006): 143.

28. Martin Fishbein et al., "Medical Problems among ICSOM Musicians: Overview of a National Survey," *Medical Problems of Performing Artists* 3, no. 1 (March 1988): 1–8.

29. Deborah Pierce, "Rising to a New Paradigm: Infusing Health and Wellness into the Music Curriculum," *Philosophy of Music Education* 20, no. 2 (Fall 2012): 165. Deborah Pierce researched library databases in an effort to understand the publications around the topic of musicians' wellness. See her article "Reaching Beyond Traditional Boundaries: The Librarian and Musicians' Health," *Notes* 67, no. 1 (September 2010): 50–67, for the history of the performing arts medicine field and how publications have evolved.

30. Chesky et al., "Health Promotion in Schools of Music," 143.

31. National Association of Schools of Music, *Handbook 2018–2019* (Reston, VA: NASM, January 2019), 67.

32. Judy Palac, "How NASM Schools Are Addressing the Music Health and Safety Standard: A Website Analysis," poster presentation, Performing Arts Medicine Association Symposium, Snowmass, CO, July 2017.

Chapter 2

1. Belle Rose Ragins and Kathy Kram, "The Roots and Meaning of Mentorship," in *The Handbook of Mentoring at Work: Theory, Research and Practice* (Thousand Oaks, CA: Sage, 2007), 3–15.

2. Tammy D. Allen et al., "Career Benefits Associated with Mentoring for Protégés: A Meta-Analysis," *Journal of Applied Psychology* 89 (2004): 127–136.

3. Kathy Kram, "Phases of the Mentor Relationship," *The Academy of Management Journal* 26, no. 4 (December 1983): 613–621.

4. Laurent A. Daloz, *Mentor: Guiding the Journey of Adult Learners* (San Francisco: Jossey-Bass, 2012).

5. Ibid., 42.

6. I consulted the following resources to create this list: Michael V. Smith, "Characteristics of Successful Mentor-Mentee Relationships: Mentoring Principles," in *Handbook for the Music Mentor*, Colleen Marie Conway, Michael V. Smith, and Thomas M. Hodgman (Chicago: GIA Publications, 2010): 293–309; Laurent A. Daloz, *Effective Teaching and Mentoring: Realizing the Transformational Power of Adult Learning Experiences* (London: Jossey-Bass, 1986).

7. Daloz, *Effective Teaching and Mentoring*, 237.

Chapter 3

1. Alan H. Lockwood, "Medical Problems in Secondary School-Aged Musicians," *Medical Problems of Performing Artists* 3, no. 4 (1988): 129–132; Lars-Goran Larsson et al., "Nature and Impact of Musculoskeletal Problems in a Population of Musicians," *Medical Problems of Performing Artists* 8, no. 3 (1993): 73–76; Kathryn E. Roach, Marcelo A. Martinez, and Nicole Anderson, "Musculoskeletal Pain in Student Instrumentalists: A Comparison with the General Student Population," *Medical Problems of Performing Artists* 9, no. 4 (1994): 125–130.

2. Ackermann Bronwen, Dianna Kenny, and James Fortune, "Incidence of Injury and Attitudes to Injury Management in Skilled Flute Players," *Work* 40 (2011): 255–259.

3. Martin Fishbein et al., "Medical Problems among ICSOM Musicians: Overview of a National Survey," *Medical Problems of Performing Artists* 3, no. 1 (March 1988): 1–8.

4. Karen Engquist, Palle Orbaek, and Kristina Jacobson, "Musculoskeletal Pain and Impact on Performance in Orchestra Musicians and Actors," *Medical Problems of Performing Artists* 19, no. 2 (June 2004): 55–61.

5. Jeremy L. Stanek, Kevin D. Komes, and Fred A. Murdock, "A Cross-Sectional Study of Pain among US College Music Students and Faculty," *Medical Problems of Performing Artists* 32, no. 1 (March 2017): 20–26.

6. Musicians with joint laxity or hypermobility (commonly known as double-jointedness) must take particular care when working on alignment, as they are at greater risk of playing-related injury (Alice G. Brandfonbrenen, "Joint Laxity and Arm Pain in a Large Clinical Sample of Musicians," *Medical Problems of Performing Artists* 17, no. 3 (September 2002): 113–115). Joint laxity is genetic and is characterized by hyperflexibility in the tendons and ligaments. Research by Alice Brandfonbrenen on a large sample of musicians defined hypermobility in the metacarpophalangeal and proximal interphalangeal finger joints as the ability to extend the joints beyond 10 degrees. In a sampling of approximately 2,400 musicians, about 35 percent of female musicians and 17 percent of male musicians had significant hypermobility associated with lower-arm pain. This indicates that hypermobility is a serious (although not the only) risk factor for injuries.

7. Eckart Altenmüller and Hans-Christian Jabusch, "Focal Dystonia in Musicians: Phenomenology, Pathophysiology, Triggering Factors, and Treatment," *Medical Problems of Performing Artists* 25, no. 1 (2010): 3–9.

8. Ibid., 3.

9. Cataldo Patruno et al., "Instrument-Related Skin Disorders in Musicians," *Dermatitis* 27, no. 1 (January–February 2016): 26–29.

10. Alan H. Watson, *The Biology of Musical Performance and Performance-Related Injury* (Lanham, MD: Scarecrow Press, 2009), 6–8.

11. Stanek et al., "A Cross-Sectional Study of Pain," 24.

12. Ackermann et al., "Incidence of Injury and Attitudes to Injury Management," 258.

13. Hunter J. H. Fry, "Overuse Syndrome of the Upper Limb in Musicians," *The Medical Journal of Australia* 144 (February 1986): 183.

14. Watson, *The Biology of Musical Performance and Performance-Related Injury*, 174–175.

15. Wendy LeBorgne and Marci Daniels Rosenberg, *The Vocal Athlete*, 2nd ed. (San Diego, CA: Plural, 2019), 110.

16. Ibid., 111.

17. Ibid., 118–119.

18. Leda Scearce, "Multidisciplinary Care of the Vocal Athlete," in *The Vocal Athlete*, 2nd ed., ed. Wendy LeBorgne and Marci Daniels Rosenberg (San Diego: Plural, 2019), 186.

19. Elizabeth Ford Baldner and Marci Rosenberg, "Interdisciplinary Management of the Professional Voice—A Hybrid Approach" (presentation at the Performing Arts Medicine & Rehabilitation Symposium, University of Michigan, Ann Arbor, MI, October 11, 2019).

20. US Department of Health and Human Services National Institute of Deafness and Other Communication Disorders, "Quick Statistics about Hearing Health, December 2016," https://www.nidcd.nih.gov/health/statistics/quick-statistics-hearing.

21. Paul Kileny and Allie Heckman, "Hearing Loss and the Performing Arts Student," (presentation at the Performing Arts Medicine & Rehabilitation Symposium, University of Michigan, Ann Arbor, MI, October 11, 2019).

22. Marshall Chasin, "Hearing Aids for Musicians: Understanding and Managing the Four Key Physical Differences between Music and Speech," *The Hearing Review* (March 2006): 24.

23. Cecil W. Hart et al., "The Musician and Occupational Sound Hazards," *Medical Problems of Performing Artists* 2, no. 3 (1987): 22–25.

24. Susan L. Phillips, Vincent C. Henrich, and Sandra T. Mace, "Prevalence of Noise-Induced Hearing Loss in Student Musicians," *International Journal of Audiology* 49, no. 4 (2010): 309–316.

25. Susan L. Phillips et al., "Environmental Factors in Susceptibility to Noise-Induced Hearing Loss in Student Musicians," *Medical Problems of Performing Artists* 23, no. 1 (March 2008): 20–28.

26. US Department of Health and Human Services, Centers for Disease Control and Prevention and National Institute for Occupational Safety, "Workplace Solutions: Reducing the Risk of Hearing Disorders among Musicians, June 2015," https://www.cdc.gov/niosh/docs/wp-solutions/2015-184/pdfs/2015-184.pdf.

27. Kris Chesky et al., "An Evaluation of Musician Earplugs with College Music Students," *International Journal of Audiology* 48, no. 9 (2009): 661–670.

Chapter 4

1. Patricia Blanco-Piñeiro, M. Pino Díaz-Pereira, and Aurora Martínez Vidal, "Variation in Posture Quality across Musical Instruments and Its Impact during Performances," *International Journal of Occupational Safety and Ergonomics* 24, no. 2 (2018): 316–323.

2. Teresia Nyman et al., "Work Postures and Neck-Shoulder Pain among Orchestra Musicians," *American Journal of Industrial Medicine* 50 (2007): 370.

3. Ibid.

4. Ann Shoebridge, Nora Shields, and Kate E. Webster, "Minding the Body: An Interdisciplinary Theory of Optimal Posture for Musicians," *Psychology of Music* 45, no. 6 (2017): 822.

5. Ibid., 821.

6. Ibid., 825.

7. Melissa Malde, MaryJean Allen, and Kurt-Alexander Zeller, *What Every Singer Needs to Know about the Body* (San Diego: Plural, 2013), 2.

8. Jan Dommerhold, "Performing Arts Medicine: Instrumentalist Musicians, Part II—Examination," *Journal of Bodywork & Movement Therapies* 14 (2010): 65–72.

9. Hankyu Park and Dongwook Han, "The Effect of the Correlation between the Contraction of the Pelvic Floor Muscles and Diaphragmatic Motion during Breathing," *Journal of Physical Therapy Science* 27, no. 7 (2015): 2113–2115.

10. Elżbieta Szczygieł et al., "The Impact of Deep Muscle Training on the Quality of Posture and Breathing," *Journal of Motor Behavior* 50, no. 2 (2018): 219–227.

11. Theodore Dimon, *The Anatomy of the Voice: An Illustrated Guide for Singers, Vocal Coaches, and Speech Therapists* (Berkeley, CA: North Atlantic Books, 2018), 17.

12. Bronwen J. Ackermann, Nicholas O'Dwyer, and Mark Halaki, "The Difference between Standing and Sitting in 3 Different Seat Inclinations on Abdominal Muscle Activity and Chest and Abdominal Expansion in Woodwind and Brass Musicians," *Frontiers in Psychology* 5, article 913 (August 2014): 1–9.

13. Ali Albarrati et al., "Effect of Upright and Slouched Sitting Postures on the Respiratory Muscle Strength in Healthy Young Males," *BioMed Research International* 10 (2018): 1–5.

14. Ibid., 4.

15. Kevin Price, Philippe Schartz, and Alan H. D. Watson, "The Effect of Standing and Sitting Postures on Breathing in Brass Players," *SpringerPlus* 3, no. 210 (2014): 1–17.

16. Daniela Ohlendorf et al., "Influence of Ergonomic Layout of Musician Chairs on Posture and Seat Pressure in Musicians of Different Playing Levels," *PLOS One* 13, no. 2 (December 11, 2018): 1–14.

Chapter 5

1. National Association of Schools of Music and Performing Arts Medicine Association, "NASM-PAMA Advisories on Neuromusculoskeletal and Vocal Health," https://nasm.arts-accredit.org/publications/brochures-advisories/nasm-pama-nms-vocal-health (accessed May 12, 2020); National Association of Schools of Music and Performing Arts Medicine Association, "NASM-PAMA Advisories on Hearing Health," https://nasm.arts-accredit.org/publications/brochures-advisories/nasm-pama-hearing-health (accessed May 12, 2020).

2. William J. Dawson, *Fit as a Fiddle: The Musician's Guide to Playing Healthy* (Lanham, MD: Rowman & Littlefield, 2008); Gerald Klickstein, *The Musician's Way: A Guide to Practice, Performance, and Wellness* (New York: Oxford University Press, 2009); Christine Zaza, "Research-Based Prevention for Musicians," *Medical Problems of Performing Artists* 9, no. 1 (March 1994): 3–6.

3. US Department of Health and Human Services, *Physical Activity Guidelines for Americans*, 2nd ed. (Washington, DC: US Department of Health and Human Services, 2018), https://health.gov/paguidelines/second-edition/pdf/Physical_Activity_Guidelines_2nd_edition.pdf.

4. Bronwen Ackermann, Dianna Kenny, and James Fortune, "Incidence of Injury and Attitudes to Injury Management in Skilled Flute Players," *Work* 40 (2011): 255–259.

5. Ibid., 258.

6. Janet Davies, "Alexander Technique Classes Improve Pain and Performance Factors in Tertiary Music Students," *Journal of Bodywork and Movement Therapies* 24, no. 1 (January 2020): 1–7.

7. Catherine Lee, "Musicians as Movers: Applying the Feldenkrais Method to Music Education," *Music Educators Journal* 104, no. 4 (June 2018): 15–19.

8. Ibid., 16.

9. Judith R. S. Stern, Sat Bir S. Khalsa, and Stefan Hofmann, "A Yoga Intervention for Music Performance Anxiety in Conservatory Students," *Medical Problems of Performing Artists* 27, no. 3 (September 2012): 123–128.

10. Sat Bir S. Khalsa et al., "Yoga Ameliorates Performance Anxiety and Mood Disturbance in Young Professional Musicians," *Applied Psychophysiological Biofeedback* 34 (2009): 279–289.

11. María Luciana Gallo, "Pilates and String Musicians: An Exploration of the Issues Addressed by the Pilates Method, an Illustrated Guide to Adapted Exercises, and a Pilates Course for University String Players" (DMA diss., Arizona State University, May 2017), 18, 20, 21, 26.

12. Michael Salvatore, "Pilates Alleviates Common Injuries Suffered by Musicians," *International Musician* 111, no. 12 (December 2013): 12–13.

13. Friedrich Molsberger and Albrecht Molsberger, "Acupuncture in the Treatment of Musculoskeletal Disorders of Orchestra Musicians," *Work* 41 (2012): 5–13.

14. Clair Davies, "Musculoskeletal Pain from Repetitive Strain in Musicians: Insights into an Alternative Approach," *Medical Problems of Performing Artists* 17, no. 1 (March 2002): 42–49.

Chapter 6

1. Sophia Dahl and Anders Friberg, "Visual Perception of Expressiveness in Musicians' Body Movements," *Music Perception* 24 (June 2007): 433–454; Bradley Vines et al., "Performance

Gestures of Musicians: What Structural and Emotional Information do they Convey?" in *Gesture-Based Communication in Human–Computer Interaction: 5th International Gesture Workshop*, eds. A. Camurri and G. Volpe (Genova, Italy: Springer-Verlag, 2004), 468–478; Marcelo Wanderley and Claude Cadoz, "Gesture-Music," in *Trends in Gestural Control of Music*, eds. Marc Battier and Marcelo Wanderley (Paris: IRCAM Research Institute, 2000), 71–94.

2. Jane W. Davidson, "Visual Perception of Performance Manner in the Movements of Solo Musicians," *Psychology of Music* 21, no. 2 (1993): 103–113.

3. Mary Broughton and Catherine Stevens, "Analyzing Expressive Qualities in Movement and Stillness: Effort-Shape Analyses of Solo Marimbists' Bodily Expression," *Music Perception* 29, no. 4 (April 2012): 339–357.

4. Dahl and Friberg, "Visual Perception of Expressiveness in Musicians' Body Movements."

5. Giuseppe di Pellegrino et al., "Understanding Motor Events: A Neurophysiological Study," *Experimental Brain Research* 91 (1992): 176–180.

6. Lois Svard, "The Musician's Guide to the Brain: How to Use Brain Science in the Study of Music," *MTNA eJournal* 1, no. 3 (February 2010): 2–11.

7. Anthony Tommasini, "Two Pianists: A Virtuoso and a Philosophizer," *New York Times*, July 24, 2009, https://www.nytimes.com/2009/07/24/arts/music/24keyboard.html.

8. Deane Juhan, *Job's Body: A Handbook for Bodywork* (Barrytown, NY: Barrytown, 1998), 234.

9. Alexander Rufsum Jensenius et al., "Musical Gestures: Concepts and Methods Research," in *Musical Gestures*, eds. Rolfe Inge Godøy and Marc Leman (New York: Routledge, 2010), 23.

10. Rudolf Laban (1879–1958)—a dancer, choreographer, and movement theoretician—laid the foundation for twentieth-century European modern dance. He was born in Bratislava and traveled extensively in European cities with his father, a military governor. Traveling exposed him to the folk dances of different countries. A true Renaissance man, he studied art, architecture, theater, and mime. His other interests included music composition, piano, crystallography, and painting. But in spite of his widely varied interests, dance was his passion. He dedicated his life to the study of movement.

11. Broughton and Stevens, "Analyzing Expressive Qualities in Movement and Stillness"; Erica Jean Neidlinger, "The Effect of Laban Effort-Shape Instruction on Young Conductors' Perception of Expressiveness Across Arts Disciplines," PhD diss., University of Minnesota (2003); Ginevra Castellano et al., "Automated Analysis of Body Movement in Emotionally Expressive Piano Performances," *Music Perception: An Interdisciplinary Journal* 26, no. 2 (December 2008): 103–119.

12. Charles Gambetta, "Conducting Outside the Box: Creating a Fresh Approach to Conducting Gesture through the Principles of Laban Movement Analysis," DMA diss., University of North Carolina at Greensboro (2005); Timothy G. Yontz, "The Effectiveness of Laban-Based Principles of Movement and Previous Musical Training on Undergraduate Beginning Conducting Students' Ability to Convey Intended Musical Content," Ph.D. diss., University of Nebraska (2001); Janine Riveire, "Bowing 'Qualities,' Laban and Motion Factors," *American String Teacher* 56, no. 4 (August 2006): 36–39.

13. Peggy Hackney, *Making Connections: Total Body Integration through Bartenieff Fundamentals* (Amsterdam: Gordon and Breach, 1998), 31.

14. Ibid., 7.

15. Linda Hartley, *Wisdom of the Body Moving: An Introduction to Body–Mind Centering* (Berkeley, CA: North Atlantic Books, 1995).

16. Hackney, *Making Connections*, 34.

17. Irmgard Bartenieff and Dori Lewis, *Body Movement: Coping with the Environment* (New York: Gordon and Breach Science, 1980), 21.

18. Hackney, *Making Connections*, 67.

19. Ibid., 174.

20. Ibid., 179.

21. Bartenieff and Lewis, *Body Movement*, 53.
22. Ibid., 56.
23. Broughton and Stevens, "Analyzing Expressive Qualities in Movement and Stillness," 343.

Chapter 7

1. Jenny K. Hyun et al., "Graduate Student Mental Health: Needs Assessment and Utilization of Counseling Services," *Journal of College Student Development* 47, no. 3 (May–June 2006): 247–266.
2. Sherry A. Benton et al., "Changes in Counseling Client Problems across 13 Years," *Professional Psychology: Research and Practice* 34, no. 1 (2003): 68–72.
3. H. Christian Bernhard II, "Burnout and the College Music Education Major," *Journal of Music Teacher Education* 15, no. 1 (Fall 2005): 43–51.
4. Hyun et al., "Graduate Student Mental Health," 255.
5. Jenny Chanfreau et al., *Predicting Wellbeing* (London: NatCen Social Research for U.K. Department of Health, August 2013), 6.
6. American Psychiatric Association, *Diagnostic and Statistical Manual of Mental Disorders*, 5th ed. [DSM-5] (Arlington, VA: American Psychiatric Association, 2013), 20.
7. David Robotham and Claire Julian, "Stress and the Higher Education Student: A Critical Review of the Literature," *Journal of Further and Higher Education* 30, no. 2 (2006): 112.
8. Roger Chaffin and Anthony F. Lemieux, "General Perspectives on Achieving Musical Excellence," in *Musical Excellence*, ed. Aaron Williamon (New York: Oxford University Press, 2004).
9. Sarath A. Nonis et al., "Influence of Perceived Control over Time on College Students' Stress and Stress-Related Outcomes," *Research in Higher Education* 39, no. 5 (1998): 587–605.
10. Helen M. Stallman, "Psychological Distress in University Students: A Comparison with General Population Data," *Australian Psychologist* 45, no. 4 (December 2010): 255.
11. Ibid., 254.
12. Dianna Kenny and Bronwen Ackermann, "Performance-Related Musculoskeletal Pain, Depression and Music Performance Anxiety in Professional Orchestral Musicians: A Population Study," *Psychology of Music* 43, no. 1 (2015): 43–60.
13. Dianna T. Kenny, *The Psychology of Music Performance Anxiety* (New York: Oxford University Press, 2011), 19.
14. Ibid., 92.
15. Michael E. Sadler and Christopher J. Miller, "Performance Anxiety: A Longitudinal Study of the Roles of Personality and Experience in Musicians," *Social Psychological and Personality Science* 1, no. 3 (2010): 280–287.
16. Aaron Williamon and Sam Thompson, "Awareness and Incidence of Health Problems among Conservatoire Students," *Psychology of Music* 34, no. 4 (2006): 411–430.
17. Margaret S. Osborne et al., "Managing Performance Anxiety and Improving Mental Skills in Conservatoire Students through Performance Psychology Training: A Pilot Study," *Psychology of Well-Being: Theory Research and Practice* 4, no. 18 (2014): 2–17.
18. Debra J. Brody et al., "Prevalence of Depression among Adults Ages 20 and Over: United States, 2013–2016," *NCHS Data Brief* 303, US Department of Health and Human Services (February 2018).
19. For more specifics on all forms of depression, see the DSM-5.
20. Claudia Spahn et al., "Health Conditions, Attitudes toward Study, and Attitudes toward Health at the Beginning of University Study: Music Students in Comparison with Other Student Populations," *Medical Problems of Performing Artists* 19, no. 1 (March 2004): 26–33; Horst Hildebrandt et al., "Increment of Fatigue, Depression and Stage Fright during the First Year of High-Level Education in Music Students," *Medical Problems of Performing Artists* 27, no. 1 (March 2012): 43–48.

21. Megan E. Cowie et al., "Perfectionism and Academic Difficulties in Graduate Students: Testing Incremental Prediction and Gender Moderation," *Personality and Individual Differences* 123 (2018): 223–228.

22. DSM-5, 53.

23. Darcy Gruttadaro and Dana Crudo, *College Students Speak: A Survey Report on Mental Health* (Arlington, VA: National Alliance on Mental Illness, 2012), 15, https://www.nami.org/About-NAMI/Publications-Reports/Survey-Reports/College-Students-Speak_A-Survey-Report-on-Mental-H.pdf.

24. Ken Duckworth, "What to Do in a Crisis," National Alliance on Mental Illness, video, accessed April 14, 2019, https://www.nami.org/Find-Support/Living-with-a-Mental-Health-Condition/What-to-Do-In-a-Crisis.

25. Gruttadaro and Crudo, *College Students Speak*, 9.

26. This exercise has been adapted from the *Wellness Handbook for the Performing Artist* by Alena Gerst (Bloomington, IN: Balboa Press, 2014).

27. This exercise has been adapted from Don Greene's *11 Strategies for Audition and Performance Success: A Workbook for Musicians* (2012), http://psi.dongreene.com.

28. This exercise has been adapted from a handout created by the Counseling and Psychological Services at the University of Michigan.

Chapter 8

1. Heather A. Wadlinger and Derek M. Isaacowitz, "Fixing Our Focus: Training Attention to Regulate Emotion," *Personality and Social Psychology Review* 15, no. 1 (2011): 75–102.

2. Susan A. Ambrose et al., *How Learning Works: 7 Research-Based Principles for Smart Teaching* (San Francisco: Jossey-Bass, 2010), 198.

3. Antoine Lutz et al., "Attention Regulation and Monitoring in Meditation," *Trends in Cognitive Sciences* 12, no. 4 (April 2008): 163–169.

4. Daniel P. Barbezat and Mirabai Bush, *Contemplative Practices in Higher Education: Powerful Methods to Transform Teaching and Learning* (San Francisco: Jossey-Bass, 2014), 23.

5. Lutz et al., "Attention Regulation and Monitoring in Meditation," 91.

6. Wadlinger and Isaacowitz, "Fixing Our Focus: Training Attention to Regulate Emotion," 75.

7. Jon Kabat-Zinn, *Wherever You Go, There You Are* (New York: Hachette Books, 1994), 4.

8. Nicole D. Anderson et al., "Mindfulness-Based Stress Reduction and Attentional Control," *Clinical Psychology and Psychotherapy* 14 (2007): 449–463.

9. Richard J. Davidson et al., "Alterations in Brain and Immune Function Produced by Mindfulness Meditation," *Psychosomatic Medicine* 65, no. 4 (2003): 564–570.

10. Sameer A. Zope and Rakesh A. Zope, "Sudarshan Kriya Yoga: Breathing for Health," *International Journal of Yoga* 6 (Jan–June 2013): 4–10.

11. Jon Kabat-Zinn, *Full Catastrophe Living* (New York: Delta, 1991), 33–40.

12. Ibid., 50.

13. Barbezat and Bush, *Contemplative Practices in Higher Education*, 90.

14. Elizabeth Larson, "Stress in the Lives of College Women: 'Lots to Do and Not Much Time,'" *Journal of Adolescent Research* 21, no. 6 (November 2006): 579–606.

15. Richard P. Brown and Patricia Gerbarg, "Sudarshan Kriya Yogic Breathing in the Treatment of Stress, Anxiety, and Depression: Part I—Neurophysiologic Model," *The Journal of Alternative and Complementary Medicine* 11, no. 1 (2005): 190.

16. Marc A. Russo, Danielle M. Santarelli, and Dean O'Rourke, "The Physiological Effects of Slow Breathing in the Healthy Human," *Breathe* 13 (2017): 298–309.

17. Thaddeus W. W. Pace et al., "Effect of Compassion Meditation on Neuroendocrine, Innate Immune and Behavioral Responses to Psychosocial Stress," *Psychoneuroendocrinology* 31, no. 1 (January 2009): 87–98.

18. Mary Helen Immordino-Yang, *Emotions, Learning and the Brain: Exploring the Educational Implications of Affective Neuroscience*, Norton Series on the Social Neuroscience of Education (New York: W. W. Norton, 2016).

19. Patricia Monaghan, *Meditation—The Complete Guide: Techniques from East and West to Calm the Mind, Heal the Body, and Enrich the Spirit* (Novato, CA: New World Library, 1999), 78.

Chapter 9

1. Benedicte Deforche et al., "Changes in Weight, Physical Activity, Sedentary Behaviour and Dietary Intake during the Transition to Higher Education: A Prospective Study," *International Journal of Behavioral Nutrition and Physical Activity* 12, no. 16 (2015): 16, https://doi.org/10.1186/s12966-015-0173-9.

2. Meg Small et al., "Changes in Eating and Physical Activity Behaviors across Seven Semesters of College: Living on or off Campus Matters," *Health Education & Behavior* 40, no. 4 (August 2013): 435–441.

3. Terry K. Huang et al., "Assessing Overweight, Obesity, Diet, and Physical Activity in College Students," *Journal of American College Health* 52 (2003): 83–86.

4. Small et al., "Changes in Eating and Physical Activity Behaviors," 440.

5. US Department of Health and Human Services, "Adult Obesity Facts," Centers for Disease Control and Prevention (February 2020), https://www.cdc.gov/obesity/data/adult.html.

6. Huang et al., "Assessing Overweight, Obesity, Diet," 84–85.

7. Deforche et al., "Changes in Weight, Physical Activity, Sedentary Behaviour and Dietary Intake during the Transition to Higher Education."

8. Bhidha Das and Ellen M. Evans, "Assessing Weight Management Barriers in First-Year College Students," *Journal of American College Health* 62, no. 7 (2014): 488–497.

9. Emily Abbott, "How College Students Access Nutrition Information: A Study on Social Media and Health Literacy," Master's thesis, California State University, Long Beach (2018).

10. Eric Buhi et al., "An Observational Study of How Young People Search for Online Sexual Health Information," *Journal of American College Health* 58, no. 2 (2009): 101–111.

11. Karin Vitzthum et al., "Eating Behavior and Nutrition Knowledge among Musical Theatre Students," *Medical Problems of Performing Artists* 28, no. 1 (March 2013): 19–23.

12. US Department of Agriculture, "Ounce-Equivalent of Protein Foods Table," www.choosemyplate.gov/eathealthy/protein-foods (accessed May 5, 2020).

13. Bill Campbell, *Sports Nutrition: Enhancing Athletic Performance* (Boca Raton, FL: CRC Press, 2014), 12–14.

14. Evan Engelstad, "Pilot Study: Does Nutrition Affect the Musical Performance Experiences of Professional Pianists?" DMA diss., University of Wisconsin–Madison (2016), 12.

15. US Department of Health and Human Services, "Probiotics: What You Need to Know," National Center for Complementary and Integrative Health, 2019, https://nccih.nih.gov/health/probiotics/introduction.htm.

16. International Food Information Council Foundation, "2018 Food & Health Survey," 2018, https://foodinsight.org/wp-content/uploads/2018/05/2018-FHS-Report-FINAL.pdf.

17. US Department of Health and Human Services and US Department of Agriculture, *2015–2020 Dietary Guidelines for Americans*, 8th Edition (Washington D. C.: December 2015), http://health.gov/dietaryguidelines/2015/guidelines/.

18. US Department of Agriculture, "ChooseMyPlate," https://www.choosemyplate.gov.

19. Floyd R. Huebner et al., "Demonstration of High Opioid-Like Activity in Isolated Peptides from Wheat Gluten Hydrolysates," *Peptides* 5, no. 6 (1984): 1139–1147.

20. Kary Woodruff, *Sports Nutrition*, ed. Katie Ferraro (New York: Momentum Press, 2016).

21. Ibid., 85.

22. Institute of Medicine, *Dietary Reference Intakes: The Essential Guide to Nutrient Requirements* (Washington, DC: The National Academies Press, 2006), 155–156.

23. Mark A. Tarnopolsky, "Caffeine and Creatine Use in Sport," *Annals of Nutrition & Metabolism* 57 (February 2010): 1–8.

24. Kathryne Pirtle, *Performance without Pain: A Step-by-Step Nutritional Program for Healing Pain, Inflammation and Chronic Ailments in Musicians, Athletes, Dancers and Everyone Else* (Washington, DC: New Trends, 2006), 49.

25. Elizabeth Claydon and Keith Zullig, "Eating Disorders and Academic Performance among College Students," *Journal of American College Health* 68, no. 3 (January 2019): 1–6.

26. Daniel Eisenberg et al., "Eating Disorder Symptoms among College Students: Prevalence, Persistence, Correlates, and Treatment-Seeking," *Journal of American College Health* 59, no. 8 (September 2011): 700–707.

27. National Council for Behavioral Health, *Mental Health First Aid™ USA* (Washington, DC: National Council for Behavioral Health and the Missouri Department of Mental Health, 2015), 90.

28. Ibid., 145.

29. Anna M. Bardone-Cone et al., "Perfectionism across Stages of Recovery from Eating Disorders," *International Journal of Eating Disorders* 43, no. 2 (2010): 139–148.

30. Ibid., 145.

31. National Council for Behavioral Health, *Mental Health First Aid™ USA*, 91.

32. Ibid., 95.

33. American College Health Association, *American College Health Association–National College Health Assessment II: Reference Group Executive Summary Spring 2019* (Silver Spring, MD: American College of Sports Medicine and the American Heart Association, 2019), 5.

34. Monica E. Hartmann and J. Roxanne Prichard, "Calculating the Contribution of Sleep Problems to Undergraduates' Academic Success," *Sleep Health* 4 (2018): 463–471.

35. Victor R. Preedy, Vinood B. Patel, and Le Lan-Anh, *Handbook of Nutrition, Diet and Sleep*, Human Health Handbooks, no. 3 (Wageningen, The Netherlands: Wageningen Academic, 2013), 14.

36. Cary A. Brown, Pei Qin, and Shaniff Esmail, "'Sleep? Maybe Later . . .': A Cross-Campus Survey of University Students and Sleep Practices," *Education Sciences* 7, no. 66 (June 2017): 1–15. doi:10.3390/educsci7030066.

37. Michael H. Bonnet and Donna L. Arand, "Insomnia," in *Handbook of Nutrition, Diet and Sleep*, ed. Victor R. Preedy, Vinood B. Patel, and Le Lan-Anh (The Netherlands: Wageningen Academic, 2013), 29–35.

38. Ibid., 35.

39. Roxanne Prichard, "Causes and Consequences of Sleep Disruption: Implications for Accurate Diagnoses and Effective Treatment Plans," Depression on College Campuses Conference, University of Michigan, Ann Arbor, MI, 2019.

40. Gideon P. Dunster et al., "Sleepmore in Seattle: Later School Start Times Are Associated with More Sleep and Better Performance in High School Students," *Science Advances* 4, no. 12 (December 2018): eaau6200. doi:10.1126/sciadv.aau6200.

41. Ibid., 140.

42. Plamen Penev, "Sleep Deprivation and Human Energy Metabolism," in *Handbook of Nutrition, Diet and Sleep*, ed. Victor R. Preedy, Vinood B. Patel, and Le Lan-Anh, (Wageningen, The Netherlands: Wageningen Academic, 2013), 195.

43. M. J. Soares, A. Macedo, and M. H. Azevedo, "Sleep Disturbances and Eating Behavior in Undergraduate Students," in *Handbook of Nutrition, Diet and Sleep*, ed. Victor R. Preedy, Vinood B. Patel, and Le Lan-Anh (Wageningen, The Netherlands: Wageningen Academic, 2013), 147–149.

44. Ibid., 151.

45. Kenneth L. Lichstein, et al., "Vitamins and Sleep: An Exploratory Study," *Sleep Medicine* 9, no. 1 (September 2007): 27.

46. Surilla Randall, "Insomnia and Sleep Medications," in *Handbook of Nutrition, Diet and Sleep*, ed. Victor R. Preedy, Vinood B. Patel, and Le Lan-Anh (Wageningen, The Netherlands: Wageningen Academic, 2013), 51.

47. John Foster, "Alcohol and Sleep," in *Handbook of Nutrition, Diet and Sleep*, ed. Victor R. Preedy, Vinood B. Patel, and Le Lan-Anh, (Wageningen, The Netherlands: Wageningen Academic, 2013), 343.

48. Shawn D. Youngstedt, "Effects of Exercise on Sleep," *Clinics in Sports Medicine* 24, no. 2 (April 2005): 355–365.

49. Feifei Wang and Szilvia Boros, "The Effect of Physical Activity on Sleep Quality: A Systematic Review," *European Journal of Physiotherapy* 19 (June 2019): 1–8, https://doi.org/10.1080/21679169.2019.1623314.

50. Richard Johnston et al., "General Health Complaints and Sleep Associated with New Injury within an Endurance Sporting Population: A Prospective Study," *Journal of Science and Medicine in Sport* 23, no. 3 (2020): 252–257.

51. Matthew D. Milewski et al., "Chronic Lack of Sleep Is Associated with Increased Sports Injuries in Adolescent Athletes," *Journal of Pediatric Orthopaedics* 34, no. 2 (March 2014): 129–133.

52. Brown, Qin, and Esmail, "'Sleep? Maybe Later. . . .'"

53. Jessica McNeil, Éric Doucet, and Jean-Philippe Chaput, "Sleep, Sedentary Activity, and Weight Gain," in *Handbook of Nutrition, Diet and Sleep*, ed. Victor R. Preedy, Vinood B. Patel, and Le Lan-Anh (Wageningen, The Netherlands: Wageningen Academic, 2013), 212.

References

Abbott, Emily. "How College Students Access Nutrition Information: A Study on Social Media and Health Literacy." Master's thesis, California State University, Long Beach, 2018.

Ackermann, Bronwen, and Roger Adams. "Physical Characteristics and Pain Patterns of Skilled Violinists." *Medical Problems of Performing Artists* 81, no. 2 (June 2003): 65–71.

Ackermann, Bronwen, Roger Adams, and Elfreda Marshall. "Strength or Endurance Training for Undergraduate Music Majors at a University?" *Medical Problems of Performing Artists* 17, no. 1 (March 2002): 33–41.

Ackermann, Bronwen, Dianna Kenny, and James Fortune. "Incidence of Injury and Attitudes to Injury Management in Skilled Flute Players." *Work* 40 (2011): 255–259.

Ackermann, Bronwen, Dianna Kenny, Ian O'Brien, and Tim Driscoll. "Sound Practice: Improving Occupational Health and Safety for Professional Orchestral Musicians in Australia." *Frontiers in Psychology* 5, article no. 973 (September 2014): 1–11.

Ackermann, Bronwen, Nicholas O'Dwyer, and Mark Halaki. "The Difference between Standing and Sitting in 3 Different Seat Inclinations on Abdominal Muscle Activity and Chest and Abdominal Expansion in Woodwind and Brass Musicians." *Frontiers in Psychology* 5, article 913 (August 2014): 1–9.

Adams, Allison Dromgold. "Yoga and Saxophone Performance: The Integration of Two Disciplines." DMA diss., Arizona State University, 2012.

Adams, Christopher M., and Ana Puig. "Incorporating Yoga into College Counseling." *Journal of Creativity in Mental Health* 3, no. 4 (2008): 357–372.

Adams, Toy B., Janet R. Bezner, Mary E. Drabbs, Robert J. Zambarano, and Mary A. Steinhardt. "Conceptualization and Measurement of the Spiritual and Psychological Dimensions of Wellness in a College Population." *Journal of American College Health* 48, no. 4 (January 2000): 165–173.

Ajaya, Swami. *Yoga Psychology: A Practical Guide to Meditation*. Honesdale, PA: Himalayan Institute Press, 2008.

Albarrati, Ali, Hamayun Zafar, Ahmad H. Alghadir, and Shahnwaz Anwer. "Effect of Upright and Slouched Sitting Postures on the Respiratory Muscle Strength in Healthy Young Males." *BioMed Research International* 10 (2018): 1–5.

Alboher, Marci. *One Person/Multiple Careers: A New Model for Work/Life Success*. New York: Business Plus, 2007.

Allen, Tammy D., Lillian T. Eby, Mark L. Poteet, Elizabeth Lentz, and Lizzette Lima. "Career Benefits Associated with Mentoring for Protégés: A Meta-Analysis." *Journal of Applied Psychology* 89 (2004): 127–136.

Alman, Donald. *One-Minute Mindfulness: 50 Simple Ways to Find Peace, Clarity, and New Possibilities in a Stressed-Out World*. Novato, CA: New World Library, 2011.

Altenmüller, Eckart, and Hans-Christian Jabusch. "Focal Dystonia in Musicians: Phenomenology, Pathophysiology, Triggering Factors, and Treatment." *Medical Problems of Performing Artists* 25, no. 1 (2010): 3–9.

Ambrose, Susan A., Michael W. Bridges, Michele DiPietro, Marsha C. Lovett, and Marie K. Norman. *How Learning Works: 7 Research-Based Principles for Smart Teaching*. San Francisco: Jossey-Bass, 2010.

American College Health Association. *American College Health Association–National College Health Assessment II: Reference Group Executive Summary Spring 2019*. Silver Spring, MD: American College of Sports Medicine and the American Heart Association, 2019.

American Psychiatric Association. *Diagnostic and Statistical Manual of Mental Disorders*. 5th ed. [DSM-5]. Arlington, VA: American Psychiatric Association, 2013.

American Tinnitus Association. "Understanding the Facts." October 2018. www.ata.org/understanding-facts.

Anderson, Nicole D., Mark A. Lau, Zindel V. Segal, and Scott R. Bishop. "Mindfulness-Based Stress Reduction and Attentional Control." *Clinical Psychology and Psychotherapy* 14 (2007): 449–463.

Andrews, Elizabeth. *Healthy Practice for Musicians.* London: Rhinegold Publishing, 1997.

Andrews, Elizabeth. *Muscle Management for Musicians.* Lanham, MD: Scarecrow Press, 2005.

Anspaugh, David J., Michael H. Hamrick, and Frank D. Rosato. *Wellness: Concepts and Applications.* New York: McGraw Hill, 2011.

Araújo, Liliana S., David Wasley, Rosie Perkins, Louise Atkins, Emma Redding, Jane Ginsborg, and Aaron Williamon. "Fit to Perform: An Investigation of Higher Education Music Students' Perceptions, Attitudes, and Behaviors toward Health." *Frontiers in Psychology* 8 (October 2018): 1–19.

Arch, Joanna J., and Michelle G. Craske. "Mechanisms of Mindfulness: Emotion Regulation Following a Focused Breathing Induction." *Behaviour Research and Therapy* 44 (2006): 1849–1858.

Ares, Gastón, Ana Giménez, Leticia Vidal, Yanfeng Zhou, Athanasios Krystallis, George Tsalis, Ronan Symoneaux, Luis M. Cunha, Ana Pinto de Moura, Anna Claret, Luis Guerrero, Armand V. Cardello, Alan Wright, Laura Jefferies, Michelle Lloyd, Denize Oliveira, and Rosires Deliza. "Do We All Perceive Food-Related Wellbeing in the Same Way? Results from an Exploratory Cross-Cultural Study." *Food Quality and Preference* 52 (2016): 62–73.

Baadjou, Vera A. E., Marjon D. F. van Eijsden-Besseling, Ans L. W. Samama-Polak, Rob J. E. M. Smeets, Valéria Lima Passos, and Klaas R. Westerterp. "Energy Expenditure in Brass and Woodwind Instrumentalists: The Effect of Body Posture." *Medical Problems of Performing Artists* 26, no. 4 (December 2011): 218–223.

Baglin, Nina. "Making or Not Making the Grade Calmly." *The Guardian* (June 30, 2003). https://www.theguardian.com/education/2003/jun/30/studentwork.students.

Baker, Nancy Coyne. "Does Daily Meditation or Coherent Breathing Influence Perceived Stress, Stress Effects, Anxiety, or Holistic Wellness in College Freshmen and Sophomores?" PhD diss., Boston College, May 2012.

Barbezat, Daniel P., and Mirabai Bush. *Contemplative Practices in Higher Education: Powerful Methods to Transform Teaching and Learning.* San Francisco: Jossey-Bass, 2014.

Bardone-Cone, Anna M., Katrina Sturm, Melissa A. Lawson, D. Paul Robinson, and Roma Smith. "Perfectionism across Stages of Recovery from Eating Disorders." *International Journal of Eating Disorders* 43, no. 2 (2010): 139–148.

Barrett, Constance E. "What Every Musician Needs to Know about the Plan for Incorporating Body Mapping in Music Instruction." *American String Teacher* 56, no. 4 (November 2006): 34–37.

Barrett, Lisa Feldman, Michael Lewis, and Jeannette M. Haviland-Jones. *Handbook of Emotions,* 4th ed. New York: Guilford Press, 2016.

Bartenieff, Irmgard, and Dori Lewis. *Body Movement: Coping with the Environment.* New York: Gordon and Breach Science, 1980.

Begley, Sharon. *Train Your Mind, Change Your Brain.* New York: Ballantine Books, 2007.

Benton, Sherry A., John M. Robertson, Wen-Chih Tseng, Fred B. Newton, and Stephen L. Benton. "Changes in Counseling Client Problems across 13 Years." *Professional Psychology: Research and Practice* 34, no. 1 (2003): 68–72.

Bergen, Teresa. "The Yoga and Dance Connection." *India Currents* 26, no. 8 (2012).

Bernhard II, Christian H. "Burnout and the College Music Education Major." *Journal of Research in Music Education* 15, no. 1 (Fall 2005): 43–51.

Blanco-Piñeiro, Patricia, M. Pino Díaz-Pereira, and Aurora Martínez Vidal. "Variation in Posture Quality across Musical Instruments and Its Impact during Performances." *International Journal of Occupational Safety and Ergonomics* 24, no. 2 (2018): 316–323.

Bonetti, Ruth. *Taking Centre-Stage: How to Survive and Enjoy Performing in Public.* Sutherland, Australia: Albatross Books, 1997.

Brach, Tara. *How to Meditate: A Guide to Formal Sitting Practice.* Cabin John, MD: Insight Meditation Community of Washington, n.d.

Brandfonbrener, Alice G. "Joint Laxity and Arm Pain in a Large Clinical Sample of Musicians." *Medical Problems of Performing Artists* 17, no. 3 (September 2002): 113–115.

Brandfonbrener, Alice G. "Orchestral Injury Prevention Intervention Study." *Medical Problems of Performing Artists* 12, no. 1 (March 1997): 9–14.

Brill, Peggy W., and Susan Suffes. *Instant Relief: Tell Me Where It Hurts and I'll Tell You What to Do.* New York: Bantam Dell, 2003.

Brody, Debra J., Laura A. Pratt, and Jeffery P. Hughes. "Prevalence of Depression among Adults Ages 20 and Over: United States, 2013–2016." *NCHS Data Brief* 303, US Department of Health and Human Services (February 2018).

Broughton, Mary, and Catherine Stevens. "Analyzing Expressive Qualities in Movement and Stillness: Effort-Shape Analyses of Solo Marimbists' Bodily Expression." *Music Perception* 29, no. 4 (April 2012): 339–357.

Broughton, Mary, and Catherine Stevens. "Music, Movement and Marimba: An Investigation of the Role of Movement and Gesture in Communicating Musical Expression to an Audience." *Psychology of Music* 37 (2009): 137–153.

Brown, Brené. *I Thought It Was Just Me (But It Isn't): Telling the Truth about Perfectionism, Inadequacy, and Power.* New York: Penguin/Gotham Books, 2007.

Brown, Brené. *The Gifts of Imperfection: Let Go of Who You Think You're Supposed to Be and Embrace Who You Are.* Center City, MN: Hazelden, 2010.

Brown, Cary A., Pei Qin, and Shaniff Esmail. "'Sleep? Maybe Later . . .': A Cross-Campus Survey of University Students and Sleep Practices." *Education Sciences* 7, no. 66 (June 2017): 1–15. doi:10.3390/educsci7030066.

Brown, Franklin C., Walter C. Buboltz Jr., and Barlow Soper. "Relationship of Sleep Hygiene Awareness, Sleep Hygiene Practices, and Sleep Quality in University Students." *Behavioral Medicine* 28, no. 1 (2002): 33–38.

Brown, Kirk Warren, J. David Creswell, Richard M. Ryan. *Handbook of Mindfulness: Theory, Research, and Practice.* New York: Guilford Publications, 2015.

Brown, Rhonda F., and Nicols S. Schutte, "Direct and Indirect Relationships between Emotional Intelligence and Subjective Fatigue in University Students." *Journal of Psychosomatic Research* 60 (2006): 585–593.

Brown, Richard P., and Patricia Gerbarg. "Sudarshan Kriya Yogic Breathing in the Treatment of Stress, Anxiety, and Depression: Part I—Neurophysiologic Model." *The Journal of Alternative and Complementary Medicine* 11, no. 1 (2005): 189–201.

Brown, Stuart, and Christopher Vaughan. *Play: How It Shapes the Brain, Opens the Imagination, and Invigorates the Soul.* New York: Penguin Group, 2009.

Bruckner, Susan. *The Whole Musician: A Multi-Sensory Guide to Practice, Performance and Pedagogy.* Santa Cruz: Effey Street Press, 2004.

Bryan, Stephanie. "Mindfulness and Nutrition in College Age Students." *Journal of Basic and Applied Science* 12 (2016): 68–74.

Buhi, Eric, Ellen Daley, Hollie J. Fuhrmann, and Sarah A. Smith. "An Observational Study of How Young People Search for Online Sexual Health Information." *Journal of American College Health* 58, no. 2 (2009): 101–111.

Buma, Lori A., Frank C. Bakker, and Raôul R. D. Oudejans. "Exploring the Thoughts and Focus of Attention of Elite Musicians under Pressure." *Psychology of Music* 42, no. 4 (2015): 459–472.

Burger, Thorsten. "Health Locus of Control and Preventive Behaviour among Students of Music." *Psychology of Music* 33, no. 3 (2005): 256–258.

Butzer, Bethany, Khalique Ahmed, and Sat Bir S. Khalsa. "Yoga Enhances Positive Psychological States in Young Adult Musicians." *Applied Psychophysiological Biofeedback* 41 (2016): 191–202.

Calais-Germain, Blandine. *Anatomy of Movement.* Seattle, WA: Eastland Press, 1993.

Campbell, Bill. *Sports Nutrition: Enhancing Athletic Performance.* Boca Raton, FL: CRC Press, 2014.

Carney, Colleen E., Jack D. Edinger, Björn Meyer, Linda Lindman, and Tai Istre. "Daily Activities and Sleep Quality in College Students." *Chronobiology International* 23 (2006): 623–637.

Castellano, Ginevra, Marcello Mortillaro, Antonio Camurri, Gualtiero Volpe, and Klaus Scherer. "Automated Analysis of Body Movement in Emotionally Expressive Piano Performances." *Music Perception: An Interdisciplinary Journal* 26, no. 2 (December 2008): 103–119.

Castillo, Linda G., and Seth J. Schwartz. "Introduction to the Special Issue on College Student Mental Health." *Journal of Clinical Psychology* 69, no. 4 (2013): 291–297.

Chaffin, Roger, and Anthony F. Lemieux. "General Perspective on Achieving Musical Excellence." In *Musical Excellence: Strategies and Techniques to Enhance Performance*, edited by Aaron Williamon, 19–40. New York: Oxford University Press, 2004.

Chan, Cliffton, and Bronwen Ackerman. "Evidence-Informed Physical Therapy Management of Performance-Related Musculoskeletal Disorders in Musicians." *Frontiers in Psychology* 5, article 706 (July 2014): 1–14.

Chan, Cliffton, Tim Driscoll, and Bronwen Ackermann. "Development of a Specific Exercise Programme for Professional Orchestral Musicians." *Injury Prevention* 19 (2013): 257–263.

Chanfreau, Jenny, Cheryl Lloyd, Christos Byron, Caireen Roberts, Rachel Craig, Danielle De Feo, and Sally McManus. "Predicting Wellbeing." London: NatCen Social Research for the Department of Health, August 2013. http://natcen.ac.uk/media/205352/predictors-of-wellbeing.pdf.

Chasin, Marshall. "Hearing Aids for Musicians: Understanding and Managing the Four Key Physical Differences between Music and Speech." *The Hearing Review* 13, no. 6 (March 2006): 1–24. Gale OneFile: Health and Medicine, https://link-gale-com.proxy.lib.umich.edu/apps/doc/A165819822/HRCA?u=umuser&sid=HRCA&xid=14842e9a (accessed April 2, 2020).

Chasin, Marshall. *Hear the Music: Hearing Loss Prevention for Musicians*. Toronto, Ontario, Canada: Musicians' Clinics of Canada, 2001.

Chawla, Kusha Pandit. "Yoga, Meditation and Stress in Student Life." *International Journal of Management Research and Reviews* 7, no. 6 (2017): 687–691.

Chesky, Kris. "Hearing Conservation and Music Education." *Seminars in Hearing* 29, no. 1 (2008): 90–93.

Chesky, Kris. "Measurement and Prediction of Sound Exposure Levels by University Wind Bands." *Medical Problems of Performing Artists* 25, no. 1 (March 2010): 29–34.

Chesky, Kris. "Preventing Music-Induced Hearing Loss." *Music Educators Journal* 94, no. 3 (January 2008): 36–41.

Chesky, Kris. "Schools of Music and Conservatories and Hearing Loss Prevention." *International Journal of Audiology* 50 (2011): S32–S37.

Chesky, Kris, William J. Dawson, and Ralph Manchester. "Health Promotion in Schools of Music: Initial Recommendations for Schools of Music." *Medical Problems of Performing Artists* 21, no. 3 (September 2006): 142–144.

Chesky, Kris, and Miriam A. Henoch. "Instrument-Specific Reports of Hearing Loss: Differences between Classical and Non-Classical Musicians." *Medical Problems of Performing Artists* 15, no. 1 (March 2000): 35–39.

Chesky, Kris, and John Hipple. "Performance Anxiety, Alcohol-Related Problems, and Social/Emotional Difficulties of College Students: A Comparative Study between Lower-Division Music and Non-Music Majors." *Medical Problems of Performing Artists* 12, no. 4 (December 1997): 126–132.

Chesky, Kris, Marla Pair, Eri Yoshimura, and Scott Landford. "An Evaluation of Musician Earplugs with College Music Students." *International Journal of Audiology* 48, no. 9 (2009): 661–670.

Chödrön, Pema. *Comfortable with Uncertainty: 108 Teachings on Cultivating Fearlessness and Compassion*. Boston, MA: Shambhala Publications, 2002.

Clark, Terry, Patricia Holmes, and Emma Redding. "Investigating the Physiological Demands of Musical Performance." In Proceedings of *the International Symposium on Performance Science 2011*, edited by Aaron Williamon, Darryl Edwards, and Lee Bartel, 24–27. Utrecht, The Netherlands: European Association of Conservatoires (AEC), August 2011.

Clark, Terry, Aaron Williamon, and Emma Redding. "The Value of Health Screening in Music Schools and Conservatoires." *Clinical Rheumatology* 32 (2013): 497–500.

Claydon, Elizabeth, and Keith Zullig. "Eating Disorders and Academic Performance among College Students." *Journal of American College Health* 68, no. 3 (January 2019): 320–325.

Cockey, Linda. "Empowering the Whole Musician: Mind and Body for a More Musical Tomorrow." *MTNA eJournal* 4, no. 1 (September 2012): 29–33.

Coffey, John K., Laura Wray-Lake, Debra Mashek, and Brittany Branard. "A Multi Study Examination of Well-being Theory in College and Community Samples." *Journal of Happiness Studies* 17 (2016): 187–211.

Conable, Barbara. *The Structures and Movement of Breathing: A Primer for Choirs and Choruses.* Portland, OR: Andover Press, 2000.

Conable, Barbara, and Benjamin J. Conable. *What Every Musician Needs to Know about the Body: The Practical Application of Body Mapping to Making Music.* Portland, OR: Andover Press, 2000.

Conway, Colleen. "Beginning Music Teacher Mentor Practices: Reflections on the Past and Suggestions for the Future." *Journal of Music Teacher Education* 24, no. 2 (2015): 88–102.

Conway, Colleen, John Eros, Kristen Pellegrino, and Chad West. "Instrumental Music Education Students' Perceptions of Tensions Experienced during Their Undergraduate Degree." *Journal of Research in Music Education* 58, no. 3 (October 2010): 260–275.

Conway, Colleen Marie, and Thomas M. Hodgman. *Handbook for the Beginning Music Teacher.* Chicago: GIA Publications, 2006.

Conway, Colleen Marie, Michael V. Smith, and Thomas M. Hodgman. *Handbook for the Music Mentor.* Chicago: GIA Publications, 2010.

Copeland, Mary Ellen. "Wellness Recovery Action Plan." *Occupational Therapy in Mental Health* 17, nos. 3–4 (2002): 127–150.

Cornett-Murtada, Vanessa. "Nurturing the Whole Musician: Mindfulness, Wellness and the Mind-Body Connection." *MTNA eJournal* 4, no. 1 (September 2012): 15–28.

Cornett, Vanessa. *The Mindful Musician: Mental Skills for Peak Performance.* New York: Oxford University Press, 2019.

Corrêa, Leticia Amaral, Luciano Teixeira dos Santos, Edmur Nelson Nogueira Paranhos, Alfredo Ignacio Minetti Albertini, Patrícia do Carmo Silva Parreira, and Leandro Alberto Calazans Nogueira. "Prevalence and Risk Factors for Musculoskeletal Pain in Keyboard Musicians: A Systematic Review." *Physical Medicine & Rehabilitation* 10 (2018): 942–950.

Cowgill, Jennifer Griffith. "Breathing for Singers: A Comparative Analysis of Body Types and Breathing Tendencies." *Journal of Singing* 66, no. 2 (November–December 2009): 141–147.

Cowie, Megan E., Logan J. Nealis, Simon B. Sherry, Paul L. Hewitt, and Gordon L. Flett. "Perfectionism and Academic Difficulties in Graduate Students: Testing Incremental Prediction and Gender Moderation." *Personality and Individual Differences* 123 (2018): 223–228.

Cox, Sandra Elaine. "Recognition, Evaluation, and Treatment Options of Performance-Related Injuries in Woodwind Musicians." DMA diss., University of Memphis, August 2009.

Craze, Richard. *Teach Yourself Alexander Technique.* Blacklick, OH: McGraw Hill, 2001.

Csikszentmihalyi, Mihaly. *Flow: The Psychology of Optimal Experience.* New York: Harper Perennial Modern Classics, 2008.

Culf, Nicola. *Musicians' Injuries: A Guide to Their Understanding and Prevention.* Guildford, UK: Parapress, 1998.

Dahl, Sophia, and Anders Friberg. "Visual Perception of Expressiveness in Musicians' Body Movements." *Music Perception* 24 (June 2007): 433–454.

Daloz, Laurent A. *Effective Teaching and Mentoring: Realizing the Transformational Power of Adult Learning Experiences.* London: Jossey-Bass, 1986.

Daloz, Laurent A. *Mentor: Guiding the Journey of Adult Learners.* San Francisco: Jossey-Bass, 2012.

Das, Bhidha, and Ellen M. Evans. "Assessing Weight Management Barriers in First-Year College Students." *Journal of American College Health* 62, no. 7 (2014): 488–497.

Das, Dipanjana. "Empirical Investigation of SAMHSA's (Substance Abuse and Mental Health Services Administration) Model of Wellness." Thesis, City University of New York (CUNY), 2015.

Davidson, Richard J., Jon Kabat-Zinn, Jessica Schumacher, Melissa Rosenkranz, Daniel Muller, Saki F. Santorelli, Ferris Urbanowski, Anne Harrington, Katherine Bonus, and John F. Sheridan. "Alterations in Brain and Immune Function Produced by Mindfulness Meditation." *Psychosomatic Medicine* 65, no. 4 (July 2003): 564–570.

Davidson, Jane W. "Visual Perception of Performance Manner in the Movements of Solo Musicians." *Psychology of Music* 21, no. 2 (1993): 103–113.

Davies, Clair. "Musculoskeletal Pain from Repetitive Strain in Musicians: Insights into an Alternative Approach." *Medical Problems of Performing Artists* 17, no. 1 (March 2002): 42–49.

Davies, Janet. "Alexander Technique Classes Improve Pain and Performance Factors in Tertiary Music Students." *Journal of Bodywork and Movement Therapies* 24, no. 1 (January 2020): 1–7.

Davies, Janet, and Sandra Mangion. "Predictors of Pain and Other Musculoskeletal Symptoms among Professional Instrumental Musicians: Elucidating Specific Effects." *Medical Problems of Performing Artists* 17, no. 4 (December 2002): 155–168.

Davis, Martha, Elizabeth Robbins Eshelman, and Matthew McKay. *The Relaxation and Stress Reduction Workbook*, 4th ed. Oakland, CA: New Harbinger, 1995.

Davoren, Martin P., Eimear Fitzgerald, Frances Shiely, and Ivan J. Perry. "Positive Mental Health and Well-being among a Third Level Student Population." *PLOS One* 8, no. 8 (August 2013): e74921. doi:10.1371/journal.pone.0074921.

Dawson, J. William. *Fit as a Fiddle: The Musician's Guide to Playing Healthy*. Lanham, MD: Rowman & Littlefield, 2008.

Dawson, J. William. "How and Why Musicians Are Different from Nonmusicians: A Bibliographic Review." *Medical Problems of Performing Artists* 26, no. 2 (2011): 65–78.

Deforche, Benedicte, Delfien Van Dyck, Tom Deliens, and Ilse De Bourdeaudhuij. "Changes in Weight, Physical Activity, Sedentary Behaviour and Dietary Intake during the Transition to Higher Education: A Prospective Study." *International Journal of Behavioral Nutrition and Physical Activity* 12, no. 16 (2015): 1–10. https://doi.org/10.1186/s12966-015-0173-9.

Deliens, Tom, Peter Clarys, Ilse De Bourdeaudhuij, and Benedicte Deforche. "Weight, Socio-Demographics, and Health Behaviour Related Correlates of Academic Performance in First Year University Students." *Nutrition Journal* 12, no. 162 (2013): 1–8. doi:10.1186/1475-2891-12-162.

Dell, Charlene. "Strings Got Rhythm: A Guide to Developing Rhythmic Skills in Beginners." *Music Educators Journal* 96, no. 3 (March 2010): 31–34.

Demirbatir, Rasim Erol. "Relationships between Psychological Well-being, Happiness, and Educational Satisfaction in a Group of University Music Students." *Educational Research and Reviews* 10, no. 15 (August 2015): 2198–2206.

Desikachar, T. K. V. *The Heart of Yoga: Developing a Personal Practice*. Rochester, VT: Inner Traditions International, 1995.

Dews, Barney C. L., and Martha S. Williams. "Student Musicians' Personality Styles, and Stresses, and Coping Patterns." *Psychology of Music and Music Education* 17 (1989): 37–47.

di Pellegrino, Giuseppe, Luciano Fadiga, Leonardo Fogassi, Vittorio Gallese, and Giacomo Rizzolatti. "Understanding Motor Events: A Neurophysiological Study." *Experimental Brain Research* 91 (1992): 176–180.

Diamond, Lisa. "The Benefits of Yoga in Improving Health." *Primary Health Care* 22, no. 2 (March 2013): 16–19.

Diener, Ed, Richard E. Lucas, and Shigehiro Oishi. "Subjective Well-being: The Science of Happiness and Life Satisfaction." In *The Oxford Handbook of Positive Psychology*, 2nd ed., edited by Shane J. Lopez and C. R. Snyder, 63–73. New York: Oxford University Press, 2009.

Dimon, Theodore. *The Anatomy of the Voice: An Illustrated Guide for Singers, Vocal Coaches, and Speech Therapists*. Berkeley, CA: North Atlantic Books, 2018.

Doherty, Sharon, and Mark Dooris. "The Healthy Settings Approach: The Growing Interest within Colleges and Universities." *Educational Health* 24 (2006): 42–43.

Dommerholt, Jan. "Performing Arts Medicine: Instrumentalist Musicians, Part II—Examination." *Journal of Bodywork and Movement Therapies* 14 (2010): 65–72.

Driskill, Kristina. "Symptoms, Causes and Coping Strategies for Performance Anxiety in Singers: A Synthesis of Research." PhD diss., West Virginia University, 2012.

Duckworth, Ken. "What to Do in a Crisis." National Alliance on Mental Health, Video, https://www.nami.org/Find-Support/Living-with-a-Mental-Health-Condition/What-to-Do-In-a-Crisis (accessed April 14, 2019).

Dunster, Gideon P., Luciano de la Iglesia, Miriam Ben-Hamo, Claire Nave, Jason G. Fleischer, Satchidananda Panda, and Horacio O. de la Iglesia. "Sleepmore in Seattle: Later School Start Times Are Associated with More Sleep and Better Performance in High School Students." *Science Advances* 4, no. 12 (December 2018): eaau6200. doi: 10.1126/sciadv.aau6200.

Eisenberg, Daniel, Emily J. Nicklett, Kathryn Roeder, and Nina E. Kirz. "Eating Disorder Symptoms among College Students: Prevalence, Persistence, Correlates and Treatment-Seeking." *Journal of American College Health* 59, no. 8 (2011): 700–707.

Engelstad, Evan. "Pilot Study: Does Nutrition Affect the Musical Performance Experiences of Professional Pianists?" DMA diss., University of Wisconsin–Madison, 2016.

Engquist, Karen, Palle Orbaek, and Kristina Jakobsson. "Musculoskeletal Pain and Impact on Performance in Orchestra Musicians and Actors." *Medical Problems of Performing Artists* 19, no. 2 (June 2004): 55–61.

Ergas, Oren. *Reconstructing "Education" through Mindful Attention: Positioning the Mind at the Center of Curriculum and Pedagogy.* London: Palgrave Macmillan, 2017.

Farnbach, Rod, and Eversley Farnbach. *Overcoming Performance Anxiety.* East Roseville, Australia: Simon & Schuster, 2001.

Feldman, Greg, Jeff Greeson, and Joanna Senville. "Differential Effects of Mindful Breathing, Progressive Muscle Relaxation, and Loving-Kindness Meditation on Decentering and Negative Reactions to Repetitive Thoughts." *Behaviour Research and Therapy* 48 (2010): 1002–1011.

Fenema, Esther van, and C. C. J. van Geel. "Mental Problems among First-Year Conservatory Students Compared with Medical Students." *Medical Problems of Performing Artists* 29, no. 2 (June 2014): 113–114.

Feuerstein, Georg. *Encyclopedic Dictionary of Yoga.* New York: Paragon House, 1990.

Fischer, Joachim E., Edgar Voltmer, Mark Zander, Brigitte M. Kudielka, Bernhard Richter, and Claudia Spahn. "Physical and Mental Health of Different Types of Orchestra Musicians Compared to Other Professions." *Medical Problems of Performing Artists* 27, no. 1 (2012): 9–14.

Fishbein, Martin, Susan E. Middlestadt, Victor Ottati, Susan Straus, and Alan Ellis. "Medical Problems among ICSOM Musicians: Overview of a National Survey." *Medical Problems of Performing Artists* 3, no. 1 (March 1988): 1–8.

Fjellman-Wiklund, Anncristine, and Gunnevi Sundelin. "Musculoskeletal Discomfort of Music Teachers: An Eight-Year Perspective and Psychosocial Work Factors." *International Journal of Occupational and Environmental Health* 4, no. 2 (1998): 89–98.

Fowler, Jane L., and John G. O'Gorman. "Mentoring Functions: A Contemporary View of the Perceptions of Mentees and Mentors." *British Journal of Management* 16 (2005): 51–57.

Frey, Rebecca, and Rosalyn Carson-DeWitt. "Bodywork Therapies." In *Gale Encyclopedia of Mental Health,* 4th ed., edited by Brigham Narins, 245–249. Famington Hills, MI: Gale Cengage Company.

Fry, Hunter J. H. "Overuse Syndrome of the Upper Limb in Musicians." *The Medical Journal of Australia* 144 (February 1986): 182–185.

Gallagher, Matthew W. "Well-being." In *The Encyclopedia of Positive Psychology,* edited by Shane J. Lopez, 1030–1034. Malden, MA: Blackwell, 2009.

Gallo, María Luciana. "Pilates and String Musicians: An Exploration of the Issues Addressed by the Pilates Method, an Illustrated Guide to Adapted Exercises, and a Pilates Course for University String Players." DMA diss., Arizona State University, May 2017.

Gambetta, Charles. "Conducting Outside the Box: Creating a Fresh Approach to Conducting Gesture through the Principles of Laban Movement Analysis." DMA diss., University of North Carolina at Greensboro, 2005.

Gates, Rachel. "Free to Sing: Encouraging Postural Release for Vocal Efficiency." *MTNA eJournal* 9, no. 4 (April 2018): 8–23.

Gates, Rachel, L., Stick Forrest, and Kerrie Obert. *The Owner's Manual to the Voice: A Guide for Singers and Other Professional Voice Users.* New York: Oxford University Press, 2013.

Georgii-Hemming, Eva, Pamela Burnard, and Sven-Erik Holgersen, eds. *Professional Knowledge in Music Teacher Education.* Burlington, VT: Ashgate, 2013.

Germer, Christopher K. *The Mindful Path to Self-Compassion: Freeing Yourself from Destructive Thoughts and Emotions.* New York: Guildford Press, 2009.

Gerst, Alena. *Wellness Handbook for the Performing Artist.* Bloomington, IN: Balboa Press, 2014.

Ginsborg, Jane, Gunter Kreutz, Mike Thomas, and Aaron Williamon. "Healthy Behaviours in Music and Non-Music Performance Students." *Health Education* 109, no. 3 (2009): 242–258.

Goleman, Daniel. *Social Intelligence: The New Science of Human Relationships.* New York: Random House/Bantam Dell, 2006.

Grace, Fran. "Learning as Path, Not a Goal: Contemplative Pedagogy—Its Principles and Practices." *Teaching Theology and Religion* 14, no. 2 (April 2011): 99–124.

Gravois, John. "Meditate on It: Can Adding Contemplation to the Classroom Lead Students to More Eureka Moments?" *Chronicle of Higher Education* 52, no. 9 (October 2015): 1–7.

Green, Barry. *The Mastery of Music: Ten Pathways to True Artistry*. New York: Broadway Books, 2003.

Greene, Don. *11 Strategies for Audition and Performance Success: A Workbook for Musicians*. 2012. http://psi.dongreene.com.

Greene, Don. *Performance Success: Performing Your Best under Pressure*. New York: Routledge, 2002.

Groneberg, David A. "Influence of Ergonomic Layout of Musician Chairs on Posture and Seat Pressure in Musicians of Different Playing Levels." *PLOS One* 13, no. 12 (December 2018): 1–14.

Gruttadaro, Darcy, and Dana Crudo. *College Students Speak: A Survey Report on Mental Health*. Arlington, VA: National Alliance on Mental Health, 2012. https://www.nami.org/About-NAMI/Publications-Reports/Survey-Reports/College-Students-Speak_A-Survey-Report-on-Mental-H.pdf.

Gunnlaugson, Olen, Edward Sarah, and Scott Charles. *Contemplative Learning and Inquiry across Disciplines*. Albany: State University of New York Press, 2014.

Guptill, Christine. "Musicians' Health: Applying the ICF Framework in Research." *Disability and Rehabilitation* 30, nos. 2–3 (July 2009): 970–977.

Guptill, Christine, and Christine Zaza. "Injury Prevention: What Music Teachers Can Do." *Music Educators Journal* 96, no. 4 (June 2010): 28–34.

Hackney, Peggy. *Making Connections: Total Body Integration through Bartenieff Fundamentals*. Amsterdam: Gordon and Breach, 1998.

Hagberg, Mats, Gunnar Thiringer, and Lars Brandström. "Incidence of Tinnitus, Impaired Hearing and Musculoskeletal Disorders among Students Enrolled in Academic Music Education: A Retrospective Cohort Study." *International Archives of Occupational and Environmental Health* 78 (2005): 575–583.

Hanna, Thomas. *Somatics: Reawakening the Mind's Control of Movement, Flexibility, and Health*. Cambridge, MA: Da Capo Press, 1988.

Hart, Cecil W., Carol L. Geltman, Joanne Schupbach, and Michael Santucci. "The Musician and Occupational Sound Hazards." *Medical Problems of Performing Artists* 2, no. 3 (1987): 22–25.

Hart, John T. "The Effects of Single Laban Effort Action Instruction on Undergraduate Conducting Students' Gestural Clarity." *Contributions to Music Education* 41 (2016): 93–111.

Hartiel, Ned, Jon Havenhand, Sat Bir Khalsa, Graham Clarke, and Anne Krayer. "The Effectiveness of Yoga for the Improvement of Well-being and Resilience to Stress in the Workplace." *Scandinavian Journal of Work, Environment and Health* 37, no. 1 (2011): 70–76.

Hartley, Linda. *Wisdom of the Body Moving: An Introduction to Body-Mind Centering*. Berkeley, CA: North Atlantic Books, 1995.

Hartmann, Monica E., and J. Roxanne Prichard. "Calculating the Contribution of Sleep Problems to Undergraduates' Academic Success." *Sleep Health* 4 (2018): 463–471.

Harvey, Pamela Lynn, Dave E. David, and Susan H. Miller. "Nutrition and the Singing Voice: Part Two." *National Association of Teachers of Singing* 54, no. 2 (November 1997): 43–49.

Hawkins, David R. *Power vs. Force: Anatomy of Consciousness*. Sedona, AZ: Veritas, 1995.

Hays, Terrence, Victor Minichiello, and Peter Wright. "Mentorship: The Meaning and the Relationship for Musicians." *Research Studies in Music Education* 15 (December 2000): 3–14.

Herbein, Jacqueline. "Piano Technique beyond the Bench: A Primer for Reducing Repetitive Strain Injury in Students." *Clavier Companion* 5, no. 1 (January–February 2013): 46–50.

Herndon, Hillary. "Balance Training for Musicians." *American String Teacher* 60, no. 4 (November 2010): 38–41.

Hildebrandt, Horst, Matthias Nübling, and Victor Candia. "Increment of Fatigue, Depression, and Stage Fright during the First Year of High-Level Education in Music Students." *Medical Problems of Performing Artists* 27, no. 1 (March 2012): 43–48.

Hogg, Karen. "Strike a Pose: How Guitarists Use Hatha Yoga to Improve Posture, Flexibility, Focus, and Stamina." *Acoustic Guitar* 12 (August 2001): 80–82.

Horvath, Janet. *Playing (Less) Hurt: An Injury Prevention Guide for Musicians*. Milwaukee, WI: Hal Leonard Books, 2010.

Horvath, Kathleen A. "Adopting a Healthy Approach to Instrumental Music Making." *Music Educators Journal* 94, no. 3 (January 2008): 30–34.

Huang, Terry K., Kari J. Harris, Rebecca E. Lee, Niaman Nazir, Wendi Born, and Harsohena Kaur. "Assessing Overweight, Obesity, Diet, and Physical Activity in College Students." *Journal of American College Health* 52 (2003): 83–86.

Huang, Wen-Shan. *Fundamentals of Tai Chi Ch'uan*. Hong Kong: South Sky, 1973.

Huebner, Floyd R., Kenneth W. Lieberman, R. P. Rubino, and Joseph S. Wall. "Demonstration of High Opioid-Like Activity in Isolated Peptides from Wheat Gluten Hydrolysates." *Peptides* 5, no. 6 (November–December 1984): 1139–1147.

Hunt, Justin, and Daniel Eisenberg. "Mental Health Problems and Help-Seeking Behaviors of College Students." *Journal of Adolescent Health* 46 (2010): 3–10.

Hyun, Jenny K., Brian C. Quinn, Temina Madon, and Steve Lustig. "Graduate Student Mental Health: Needs Assessment and Utilization of Counseling Services. *Journal of College Student Development* 47, no. 3 (May–June 2006): 247–266.

Immordino-Yang, Mary Helen. *Emotions, Learning and the Brain: Exploring the Educational Implications of Affective Neuroscience*. Norton Series on the Social Neuroscience of Education. New York: W. W. Norton, 2016.

Institute of Medicine. *Dietary Reference Intakes: The Essential Guide to Nutrient Requirements*. Washington, DC: The National Academies Press, 2006.

International Food Information Council Foundation. "2018 Food & Health Survey." 2018. https://foodinsight.org/wp-content/uploads/2018/05/2018-FHS-Report-FINAL.pdf.

International Society for the Study of Tension in Performance. "History of ISSTIP." Middlesex, UK. http://isstip.org/history.html (accessed November 2, 2019).

Ioannou, Christos, and Eckhart Altenmüller. "Approaches to and Treatment Strategies for Playing-Related Pain Problems among Czech Instrumental Music Students: An Epidemiological Study." *Medical Problems of Performing Artists* 30, no. 3 (September 2015): 135–142.

Iyengar, B. K. S. *Light on Yoga*. New York: Schocken Books, 1960.

Jabusch, Hans-Christian, and Eckart Altenmüller. "Anxiety as an Aggravating Factor during Onset of Focal Dystonia in Musicians." *Medical Problems of Performing Artists* 19, no. 2 (June 2004): 75–81.

Jahn, Anthony, ed. *The Singer's Guide to Complete Health*. New York: Oxford University Press, 2013.

Jameson, Timothy J. D. C. *Repetitive Strain Injuries: The Complete Guide to Alternative Treatments and Prevention*. New Canaan, CT: Keats, 1998.

Jensenius, Alexander R., and Marcelo M. Wanderley. "Musical Gestures: Concepts and Methods Research." In *Musical Gestures*, edited by Rolfe Inge Godøy and Marc Leman, 24–47. New York: Routledge, 2010.

Jin, P. "Efficacy of Tai Chi, Brisk Walking, Meditation, and Reading in Reducing Mental and Emotional Stress." *Journal of Psychosomatic Research* 36, no. 4 (May 1992): 361–370.

John, Jennifer. "Pilates for Musicians." *American String Teacher* 53, no. 3 (August 2003): 78–80.

Johnston, Richard, Roisin Cahalan, Laura Jayne Bonnett, Matthew Maguire, Philip D. Glasgow, Sharon M. Madigan, Kieran James O'Sullivan, and Thomas Comyuns. "General Health Complaints and Sleep Associated with New Injury within an Endurance Sporting Population: A Prospective Study." *Journal of Science and Medicine in Sport* 23, no. 3 (2020): 252–257.

Jones, Carol Anne. "Music and Medicine: Preventing Performance Injuries." *Teaching Music* 9, no. 2 (October 2001): 23–30.

Jones, Matthew. "Positive Action: Holistic Approach to Music-Making." *Music Teacher* 84 (October 2005): 30–31.

Juhan, Deane. *Job's Body: A Handbook for Bodywork*. Barrytown, NY: Barrytown, 1998.

Kabat-Zinn, Jon. *Full Catastrophe Living*. New York: Delta, 1991.

Kabat-Zinn, Jon. "Mindfulness-Based Interventions in Context: Past, Present and Future." *Clinical Psychology: Science and Practice* 10 (2003): 144–156.

Kabat-Zinn, Jon. *Wherever You Go, There You Are*. New York: Hatchette Books, 1994.

Kaminoff, Leslie, and Amy Matthews. *Yoga Anatomy*. Champaign, IL: Human Kinetics, 2012.

Kapsetaki, Marianna Evangelia, and Charlie Easmon. "Eating Disorders in Non-Dance Performing Artists: A Systematic Literature Review." *Medical Problems of Performing Artists* 32, no. 4 (December 2017): 227–234.

Kemp, Anthony. *The Musical Temperament: Psychology and Personality of Musicians*. New York: Oxford University Press, 2000.

Kempter, Susan. *How Muscles Learn: Teaching the Violin with the Body in Mind*. Los Angeles: Summy-Birchard, 2003.

Kenny, Dianna. *The Psychology of Music Performance Anxiety*. New York: Oxford University Press, 2011.

Kenny, Dianna, and Bronwen Ackermann. "Performance-Related Musculoskeletal Pain, Depression and Music Performance Anxiety in Professional Orchestral Musicians: A Population Study." *Psychology of Music* 43 (2015): 43–60.

Kenny, Dianna, Pamela Davis, and Jenni Oates. "Music Performance Anxiety and Occupational Stress amongst Opera Chorus Artists and their Relationship with State and Trait Anxiety and Perfectionism." *Anxiety Disorders* 18 (2004): 757–777.

Keyes, Corey L. M. "Promoting and Protecting Mental Health as Flourishing: A Complementary Strategy for Improving National Mental Health." *American Psychologist* 62, no. 2 (February–March 2007): 95–108.

Khalsa, Sat Bir, Bethany Butzer, Stephanie M. Shorter, Kirsten M. Reinhardt, and Stephen Cope. "Yoga Reduces Performance Anxiety in Adolescent Musicians." *Alternative Therapies* 19, no. 2 (March/April 2013): 34–45.

Khalsa, Sat Bir, Stephanie M. Shorter, Stephen Cope, Grace Wyshak, and Elyse Sklar. "Yoga Ameliorates Performance Anxiety and Mood Disturbance in Young Professional Musicians." *Applied Psychophysiological Biofeedback* 34 (2009): 279–289.

Kiesgen, Paul. "Voice Pedagogy: Breathing." *Journal of Singing* 62, no. 2 (November 2005): 169–171.

Kileny, Paul, and Allie Heckman. "Hearing Loss and the Performing Arts Student." Presentation, Performing Arts Medicine and Rehabilitation Symposium, University of Michigan, Ann Arbor, MI, October 2019.

Kjellgren, Anette, Sven Å Bood, Kajsa Axelsson, Torsten Norlander, and Fahri Saatcioglu. "Wellness through a Comprehensive Yogic Breathing Program: A Controlled Pilot Trial." *BMC Complementary and Alternative Medicine* 7, no. 43 (January 2007): 1–8.

Klein, Sabine D., Claudine Bayard, and Ursula Wolf. "The Alexander Technique and Musicians: A Systematic Review of Controlled Trials." *BMC Complementary and Alternative Medicine* 14 (2014): 414. doi: 10.1186/1472-6882-14-414.

Klickstein, Gerald. *The Musician's Way: A Guide to Practice, Performance, and Wellness*. New York: Oxford University Press, 2009.

Kochem, Frederico Barreto, and Julio Guilherme Silva. "Prevalence of Playing-Related Musculoskeletal Disorders in String Players: A Systematic Review." *Journal of Manipulative and Physiological Therapeutics* 41, no. 6 (July 2018): 540–549.

Kok, Laura M., Theodora P. M. Vliet Vlieland, Marta Fiocco, Ad A. Kaptein, and Rob G. H. H. Nelissen. "Musicians' Illness Perceptions of Musculoskeletal Complaints." *Clinical Rheumatology* 32 (2013): 487–492.

Kram, Kathy. "Phases of the Mentor Relationship." *The Academy of Management Journal* 26, no. 4 (December 1983): 608–625.

Kreutz, Gunter, Jane Ginsborg, and Aaron Williamon. "Health-Promoting Behaviours in Conservatoire Students." *Psychology of Music* 37 (2009): 47–60.

Kreutz, Gunter, Aaron Williamon, and Jane Ginsborg. "Music Students' Health Problems and Health-Promoting Behaviours." *Medical Problems of Performing Artists* 23, no. 1 (2008): 3–11.

Kropff, Kris, ed. *A Symposium for Pianists and Teachers: Strategies to Develop the Mind and Body for Optimal Performance*. Dayton, OH: Heritage Music Press, 2002.

Lanzer, Katie. "Yoga and Piano: Learning to Unify Musical Intentions with Easeful Actions." *American Music Teacher* (June–July 2009): 26–30.

Larson, Elizabeth A. "Stress in the Lives of College Women: 'Lots to Do and Not Much Time.'" *Journal of Adolescent Research* 21, no. 6 (November 2006): 579–606.

Larsson, Lars-Goran, John Baum, Govind S. Mudholkar, and Georgia D. Kollia. "Nature and Impact of Musculoskeletal Problems in a Population of Musicians." *Medical Problems of Performing Artists* 8, no. 3 (1993): 73–76.

Leanderson, Rolf, and Sundberg, Johan. "Breathing for Singing." *Journal of Voice* 2, no. 1 (1988): 2–12.

LeBorgne, Wendy, and Marci Daniels Rosenberg. *The Vocal Athlete*, 2nd ed. San Diego: Plural, 2019.

Lederman, Richard J., and Stephan U. Schuele. "Occupational Disorders in Instrumental Musicians." *Medical Problems of Performing Artists* 19, no. 3 (2004): 123–128.

Lee, Catherine. "Musicians as Movers: Applying the Feldenkrais Method to Music Education." *Music Educators Journal* 104, no. 4 (June 2018): 15–19.

Lee, Sang-Hie, Stephanie Carey, Rajiv Dubey, and Rachel Matz. "Intervention Program in College Instrumental Musicians, with Kinematics Analysis of Cello and Flute Playing: A Combined Program of Yogic Breathing and Muscle Strengthening-Flexibility Exercises." *Medical Problems of Performing Artists* 27, no. 2 (June 2012): 85–94.

Lehmann, Andreas C., John A. Sloboda, and Robert H. Woody. *Psychology for Musicians: Understanding and Acquiring the Skills*. New York: Oxford University Press, 2007.

Lerner, Daniel, and Alan Schlechter. *U Thrive: How to Succeed in College (and Life)*. New York: Little, Brown, 2017.

Levinson, Daniel J., Charlotte N. Darrow, Edward B. Klein, Mariah H. Levinson, and Braxton McKee. *The Seasons of a Man's Life*. New York: Random House, 1978.

Lichstein, Kenneth L., Kristen L. Payne, James P. Soeffing, H. Heith Durrence, Daniel J. Taylor, Brant W. Riedel, and Andrew J. Bush. "Vitamins and Sleep: An Exploratory Study." *Sleep Medicine* 9, no. 1 (September 2007): 27–32.

Lieberman, Julie Lyonn. *You Are Your Instrument: The Definitive Musician's Guide to Practice and Performance*. New York: Huiksi Music, 1997.

Lockwood, Alan, H. "Medical Problems in Secondary School-Aged Musicians." *Medical Problems of Performing Artists* 3, no. 4 (1988): 129–132.

Longo, Lucia, Arianna Di Stadio, Massimo Ralli, Irene Marinucci, Giovanni Ruoppolo, Laura Dipietro, Marco de Vincentiis, and Antonio Greco. "Voice Parameter Changes in Professional Musician-Singers Singing with and without an Instrument: The Effect of Body Posture." *Folia Phoniatrica et Logopaedica* (July 2019): 1–7.

Luna, Gaye, and Deborah L. Cullen. "Empowering the Faculty: Mentoring Redirected and Renewed." ASHE-ERIC Higher Education Report, no. 3. Washington, DC: George Washington University, Graduate School of Education and Human Development, 1995.

Lund, Hannah G., Brian D. Reider, Annie B. Whiting, and J. Roxanne Prichard. "Sleep Patterns and Predictors of Disturbed Sleep in a Large Population of College Students." *Journal of Adolescent Health* 46 (2010): 124–132.

Lutz, Antoine, Heleen A. Slagter, John D. Dunne, and Richard J. Davidson. "Attention Regulation and Monitoring in Meditation." *Trends in Cognitive Sciences* 12, no. 4 (April 2008): 163–169.

Mackworth-Young, Lucinda. *Music and Movement: Tuning in Practical Psychology for Musicians Who Are Teaching, Learning and Performing*. Norfolk, UK: MMM Publications, 2000.

Magrath, Jane, and Douglas Weeks. "Polyphony: Emotional Health and the Musician." *American Music Teacher* 53, no. 6 (2004): 78, 79, 83.

Malde, Melissa, Mary Jean Alien, and Kurt-Alexander Zeller. *What Every Singer Needs to Know about the Body*. San Diego: Plural, 2009.

Manchester, Ralph A. "Energy Expenditure in the Performing Arts." *Medical Problems of Performing Artists* 26, no. 4 (December 2011): 183–184.

Manchester, Ralph A. "Health Promotion Courses for Music Students: Part 1." *Medical Problems of Performing Artists* 22, no. 1 (2007): 26–29.

Mark, Thomas. *What Every Pianist Needs to Know about the Body*. Chicago: GIA Publications, 2003.

Matvienko, Oksana, Douglas S. Lewis, and Elisabeth Schafer. "A College Nutrition Science Course as an Intervention to Prevent Weight Gain in Female College Freshmen." *Journal of Nutrition Education and Behavior* 33 (2001): 95–101.

McAllister, Lesley Sisterhen. *The Balanced Musician: Integrating Mind and Body for Peak Performance*. Lanham, MD: Scarecrow Press, 2013.

McBrien, Robert. "The Mind-Body Connection Stress Reduction for Musicians." *American Music Teacher* 55, no. 2 (October–November 2005): 34–35.

McCaw, Dick. "Yoga and Actor Training." *Theatre, Dance and Performance Training* 7, no. 1 (2016): 124–126.

McCowen, Heather V. "Mentoring in Higher Education Music Study: Are Good Teachers Mentors?" PhD diss., University of North Texas, 2010.

McCoy, Scott. "On Breathing and Support." *Journal of Singing* 70, no. 3 (January–February 2014): 321–324.

Medeiros, Joshua T. "The Role of a University in Shaping College Students' Nutrition and Physical Activity Behaviors: A Qualitative Case Study." PhD diss., University of Hartford, 2017.

Meiselman, Herbert L. "Quality of Life, Well-being and Wellness: Measuring Subjective Health for Foods and Other Products." *Food Quality and Preference* 54 (2016): 101–109.

Meitlis, Rebecca. "Connecting through the Breath towards Expressive Communication in Performance: An Enquiry into the Training of Opera Singers." *Theatre, Dance and Performance Training* 6, no. 2 (2015): 187–199.

Milewski, Matthew D., David Skaggs, Gregory Bishop, J. Lee Pace, David A. Ibrahim, Tishya A. L. Wren, and Audrius Barzdukas. "Chronic Lack of Sleep Is Associated with Increased Sports Injuries in Adolescent Athletes." *Journal of Pediatric Orthopaedics* 34, no. 2 (March 2014): 129–133.

Miller, Fred L. *How to Calm Down: Three Deep Breaths to Peace of Mind*. New York: Warner Books, 2002.

Miller, John P. *The Holistic Curriculum*, 2nd ed. Toronto, Ontario: University of Toronto Press, 2007.

Miller, Richard. *Solutions for Singers: Tools for Performers and Teachers*. New York: Oxford University Press, 2004.

Miller, William R., and Stephen Rollnick. *Motivational Interviewing: Helping People Change*, 3rd ed. New York: Guilford Press, 2013.

Molsberger, Fiedrich, and Albrecht Molsberger. "Acupuncture in Treatment of Musculoskeletal Disorders of Orchestra Musicians." *Work* 41 (2012): 5–13.

Monaghan, Patricia. *Meditation—The Complete Guide: Techniques from East and West to Calm the Mind, Heal the Body, and Enrich the Spirit*. Novato, CA: New World Library, 1999.

Morton, Jennie. *The Authentic Performer: Wearing a Mark and the Effect on Health*. Devon, UK: Compton, 2015.

Mullangi, Samyukta, and Reshma Jagsi. "Imposter Syndrome: Treat the Cause, Not the Symptom." *Journal of the American Medical Association* 322, no. 5 (August 2019): 403–404.

Naar-King, Sylvie, and Mariann Suarez. *Motivational Interviewing with Adolescents and Young Adults*. New York: Guilford Press, 2011.

Nagel, Julie Jafee. "How to Destroy Creativity in Music Students: The Need for Emotional and Psychological Support Services in Music Schools." *Medical Problems of Performing Artists* 24, no. 1 (2009): 15–17.

Nagel, Julie Jafee. *Managing Stage Fright: A Guide for Musicians and Music Teachers*. New York: Oxford University Press, 2017.

National Association of Schools of Music. "NASM Handbook 2018–19." Reston, VA: National Association of Schools of Music, January 2019. https://nasm.arts-accredit.org/wp-content/uploads/sites/2/2019/01/M-2018-19-Handbook-Current-09-30-2019.pdf.

National Association of Schools of Music and Performing Arts Medicine Association. "NASM-PAMA Advisories on Neuromusculoskeletal and Vocal Health." https://nasm.arts-accredit.org/publications/brochures-advisories/nasm-pama-nms-vocal-health (accessed May 12, 2020).

National Association of Schools of Music and Performing Arts Medicine Association. "NASM-PAMA Advisories on Hearing Health." https://nasm.arts-accredit.org/publications/brochures-advisories/nasm-pama-hearing-health (accessed May 12, 2020).

National Council for Behavioral Health. *Mental Health First Aid™ USA*. Washington, DC: National Council for Behavioral Health and the Missouri Department of Mental Health, 2015.

Neely, Dawn Wells. "Body Consciousness and Singers: Do Voice Teachers Use Mind-Body Methods with Students and in Their Own Practice?" *Journal of Singing* 73, no. 2 (November–December 2016): 137–147.

Neidlinger, Erica Jean. "The Effect of Laban Effort-Shape Instruction on Young Conductors' Perception of Expressiveness Across Arts Disciplines." PhD diss., University of Minnesota, 2003.

Nelson, Samuel H., and Elizabeth Blades-Zeller. *Singing with Your Whole Self: The Feldenkrais Method and Voice*. Lanham, MD: Scarecrow Press, 2002.

Newlove, Jean, and John Dalby. *Laban for All*. London: Nick Hern Books, 2004.

Nonis, Sarath A., Gail I. Hudson, Laddie B. Logan, and Charles W. Ford. "Influence of Perceived Control over Time on College Students' Stress and Stress-Related Outcomes." *Research in Higher Education* 39, no. 5 (1998): 587–605.

Norris, Richard. *The Musician's Survival Manual: A Guide to Preventing and Treating Injuries in Instrumentalists*. Saint Louis, MO: MMB Music, 1997.

Nussek, Manfred, and Marcelo M. Wanderley. "Music and Motion: How Music-Related Ancillary Body Movements Contribute to the Experience of Music." *Music Perception* 25, no. 4 (2009): 335–353.

Nyman, Teresia, Christina Wikorin, Marie Mulder, and Yvonne Liljeholm Johansson. "Work Postures and Neck-Shoulder Pain among Orchestra Musicians." *American Journal of Industrial Medicine* 50 (2007): 370–376.

Ohlendorf, Daniela, Christian Maurer, Elisabeth Bolender, Veronica Kocis, Martha Song, and David A. Groneberg. "Influence of Ergonomic Layout of Musician Chairs on Posture and Seat Pressure in Musicians of Different Playing Levels." *PLOS One* 13, no. 2 (December 11, 2018): 1–14.

Oliver, Gretchen, and Heather Adams-Blair. "Improving Core Strength to Prevent Injury." *Journal of Physical Education, Recreation and Dance* 81, no. 7 (2010): 15–19.

Olson, Mia. *Musician's Yoga: A Guide to Practice, Performance, and Inspiration*. Boston, MA: Berklee Press, 2009.

Orza, Heather. "Assessing the Nutritional Knowledge and Exercise Habits of Community College Students." *Undergraduate Research Journal for the Human Sciences* 6 (2007). https://www.kon.org/urc/v6/orza.html.

Orzech, Kathryn M., David B. Salafsky, and Lee Ann Hamilton. "The State of Sleep among College Students at a Large Public University." *Journal of American College Health* 59, no. 7 (2011): 612–619.

Osborne, Margaret S., Don J. Greene, and Don T. Immel. "Managing Performance Anxiety and Improving Mental Skills in Conservatoire Students through Performance Psychology Training: A Pilot Study." *Psychology of Well-Being* 4, no. 18 (2014): 2–17.

Pace, Thaddeus W. W., Lobsang Tenzin Negi, Daniel D. Adame, Steven P. Cole, Teresa I. Sivilli, Timothy D. Brown, Michael J. Issa, and Charles L. Raison. "Effect of Compassion Meditation on Neuroendocrine, Innate Immune and Behavioral Responses to Psychosocial Stress." *Psychoneuroendocrinology* 31, no. 1 (January 2009): 87–98.

Pal, Gopal Krushna, Subramaniyam Velkumary, and Trakroo Madanmohan. "Effect of Short-Term Practice of Breathing Exercises on Automatic Functions in Normal Human Volunteers." *Indian Journal of Medical Research* 120 (2004): 115–121.

Palac, Judy. "Promoting Musical Health, Enhancing Musical Performance: Wellness for Music Students." *Music Educators Journal* 94, no. 3 (2008): 18–22.

Palac, Judy. "How NASM Schools Are Addressing the Music Health and Safety Standard: A Website Analysis." Poster presentation, Performing Arts Medicine Association Symposium, Snowmass, CO, July 2017.

Papageorgi, Ioulia, Andrea Creech, and Graham Frederick Welch. "Perceived Performance Anxiety in Advanced Musicians Specializing in Different Musical Genres." *Psychology of Music* 41, no. 1 (2013): 18–41.

Pargman, David. *Managing Performance Stress: Models and Methods*. New York: Routledge, 2006.

Park, Hankyu, and Dongwook Han. "The Effect of the Correlation between the Contraction of the Pelvic Floor Muscles and Diaphragmatic Motion during Breathing." *Journal of Physical Therapy Science* 27, no. 7 (2015): 2113–2115.

Park, Jung-Eun. "The Relationship between Musical Performance Anxiety, Healthy Lifestyle Factors, and Substance Use among Young Adult Classical Musicians: Implications for Training and Education." PhD diss., Columbia University, 2010.

Parnes, Karen, and Dovrat Dagan. "Yoga as an Adventure." *Scholastic Parent and Child* (April–May 2005): 54–57.

Pascual-Leone, Alvaro, Amir Amedi, Felipe Fregni, and Lotfi B. Merabet. "The Plastic Human Brain Cortex." *Annual Review of Neuroscience* 28 (July 2005): 377–401.

Patruno, Cataldo, Maddalena Napolitano, Serena La Bella, Fabio Ayala, Nicola Balato, Mariateresa Cantelli, and Anna Balato. "Instrument-Related Skin Disorders in Musicians." *Dermatitis* 27, no. 1 (January–February 2016): 26–29.

Paull, Barbara, and Christine Harrison. *The Athletic Musician: A Guide to Playing without Pain.* Lanham, MD: Scarecrow Press, 1997.

Pećina, Marko, and Ivan Bojanić. *Overuse Injuries of the Musculoskeletal System,* 2nd ed. Boca Raton, FL: CRC Press, 2004.

Perkins, Rosie, Helen Reid, Lilian S. Araújo, Terry Clark, and Aaron Williamon. "Perceived Enablers and Barriers to Optimal Health among Music Students: A Qualitative Study in the Music Conservatoire Setting." *Frontiers in Psychology* 8, article 968 (June 2017): 1–15.

Peterson, Patti H. "On the Voice: Alexander or Feldenkrais: Which Method Is Best?" *The Choral Journal* 48, no. 11 (May 2008): 67–72.

Pherigo, Johnny L. "Science and Medicine: What Every Musician Needs to Know about the Body— An Introduction to Body Mapping." *Journal of the International Horn Society* 45, no. 1 (October 2014): 90–93.

Phillips, Andrew J. K., William M. Clerx, Conor S. O'Brien, Akane Sano, Laura K. Barger, Rosalind W. Picard, Steven W. Lockley, Elizabeth B. Klerman, and Charles A. Czeisler. "Irregular Sleep/Wake Patterns Are Associated with Poorer Academic Performance and Delayed Circadian and Sleep/ Wake Timing." *Scientific Reports* 7, no. 3216 (2017): 1–13.

Phillips, Susan L., Vincent C. Henrich, and Sandra T. Mace. "Prevalence of Noise-Induced Hearing Loss in Student Musicians." *International Journal of Audiology* 49, no. 4 (2009): 309–316.

Phillips, Susan L., Julie Shoemaker, Sandra T. Mace, and Donald A. Hodges. "Environmental Factors in Susceptibility to Noise-Induced Hearing Loss in Student Musicians." *Medical Problems of Performing Artists* 23, no. 1 (March 2008): 20–28.

Pierce, Deborah L. "Reaching beyond Traditional Boundaries: The Librarian and Musicians' Health." *Notes* 67, no. 1 (September 2010): 50–67.

Pierce, Deborah L. "Rising to a New Paradigm: Infusing Health and Wellness into the Music Curriculum." *Philosophy of Music Education Review* 20, no. 2 (Fall 2012): 155–176.

Pirtle, Kathryne. *Performance without Pain: A Step-by-Step Nutritional Program for Healing Pain, Inflammation and Chronic Ailments in Musicians, Athletes, Dancers and Everyone Else.* Washington, DC: New Trends, 2006.

Popa, Ana Sorna. "You Become What You Practice: Application of Tai Chi Principles to Piano Playing." DMA diss., Boston University, 2012.

Popkin, Barry M., Kristen E. D'Anci, and Irwin H. Rosenberg. "Water, Hydration, and Health." *Nutrition Reviews* 68, no. 8 (2010): 439–458.

Powell, Trevor. *The Mental Health Handbook.* New York: Routledge, 2008.

Preedy, Victor R., Vinood B. Patel, and Le Lan-Anh. *Handbook of Nutrition, Diet and Sleep.* Human Health Handbooks, no. 3. Wageningen, The Netherlands: Wageningen Academic, 2013.

Price, Kevin, Philippe Schartz, and Alan H. D. Watson. "The Effects of Standing and Sitting Postures on Breathing in Brass Players." *SpringerPlus* 3, no. 210 (2014): 1–17.

Prichard, Roxanne J. "Causes and Consequences of Sleep Disruption: Implications for Accurate Diagnoses and Effective Treatment Plans." Presentation, Depression on College Campuses Conference, Ann Arbor, MI, 2019.

Pruett, Kyle D. "First Patrons: Parenting the Musician." *Medical Problems of Performing Artists* 19, no. 4 (2004): 154–159.

Radionoff, Sharon L. *The Vocal Instrument.* San Diego: Plural, 2008.

Ragins, Belle Rose, and Kathy Kram. "The Roots and Meaning of Mentoring." In *The Handbook of Mentoring at Work: Theory, Research, and Practice,* edited by Belle Rose Ragins and Kathy E. Kram, 3–15. Thousand Oaks, CA: Sage Publications, 2007.

Ramsay, Nicky, and Janet Free. *Holistic Bodywork for Performers: A Practical Guide.* Wiltshire, UK: Crowood Press, 2004.

Raymond, Delbert M., III, June Hart Romeo, and Karoline V. Kumke. "A Pilot Study of Occupational Injury and Illness Experienced by Classical Musicians." *Workplace Health and Safety* 60, no. 1 (2012): 19–24.

Rennie-Salonen, Bridget, and Frelét de Villiers. "Towards a Model for Musicians' Occupational Health Education at Tertiary Level in South Africa." *Journal of Music Research in Africa* 13, no. 2 (2016): 130–151.

Riley, Kristen, and Crystal Park. "How Does Yoga Reduce Stress? A Systematic Review of Mechanisms of Change and Guide to Future Inquiry." *Health Psychology Review* 9, no. 3 (2015): 379–396.

Riveire, Janine. "Bowing 'Qualities,' Laban and Motion Factors." *American String Teacher* 56, no. 3 (August 2006): 36–39.

Roach, Kathryn E., Marcelo A. Martinez, and Nicole Anderson. "Musculoskeletal Pain in Student Instrumentalists: A Comparison with the General Student Population." *Medical Problems of Performing Artists* 9, no. 4 (1994): 125–130.

Roberts, Ron, John Golding, Tony Towell, Steven Reid, Sally Woodford, Arlene Vetere, and Irene Weinreb. "Mental and Physical Health in Students: The Role of Economic Circumstances." *British Journal of Health Psychology* 5 (2000): 289–297.

Robinson, Dan, Joanna Zander, and British Columbia Research. *Preventing Musculoskeletal Injury (MSI) for Musicians and Dancers: A Resource Guide.* Vancouver, BC: Safety and Health in Arts Production and Entertainment (SHAPE), 2002.

Robotham, David, and Claire Julian. "Stress and the Higher Education Student: A Critical Review of the Literature." *Journal of Further and Higher Education* 30, no. 2 (2006): 107–117.

Rodrigues, Matilde Alexandra, Marisa Alexandra Freitas, Maria Paula Neves, and Manuela Viera Silva. "Evaluation of the Noise Exposure of Symphonic Orchestra Musicians." *Noise and Health* 16, no. 68 (January–February 2014): 40–46.

Roman-Liu, Danuta, Iwona Grabarek, Paweł Bartuzi, and Włodzimierz Choromański. "The Influence of Mental Load on Muscle Tension." *Ergonomics* 56, no. 7 (2013): 1125–1133.

Romeo, June Hart, Karoline V. Kumke, and Delbert M. Raymond. "A Pilot Study of Occupational Injury and Illness Experienced by Classical Musicians." *Workplace Health and Safety* 60, no. 1 (2012): 19.

Rose, Gail L. "Group Differences in Graduate Students' Concepts of the Ideal Mentor." *Research in Higher Education* 46, no. 1 (February 2005): 53–80.

Rosenberg, Marci Daniels, and Elizabeth Baldner. "Interdisciplinary Management of the Professional Voice: A Hybrid Approach." Performing Arts Medicine and Rehabilitation Symposium, University of Michigan, Ann Arbor, MI, October 2019.

Roskell, Penelope. "Balancing Act." *Piano* (2000): 33–35.

Rosset i Llobet, Jaume, and George Odam. *The Musician's Body: A Maintenance Manual for Peak Performance.* London: Guildhall School of Music and Drama; Burlington, VT: Ashgate, 2007.

Rush, Mark. *Playing the Violin: An Illustrated Guide.* New York: Routledge, 2006.

Russo, Marc A., Danielle M. Santarelli, and Dean O'Rourke. "The Physiological Effects of Slow Breathing in the Healthy Human." *Breathe* 13 (2017): 298–309.

Ryan, Richard M., and Edward L. Deci. "On Happiness and Human Potentials: A Review of Research on Hedonic and Eudaimonic Well-Being." *Annual Review of Psychology* 52 (2001): 141–166.

Ryan, Richard M., and Edward L. Deci. "Self-Determination Theory and the Facilitation of Intrinsic Motivation, Social Development and Well-being." *American Psychologist* 55, no. 1 (January 2000): 68–78.

Sadler, Michael E., and Christopher J. Miller. "Performance Anxiety: A Longitudinal Study of the Roles of Personality and Experience in Musicians." *Social Psychological and Personality Science* 1, no. 3 (2010): 280–287.

Salazar, Stephanie, and Lizelle Salazar. "Peer-to-Peer Depression Awareness Campaign: Mentor Manual." University of Michigan Depression Center, Ann Arbor, MI, 2018.

Salomoni, Sauro, Wolbert van den Hoorn, and Paul Hodges. "Breathing and Singing: Objective Characterization of Breathing Patterns in Classical Singers." *PLOS One* 11, no. 5 (May 2016): 1–18.

Salvatore, Michael. "Pilates Alleviates Common Injuries Suffered by Musicians." *International Musician* 111, no. 12 (December 2013): 12–13.

Sarath, Ed. "Meditation, Creativity, and Consciousness: Charting Future Terrain within Higher Education." *Teachers College Record* 108, no. 9 (September 2006): 1816–1841.

Sarath, Edward, David Myers, and Patricia Shehan Campbell. *Redefining Music Studies in an Age of Change: Creativity, Diversity and Integration.* New York: Routledge, 2016.

Schlinger, Marcy. "Feldenkrais Method, Alexander Technique and Yoga-Body Awareness Therapy in the Performing Arts." *Physical Medicine and Rehabilitation Clinics of North America* 17, no. 4 (2006): 865–875.

Schmalzl, Laura, Mardi A. Crane-Godreau, and Peter Payne. "Movement-Based Embodied Contemplative Practices: Definitions and Paradigms." *Frontiers in Human Neuroscience* 8 (April 2014): 205. doi:10.3389/fnhum.2014.00205.

Schmidt, Norman B., J. Anthony Richey, Michael J. Zcolensky, and Jon K. Maner. "Exploring Human Freeze Responses to a Threat Stressor." *Journal of Behavior Therapy and Experimental Psychiatry* 39, no. 3 (2009): 292–304.

Schoeb, Veronika, and Amélie Zosso. "You Cannot Perform Music without Taking Care of Your Body: A Qualitative Study on Musicians' Representation of Body and Health." *Medical Problems of Performing Artists* 27, no. 3 (2012): 129–136.

Schoen, Eva, Rebecca Brock, and Jennifer Hannon. "Gender Bias, Other Specified and Unspecified Feeding and Eating Disorders, and College Students: A Vignette Study." *Eating Disorders: The Journal of Treatment and Prevention* (May–June 2019): 291–304.

Schuele, Stephan U., and Richard J. Lederman. "Occupational Disorders in Instrumental Musicians." *Medical Problems of Performing Artists* 19, no. 3 (September 2004): 123–128.

Schueller, Stephen M., and Martin E. P. Seligman. "Pursuit of Pleasure, Engagement, and Meaning: Relationships to Subjective and Objective Measures of Well-being." *The Journal of Positive Psychology* 5, no. 4 (2010): 253–263.

Scott, Joe. "The Effect of Perfectionism and Unconditional Self-Acceptance on Depression." *Journal of Rational-Emotive and Cognitive-Behavior Therapy* 25, no. 1 (2007): 35–64.

Seligman, Martin. "The New Era of Positive Psychology." TED talk 23:30, 2004. https://www.ted.com/talks/martin_seligman_on_the_state_of_psychology?language=en#t-386324

Seligman, Martin. "PERMA and the Building Blocks of Well-being." *The Journal of Positive Psychology* 13, no. 4 (2018): 333–335.

Sexton, Natasia. "Body Alignment and Awareness for Conductors: What's Good for the Conductor Is Good for the Ensemble." *MTNA eJournal* 10, no. 1 (September 2018): 2–13.

Sheridan, John F. "Alterations in Brain and Immune Function Produced by Mindfulness Meditation." *Psychosomatic Medicine* 65 (2003): 564–570.

Shoebridge, Ann, Nora Shields, and Kate E. Webster. "Minding the Body: An Interdisciplinary Theory of Optimal Posture for Musicians." *Psychology of Music* 45, no. 6 (2017): 821–838.

Small, Meg, Lisa Bailey-Davis, Nicole Morgan, and Jennifer Maggs. "Changes in Eating and Physical Activity Behaviors across Seven Semesters of College: Living on or off Campus Matters." *Health Education and Behavior* 40, no. 4 (August 2013): 435–441.

Smith, Gareth Dylan, and Adele Teague. "Portfolio Careers and Work-Life Balance among Musicians: An Initial Study into Implications for Higher Music Education." *British Journal of Music Education* 32, no. 2 (2015): 177–193.

Smith, Michael V. "Modern Mentoring: Ancient Lessons for Today." *Music Educators Journal* 92, no. 2 (November 2005): 62–67.

Sneed, Bonnie Borshay. "On the Voice: Teaching Good Breath Technique: It Starts in the Warmup." *The Choral Journal* 40, no. 9 (April 2000): 51–55.

Sondra, Fraleigh. *Moving Consciously: Somatic Transformations through Dance, Yoga and Touch.* Champaign, IL: University of Illinois Press, 2015.

Spahn, Claudia, Horst Hildebrandt, and Karin Seidenglanz. "Effectiveness of a Prophylactic Course to Prevent Playing-Related Health Problems of Music Students." *Medical Problems of Performing Artists* 16, no. 1 (2001): 24–31.

Spahn, Claudia, Bernhard Richter, and Ina Zchocke. "Health Attitudes, Preventive Behavior, and Playing-Related Health Problems among Music Students." *Medical Problems of Performing Artists* 17, no. 1 (2002): 22–28.

Spahn, Claudia, Sandra Strukely, and Andreas Lehmann. "Health Conditions, Attitudes toward Study, and Attitudes toward Health at the Beginning of University Study: Music Students in Comparison with Other Student Populations." *Medical Problems of Performing Artists* 16, no. 1 (March 2004): 26–33.

Stallman, Helen M. "Psychological Distress in University Students: A Comparison with General Population Data." *Australian Psychologist* 45, no. 4 (December 2010): 249–257.

Stanek, Jeremy L., Kevin D. Komes, and Fred A. Murdock. "A Cross-Sectional Study of Pain among US College Music Students and Faculty." *Medical Problems of Performing Artists* 32, no. 1 (March 2017): 20–26.

Stanhope, Jessica. "Physical Performance and Musculoskeletal Disorders: Are Musicians and Sportspeople on a Level Playing Field?" *Performance Enhancement and Health* 4 (2016): 18–26.

Stanley, Nicky, and Jill Manthrope, eds. *Students' Mental Health Needs*. New York: Jessica Kingsley, 2002.

Steinmetz, Anke, Heiko Moller, Wolfram Seidel, and Thomas Rigotti. "Playing-Related Musculoskeletal Disorders in Music Students: Associated Musculoskeletal Signs." *European Journal of Physical Rehabilitation Medicine* 48 (2012): 625–633.

Steinmetz, Anke, Wolfram Siedel, and Burkhard Muche. "Impairment of Postural Stabilization Systems in Musicians with Playing-related Musculoskeletal Disorders." *Journal of Manipulative and Physiological Therapeutics* 33, no. 8 (October 2010): 603–611.

Stern, Judith, Sat Bir Khalsa, and Stefan Hofmann. "A Yoga Intervention for Music Performance Anxiety in Conservatory Students." *Medical Problems of Performing Artists* 27, no. 3 (2012): 123–128.

Stewart-Brown, Sarah, Julie Evans, Jacoby Patterson, Sophie Peterson, Helen Doll, John Balding, and David Regis. "The Health of Students in Institutes of Higher Education: An Important and Neglected Public Health Problem?" *Journal of Public Health* 22, no. 4 (December 1, 2000): 492–499.

Stoewen, Debbie L. "Dimensions of Wellness: Change Your Habits, Change Your Life." *The Canadian Veterinary Journal* 58, no. 8 (2017): 861–862.

Substance Abuse and Mental Health Services Administration. "Creating a Healthier Life: A Step-by-Step Guide to Wellness." 2016. https://store.samhsa.gov/system/files/sma16-4958.pdf.

Sundberg, Joan, and Monica Thomasson. "Consistency of Inhalatory Breathing Patterns in Professional Operatic Singers." *Journal of Voice* 15, no. 3 (September 2001): 373–383.

Svard, Lois. "The Musician's Guide to the Brain: How to Use Brain Science in the Study of Music." *MTNA eJournal* 1, no. 3 (February 2010): 2–11.

Swarbrich, Margaret. "A Wellness Approach." *Psychiatric Rehabilitation Journal* 29, no. 4 (Spring 2006): 311–314.

Szczygieł, Elżbieta, Jędrzej Blaut, Katarzyna Zielonka-Pycka, Krzysztof Tomaszewski, Joanna Golec, Dorota Czechowska, Agata Masłoń, and Edward Golec. "The Impact of Deep Muscle Training on the Quality of Posture and Breathing." *Journal of Motor Behavior* 50, no. 2 (2018): 219–227.

Tarnopolsky, Mark A. "Caffeine and Creatine Use in Sport." *Annals of Nutrition and Metabolism* 57 (2010): 1–8.

Taylor, Nancy. *Teaching Healthy Musicianship: The Music Educator's Guide to Injury Prevention and Wellness*. New York: Oxford University Press, 2016.

Thompson, Sam. "Awareness and Incidence of Health Problems among Conservatoire Students." *Psychology of Music* 34, no. 4 (2006): 411–430.

Titze, Ingo R. "Vocal Straw Exercise." The National Center for Voice and Speech video, 4:37, www.ncvs.org/videos.html.

Tommasini, Anthony. "Two Pianists: A Virtuoso and a Philosophizer." *New York Times*, July 24, 2009. https://www.nytimes.com/2009/07/24/arts/music/24keyboard.html.

Tran, Mark, Robert Holly, Jake Lashbrook, and Ezra A. Amsterdam. "Effects of Hatha Yoga Practice on the Health-Related Aspects of Physical Fitness." *Preventive Cardiology* (Fall 2010): 165–170.

Tse, Michael. *Qigong for Health and Vitality*. New York: St. Martin's Press, 1996.

US Department of Agriculture. "Ounce-Equivalent of Protein Foods Table." www.choosemyplate.gov/eathealthy/protein-foods (accessed May 5, 2020).

US Department of Health and Human Services. *Physical Activity Guidelines for Americans*, 2nd ed. Washington, DC: US Department of Health and Human Services, 2018. https://health.gov/paguidelines/second-edition/pdf/Physical_Activity_Guidelines_2nd_edition.pdf.

US Department of Health and Human Services, Centers for Disease Control and Prevention. "Adult Obesity Facts." February 2020. https://www.cdc.gov/obesity/data/adult.html.

US Department of Health and Human Services, Centers for Disease Control and Prevention and National Institute for Occupational Safety. "Workplace Solutions: Reducing the Risk of Hearing

Disorders among Musicians." June 2015. https://www.cdc.gov/niosh/docs/wp-solutions/2015-184/pdfs/2015-184.pdf.

US Department of Health and Human Services, National Center for Complementary and Integrative Health. "Probiotics: What you Need to Know." 2019. https://nccih.nih.gov/health/probiotics/introduction.htm.

US Department of Health and Human Services, National Institute on Deafness and Other Communication Disorders. "Quick Statistics about Hearing Health." 2016. https://www.nidcd.nih.gov/health/statistics/quick-statistics-hearing.

US Department of Health and Human Services, Public Health Service, Centers for Disease Control and Prevention, National Institute for Occupational Safety and Health. *Criteria for a Recommended Standard: Occupational Noise Exposure.* Cincinnati, OH: DHHS (NIOSH) Publication 98-126 (June 1998).

US Department of Health and Human Services and US Department of Agriculture. *2015–2020 Dietary Guidelines for Americans*, 8th Edition. Washington, DC. December 2015. http://health.gov/dietaryguidelines/2015/guidelines/.US Department of Labor. "Occupational Safety and Health Administration." https://www.osha.gov. (accessed May 1, 2020).

Vaag, Jonas, Ingvild Saksvik-Lehouillier, Johan Håkon Bjørngaard, and Ottar Bjerkeset. "Sleep Difficulties and Insomnia Symptoms in Norwegian Musicians Compared to the General Population and Workforce." *Behavioral Sleep Medicine* 14, no. 3 (2015): 25–342.

Valentine, Elizabeth R., David F. P. Fitzgerland, Tessa L. Gorton, Jennifer A. Hudson, and Elizabeth R. C. Symonds. "The Effect of Lessons in the Alexander Technique on Music Performance in High and Low Stress Situations." *Psychology of Music* 23 (1995): 129–141.

Van Fenema, Esther, Jolien E. Julsin, Ingrid V. Carlier, Martijn S. van Noorden, Erik J. Giltay, Nic J. A. van der Wee, and Frans G. Zitman. "Musicians Seeking Psychiatric Help: A Preliminary Study of Psychiatric Characteristics." *Medical Problems of Performing Artists* 28, no. 1 (2013): 9–18.

Van Vugt, Floris T., Laurent Boullet, Hans-Christian Jabusch, and Eckhart Alternmüller. "Musician's Dystonia in Pianists: Long-Term Evaluation of Retraining and Other Therapies." *Parkinsonism and Related Disorders* 20 (2014): 8–12.

Vervainioti, Angeliki, and Evangelos C. Alexopoulos. "Job-Related Stressors of Classical Instrumental Musicians: A Systematic Qualitative Review." *Medical Problems of Performing Artists* 30, no. 4 (December 2015): 197–202.

Vines, Bradley, Marcelo M. Wanderley, Carol Krumhansl, Regina Nuzzo, and Daniel Levitin. "Performance Gestures of Musicians: What Structural and Emotional Information Do They Convey?" In *Gesture-Based Communication in Human-Computer Interaction, 5th International Gesture Workshop*, edited by A. Camurri and G. Volpe, 468–478. Genova, Italy: Springer-Verlag, 2004.

Vitzthum, Karin, Eva Endres, Franziska Koch, David A. Groneberg, David Quarcoo, Eileen Wanke, and Stefanie Mache. "Eating Behavior and Nutrition Knowledge among Musical Theatre Students." *Medical Problems of Performing Artists* 28, no. 1 (March 2013): 19–23.

Voltmer, Edgar. "Health Promotion and Prevention in Higher Music Education: Results of a Longitudinal Study." *Medical Problems of Performing Artists* 25, no. 2 (2010): 54–65.

Voltmer, Edgar, Mark Zander, Joachim E. Fischer, Brigitte M. Kudielka, Bernhard Richter, and Claudia Spahn. "Physical and Mental Health of Different Types of Orchestra Musicians Compared to Other Professions." *Medical Problems of Performing Artists* 27, no. 1 (March 2012): 9–14.

Wachter, Claire. "A Rolfer Can Tune Your Body." *Piano and Keyboard* 206 (September–October 2000): 22–27.

Wadlinger, Heather A., and Derek M. Isaacowitz. "Fixing Our Focus: Training Attention to Regulate Emotion." *Personality and Social Psychology Review* 15, no. 1 (2011): 75–102.

Walker, Brad. *The Anatomy of Stretching.* Berkley, CA: North Atlantic Books, 2007.

Wan, Agnes. "What Relaxation Means for Musicians." *American Music Teacher* 65, no. 6 (June–July 2016): 8–11.

Wanderley, Marcelo, and Claude Cadoz. "Gesture-Music." In *Trends in Gestural Control of Music*, edited by Marc Battier and Marcelo Wanderley, 71–94. France: IRCAM Research Institute, 2000.

Wang, Feifei, and Szilvia Boros. "The Effect of Physical Activity on Sleep Quality: A Systematic Review." *European Journal of Physiotherapy* 19 (June 2019): 1–8. https://doi.org/10.1080/21679169.2019.1623314.

Waterman, Alan S. "Two Conceptions of Happiness: Contrasts of Personal Expressiveness (Eudaimonia) and Hedonic Enjoyment." *Journal of Personality and Social Psychology* 64, no. 4 (1993): 678–691.

Waterman, Alan S., Seth J. Schwartz, and Regina Conti. "The Implications of Two Conceptions of Happiness (Hedonic Enjoyment and Eudaimonia) for the Understanding of Intrinsic Motivation." *Journal of Happiness Studies* 9 (2008): 41–79.

Watson, Alan H. *The Biology of Musical Performance and Performance-Related Injury.* Lanham, MD: Scarecrow Press, 2009.

West, Delia S., Zoran Bursac, Donna Quimby, T. Elaine Prewitt, Thea Spatz, Creshelle Nash, and Kenya Eddings. "Self-Reported Sugar-Sweetened Beverage Intake among College Students." *Obesity* 14 (2006): 1825–1831.

Williamon, Aaron, and Sam Thompson. "Awareness and Incidence of Health Problems among Conservatoire Students." *Psychology of Music* 34, no. 4 (2006): 411–430.

Wilson, Paul. *Completely Calm.* Victoria, Australia: Penguin Books, 1998.

Wilter, Willett C. *Eat, Drink, and Be Healthy: The Harvard Medical School Guide to Healthy Eating.* New York: Simon and Schuster Source, 2001.

Woodard, Kathryn. "Recovering Disembodied Spirits: Teaching Movement to Musicians." *British Journal of Music Education* 26, no. 2 (2009): 153–172.

Woodruff, Kary. *Sports Nutrition.* Edited by Katie Ferraro. New York: Momentum Press, 2016.

Workman, Darin. *The Percussionists' Guide to Injury Treatment and Prevention: The Answer Guide for Drummers in Pain.* New York: Routledge, 2006.

World Health Organization. *Constitution of the World Health Organization.* September 2005. https://www.who.int/governance/eb/who_constitution_en.pdf.

World Health Organization. *Health Promotion Glossary Update.* 2000. https://www.who.int/health-promotion/about/HPR%20Glossary_New%20Terms.pdf.

Wristen, Brenda G. "Depression and Anxiety in University Music Students." *Update: Applications of Research in Music Education* 31, no. 2 (2013): 20–27.

Yardley Beers, Deborah. "A Mind-Body Approach." *American Piano Teacher* 56, no. 1 (August–September 2006): 24–27.

Yontz, Timothy, G. "The Effectiveness of Laban-Based Principles of Movement and Previous Musical Training on Undergraduate Beginning Conducting Students' Ability to Convey Intended Musical Content." PhD diss., University of Nebraska, 2001.

Youngstedt, Shawn D. "Effects of Exercise on Sleep." *Clinics in Sports Medicine* 24, no. 2 (April 2005): 355–365.

Zander, Voltmer, and Claudia Spahn. "Health Promotion and Prevention in Higher Music Education: Results of a Longitudinal Study." *Medical Problems of Performing Artists* 25, no. 2 (June 2010): 54–65.

Zaza, Christine. "Research-Based Prevention for Musicians." *Medical Problems of Performing Artists* 9, no. 1 (March 1994): 3–6.

Zope, Sameer A., and Rakesh A. Zope. "Susharshan Kriya Yoga: Breathing for Health." *International Journal of Yoga* 6 (January–June 2013): 4–10.

Index

Figures, tables and, notes, are indicated by *f*, *t*, and n following the page numbers.